POT INC.

INSIDE MEDICAL MARIJUANA, AMERICA'S MOST OUTLAW INDUSTRY

GREG CAMPBELL

Greg Campbell

STERLING
New York

STERLING
New York

An Imprint of Sterling Publishing
387 Park Avenue South
New York, NY 10016

ISBN 978-1-4027-7925-1 (hardcover)
ISBN 978-1-4027-8967-0 (ebook)

Distributed in Canada by Sterling Publishing
c/o Canadian Manda Group, 165 Dufferin Street
Toronto, Ontario, Canada M6K 3H6
Distributed in the United Kingdom by GMC Distribution Services
Castle Place, 166 High Street, Lewes, East Sussex, England BN7 1XU
Distributed in Australia by Capricorn Link (Australia) Pty. Ltd.
P.O. Box 704, Windsor, NSW 2756, Australia

For information about custom editions, special sales, and premium and
corporate purchases, please contact Sterling Special Sales at 800-805-5489
or specialsales@sterlingpublishing.com.

Manufactured in the United States of America

2 4 6 8 10 9 7 5 3 1

www.sterlingpublishing.com

To the memory of Cynthia Malara

◆

It is one of the happy accidents of the federal system that a single courageous state may, if its citizens choose, serve as a laboratory; and try novel social and economic experiments without risk to the rest of the country.

—JUSTICE LOUIS D. BRANDEIS[1]

CONTENTS

A Note About Stoners and Potheads

Spend any significant amount of time immersed in cannabis culture, and you will run across some very sensitive and grumpy people. On one hand, this is understandable. Marijuana users have been viewed as among the most worthless deadbeats American society has produced, a population of soft-brained morons who can't cook soup or remember what day it is and who watch TV all day when they should be out looking for a job that doesn't require peeing in a cup. That's actually an improvement over the popular viewpoint of the 1930s and 1940s, when pot smokers were considered to be murderous perverts who would hump, kill, or corrupt any stray pet or wayward child that crossed their paths.

So it's hardly surprising that marijuana advocates—whether suited or in pajamas, employed or freeloading—can be touchy about the language used to discuss them and their habits. The trouble is, no one can agree on which words are offensive and which aren't. A certain faction considers *marijuana* itself pejorative and racist, based on a longstanding theory that narcotics agents in the 1930s chose that word over the more scientific *cannabis* when crafting drug laws; the word is of Mexican-Spanish origin and thus, the belief is, sounded more exotic and sinister. For others, *cannabis* is too pretentious to take seriously. Some get annoyed at being called *stoners* but don't mind being called *potheads*. For others, the opposite is true. And some—those who don't consider a hit or two a day to be a big deal—would just prefer to be called *recreational users* if they must be called anything at all. The act of actually inhaling is also a linguistic minefield. In the modern world of *medical* marijuana, to talk of "getting stoned" is an immediate giveaway that you're an ignorant square who doesn't really buy this whole medical argument. That, or you're a pothead who's gaming the system but hasn't yet learned to cover your tracks by adopting the correct lexicon. Patients *medicate*, even if the need to do so is no more pressing than that *South Park* comes on in fifteen minutes.

Obviously, there is a desire among those in the medical marijuana field to create some distance between them and Snoop Dogg, who is proud to smoke weed onstage during performances, or the daily user who greets the day with a wake-and-bake. Theirs is a much less flamboyant battle of perception, whether in a sprawling metropolis like L.A. or a puny high-plains town like Windsor, Colorado, population eighteen thousand. In 2009, marijuana and its colorful culture came into the mainstream more prominently than at any other time in history, but the old perceptions of those who use it—whether for cancer or before a Phish concert—linger in the minds of politicians, bankers, cops, and every other nonsmoker being asked to accept this formerly underground lifestyle now that it's taken up residence in the storefront next to the local Starbucks.

Ergo, *medicating* is preferable to *getting baked*.

Still, you can't mistake the irony in this argument over the vocabulary. Pot smokers themselves are responsible for the most colorful terminology in circulation. Dispensaries are named with little thought (or care) as to how they might sound to those who are already dubious about the industry's legitimacy: CannaMart, Smokin Coffin, Dr.

viii   •   *A Note About Stoners and Potheads*

Reefer, The Health Joint, House of Kush, Daddy Fat Sacks. And the strains: Durban Poison, AK-47, Green Crack, Matanuska Thunder-fuck. You'd think *pothead* would be the least of anyone's worries.

Because these sensitivities are different from person to person, trying to avoid controversy in this realm can quickly become an exercise in futility—use the wrong word in the wrong crowd and you're likely to start a fight. It's best just to speak as plainly as possible and hope everyone knows you mean no harm. Therefore, this disclaimer:

The words *pothead*, *stoner*, *toker*, and the like are used loosely and colloquially throughout this book, and if it's not clear in the context in which they are used, no offense is intended. Except, on occasion, when it is. Those terms are *not* meant to refer to medical marijuana patients, those people who have turned to marijuana because of a dire medical need. Generally, unless a direct quotation required it, I've avoided the words *dope* and *doper*, which are generally agreed in modern usage to refer to hard drugs and their users—substances like methamphetamine, cocaine, and heroin, all of which are far more dangerous, destructive, and deadly than marijuana. People who've made their reputations by illegally transporting tons of marijuana into the United States are surprisingly immune to offense—unless you call them dope smugglers. *Marijuana*, *cannabis*, *pot*, *reefer*, *bud*, *weed*, and the like are all used more or less interchangeably here. *Marihuana*, spelled with an *h*, is used when quoting people, newspaper articles, and documents from the time when that was the common spelling, roughly from the 1920s to the 1940s.

Finally, many of the people quoted or described in the following pages are only vaguely identified. The reasons why should be readily apparent.

—*Greg Campbell*
Fort Collins, Colorado

Prologue

"Living the Dream"

"The first rule of Fight Club is you do not talk about Fight Club."

—Brad Pitt as Tyler Durden, *Fight Club*, 1999

When Jeff Sweetin, the Special Agent in Charge of the Drug Enforcement Administration's Denver field office, first heard of Chris Bartkowicz on February 12, 2010, he thought Bartkowicz was nuts.

It was early on a cold, bright Friday in Colorado when Sweetin's assistant, Kevin Merrill, stepped into Sweetin's office and suggested he check out the Web site for the local NBC affiliate, 9News. The night before, Merrill had been watching TV when 9News teased a story scheduled to air Friday night, about a man who was extremely proud of his massive clandestine marijuana growing operation. The promo clip was online and, sure enough, there was this pretty jovial guy, Bartkowicz, confiding to the world that none of his suburban neighbors had any idea of the miniature rainforest of marijuana he was cultivating in his two-thousand-square-foot basement. He showed off for the cameras hundreds of pot plants growing under bright lights and estimated that the crop would yield him in the neighborhood of $400,000.

You didn't need to be a DEA agent to know that Bartkowicz was violating every rule of common sense that applied to people breaking state and federal drug laws, a set of "keep a low profile" reminders that, if they didn't come to you naturally, are printed on the first pages of nearly every marijuana gardening book ever written.

Jorge Cervantes's popular *Marijuana Horticulture: The Indoor/ Outdoor Medical Grower's Bible* bears this admonishment: "Successful indoor growers are good citizens and keep a low profile. They keep their yard and home clean and in excellent repair. They always drive a street-legal car and there are no outstanding warrants on the drivers. . . . Smart growers pay bills on time, are nice to neighbors, and do not throw noisy, wild, crazy parties. . . . The cardinal rule of growing is: Never tell anybody about any garden."[1]

Cervantes surely didn't think it necessary to add, "And don't go on the local television news with your real name spelled out in big letters under your un-obscured face, wearing a 'Got Weed' T-shirt bragging about how no one knows what you're doing and that you hope to clear nearly a half million dollars with your crop of illegal drugs." But maybe he should have.

"Definitely, I'm living the dream now," Bartkowicz chuckled to the reporter, who himself was probably dreaming of the big ratings Bartkowicz's unusual candor would deliver.

"My first thought was, 'This guy's crazy,'" said Sweetin, a twenty-three-year veteran of the DEA whose whole career has been dedicated to busting drug dealers, a pursuit that usually involved more legwork than watching the nightly news. "He's giving me and everyone else his real name and neighborhood."

A quick search of public records databases showed that not only did Bartkowicz indeed live at 2006 Glenhaven Drive in Highlands Ranch, a quiet and well-to-do community of trophy homes southwest of downtown Denver, but that his house was within a few dozen yards of an elementary school, an automatic sentence enhancement to the felonies Bartkowicz admitted committing on TV.

"The best information I have ever gotten as a DEA agent came from [that] news station," Sweetin recalled in 2011, still sounding somewhat amazed more than a year later. All that was left to do that day was send some agents to be sure the report wasn't some sort of weird hoax.

The DEA's visit that afternoon was less of a raid than is typical in such a situation, but so too was the way in which Bartkowicz came to the feds' attention. Just as there were no undercover drug buys or paid snitches, there were also no battering rams or SWAT cops with rifles at the ready. Instead, fewer than a dozen DEA agents and police officers with the South Metro Drug Task Force approached Bartkowicz as he was leaving his palatial house and asked permission to look inside. Bartkowicz agreed, and before the original story could air that night, 9News had another one to report—Bartkowicz was arrested and charged with enough federal drug crimes to add up to a maximum possible sentence of forty years in prison, a $2 million fine, and the forfeiture of his $637,000 house. His crop of 244 marijuana plants were chopped down by federal agents, dragged out to the driveway, and hauled off in sixteen large moving boxes. He went from living the dream one minute to living every pot grower's nightmare the next.

No one seemed surprised at the outcome except Bartkowicz, who, even in handcuffs and on his way to lockup, argued that he'd done nothing wrong.

"He actually was very vocal about that when he arrived at the jail," Sweetin said. "This is a guy who didn't fully get what he'd done."

Bartkowicz was not the only marijuana cultivator in Colorado feeling cocky at the time, although he is the only one who thought it safe to document his activities on the evening news. He was one of the thousands of Coloradans enrolled in the state's decade-old medical marijuana program, which makes it legal—under state law, at least—for qualifying patients to grow, use, and possess as many as six cannabis plants and up to two ounces of manicured pot. The law also allows patients to assign their plant-growing privileges to someone with a green thumb, which is how Bartkowicz explained the presence of forty times the allowable number of plants in his basement—he said he was growing them for himself (a car accident in the 1990s left him with an injured back that qualified him for pot therapy) and other patients who'd enrolled in the program. Unfortunately, he hadn't been able to produce all the paperwork listing all the patients he was growing for when he was arrested.

Not that it would have mattered.

"This would have risen to our attention based on what we saw with or without medical marijuana," Sweetin said. "This was what we would consider to be a significant indoor grow for a suburban location."

Any type of grow involving the plant genus *Cannabis L.*—whether indoors or outdoors, in suburbia or a ghetto, in a medically permissive state like Colorado or a draconian gulag like Oklahoma, which regularly hands out mind-blowing sentences for marijuana convicts—could not possibly be more illegal under federal drug laws, which supersede state laws. In fact, marijuana is illegal in nearly every corner of the planet, with the exception, since 1996, of some states where it's not—by state law, that is.

By the time of Bartkowicz's arrest in 2010, fourteen states and the District of Columbia had passed some form of law allowing patients with certain medical ailments the right to smoke or consume marijuana to deal with their symptoms, beginning in 1996 with California's passage of the Compassionate Use Act, Proposition 215. Usually written by marijuana activists with little or no input from cops and politicians, the various state laws allowing the medical use of pot differ greatly from one another—what the authors of such measures deemed to be palpable to voters in California, for example, varies from what backers thought they would approve in Montana or Maine or New Mexico. The result is a confusing set of regulations from state to state that vary in the number of plants one can grow, the requirements for applying as a medical marijuana patient, how and under what circumstances a person can sell pot to others, and even the types of ailments that qualify one as a medical pot smoker. For example, in Colorado, voters didn't just pass a new law to legalize medical marijuana in 2000, they amended the state constitution to allow it. That meant it was more ironclad than in other states because politicians couldn't revoke it—that would take another full vote of the electorate—and any legislative tinkering they might try to impose would have to pass a constitutional legal test. Regulations and bureaucratic policies were susceptible to legal review to be sure they jibed with the amendment voters passed. In Colorado, the right to smoke pot for reasons as vague as suffering "severe pain" was as locked in as it could get.

Regardless, as in every other state that had passed something similar, federal law trumped Colorado's. And federal law resolutely forbids—at the cost of great penalties to personal freedom and fortune—the use of marijuana for any reason at all.

Because of this unavoidable fact, for most of the past ten to fifteen years, the laws in these various states were considered by most Americans as little more than legal oddities, like those old statutes that sometimes make the news about how it's illegal to tether your horse outside a post office on Sundays during the sugar beet harvest. While the laws existed, relatively few took advantage of them, because in their early days, many of the brave souls who'd tested the waters with overt moves to open storefront dispensaries or run less-than-secret growing operations were busted and prosecuted under the federal law. Not many wanted to follow in their footsteps. Federal agents didn't hesitate to crush under their heels any attempt to make mainstream the concept that marijuana could be anything but a dangerous and deadly scourge on the nation. No matter what the voters of any individual state said, the federal government was—and is—determined to deny that the concept of "medical" marijuana is anything other than a ruse used by perfectly healthy pot smokers to get stoned with impunity.

The problem for those insisting otherwise was lack of critical mass—in spite of activists' successes passing laws in a third of the states, there was almost no national debate about the issue. At best, the topic was a punch line for late-night talk show hosts, and it was hard for true believers to get taken seriously by anyone who hadn't given much thought to marijuana since their days of experimenting in college dorm rooms. If pot can be medicinal, the sentiment ran among those who barely gave it a thought, then so can vodka.

The tipping point came in October 2009, when, seemingly out of the blue, the U.S. Justice Department issued an advisory memo to federal prosecutors suggesting they make busting medical marijuana patients and businesses a low priority. The memo was a make-good on a campaign promise by President Barack Obama, who, as a senator from Illinois, said in 2004 that the War on Drugs had been an "utter failure" and that we need to "rethink" our marijuana laws.

"I would not have the Justice Department prosecuting and raiding medical marijuana [patients]," he said on the campaign trail in 2007. "That's not a good use of our resources."[2]

When that sentiment was put into a memo and publicized by the media, it was as if a nation's worth of sleeper cells had been activated. Pot smokers came out of the woodwork and, in Colorado, as elsewhere, they bum-rushed the state-run registry to declare their medical infirmities—which, nine times out of ten, were suspiciously unobvious—in order to qualify as medical marijuana users. Since Colorado's law was silent on where all these new patients were to get their medicine, "ganjapreneurs" filled the legal vacuum with marijuana dispensaries, which are like Baskin-Robbins for potheads and usually with more than thirty-one flavors to choose from. Predictably, people who believe cannabis's roots run through the earth straight to Satan's doorstep practically barricaded their homes in fear that their neighborhoods would soon be overrun with drug-addled degenerates.

Cops and politicians didn't know which way was up. What came to be known as the Great Green Rush of 2009 detonated while the

Colorado state legislature was out of session, meaning that for several long weeks the lunatics were running the asylum, at least from lawmakers' perspectives. Politicians were so unhinged that one of them, State Sen. Scott Renfroe, suggested that the governor mobilize the Colorado National Guard to confiscate medical marijuana licenses from the estimated ten thousand potheads who gather to burn some weed in front of the capitol building every April 20—international marijuana smoke-out day, during which people around the world toke up in public.[3] He clearly had no concept that such a thing happens every year on the same day, from pole to pole, and has nothing to do with medical marijuana. But imagine his revulsion in thinking that *this* is what the citizen initiative process has wrought on his fine state—smelly hippies jammed up against the state capitol building and spread out as far as the eye can see, banging their bongos and playing with Hula-Hoops, dancing in the sunshine and having fun.

From the marijuana advocates' point of view, people like Renfroe were silly idiots who provided the comic relief while they raced to invent an entirely new industry in American history—the for-profit retail sale of a drug that's not recognized by the federal government as having any legitimate therapeutic uses—before lawmakers could pass any new laws to rein in the rights afforded by the state constitution.

Practically overnight, medical marijuana dominated the news, not only in the places where it had been legalized and which were experiencing an unprecedented surge of overt ganja-related activity, but on the national scene as well. For many people, the idea that smoking pot could ease the symptoms of serious illnesses was a new one, one that contradicted everything they'd been told for decades. But it's not a new concept at all. Even in the darkest days of prohibition, and in places in the country where getting caught could mean a possible life sentence in prison, sick people grew pot to ease their pain, not to get high for fun.

And many who were a lot less flamboyant than Chris Bartkowicz paid a hefty price for doing so.

FIFTEEN YEARS BEFORE Bartkowicz became a central figure in the debate over how states handle claims of marijuana's medical efficacy, the police raided the home of a much quieter grower on a similarly sleepy street in Tulsa, Oklahoma. That's where Will Foster had the perfect place to grow marijuana. His 1950s-era house came with a Cold War bomb shelter off the laundry room, a little space that was accessed through a broom closet and a big metal door. It was very plain, just a twelve-by-twelve-foot concrete cube of a room, but it was well hidden and it had thick walls and its own ventilation system. He bought a grow light and raised about twenty or twenty-five marijuana plants in a five-by-five corner of the room.

Foster was in his mid-thirties at the time, a beefy Midwesterner with a walrus mustache and a big bald forehead that reached nearly to the crown of his head, fringed with a fluffy semicircle of hair reaching around from the back, like a cloud wrapping itself around a bare mountaintop. He was a software engineer who owned his own business developing unique programs for the medical industry. Divorced with two kids and dating a woman with two of her own, Foster was not the first person to come to mind when imaging an underground marijuana cultivator. He's the sort of person you picture when you need car insurance.

Foster wasn't a drug dealer. He raised the crop of cannabis plants for his own use, to help him cope with the pain of chronic arthritis in his feet and ankles. It was a condition that first began when he was twenty-five or twenty-six, with painful swelling and inflammation of his lower legs, feet, and toes. He was in the army when he was diagnosed, and doctors attributed it to Foster's unfortunate history of sports injuries as a teen. He'd been banged up on the high school football team, where he was an all-conference running back in his junior and senior years, and he broke his ankles twice playing basketball.

The pain in his deteriorating joints never went away; in fact, as he got older and went back to civilian life, it got progressively worse. It felt like he was grinding glass in his ankles, and the pain often intensified when he ate certain foods or spent too much time on his feet. Doctors prescribed a battery of anti-inflammatory drugs and painkillers, such as Percodan, Percocet, Lorcet, Darvocet, and Vicodin, among others. His medicine chest looked like a small pharmacy, but the drugs only masked the pain. Worse, they made him lethargic and sleepy, which is not good for arthritis. Exercise is a crucial treatment for stiff, painful joints, but Foster's pharmacological regimen only made him want to crawl into bed.

"Taking all these painkillers is probably the worst thing for you because the last thing you want to do is be active," Foster said in his distinct heartland twang. The painkillers also had a host of potentially dangerous side effects, including addiction and the potential to die from overdose. It was a miserable existence. To keep the pain at bay, he needed the pills. But the pills made him groggy and unable to exercise, which made the condition worse. The arthritis eventually spread to his hips, lower back, and hands.

In the late 1980s or early 1990s, Foster finally found a drug that dulled the pain to manageable levels without making him lethargic. No one had ever died from it, and it was about as addictive as a cup of coffee. It allowed him to work without getting fatigued, and he had the energy to enjoy hanging out with his family, a definite quality-of-life improvement. The trouble was, this life-changing drug didn't come from a pharmacist, but from a street dealer. Foster said it was his grandmother, who died at the age of ninety-eight in 1987, who first taught him about marijuana's medicinal effects.

"One day she was talking about cannabis and how it treated everything when she was growing up and that we did not need all these medicines to take care of us," Foster remembers. "She didn't realize that marijuana and cannabis were the same plant at the time. She had arthritis, and cannabis is what she would have preferred to use as a treatment. But it wasn't available in the drugstore anymore."

It certainly wasn't available in the drugstore when Foster developed his own arthritis. Because he had to turn to the black market for his supply, it typically wasn't very good.

"It was horrible ditchweed that looked sometimes like it was soaked in diesel," he says of the marijuana he scored on the streets of Tulsa in the mid-1990s. "It was Mexican weed that was smuggled across the border, you know. I've seen some interesting stuff."

In fact, it was a little too interesting. Foster got tired of the poor quality and of not knowing exactly what he was smoking or where it came from. So he decided to grow his own.

"For more safe and effective medicine, it seemed like the thing to do was to cultivate it instead of rely on the black market," he says. "That way I knew what was done with it, what was introduced to it, what pesticides if any had been used on it."

It's impossible to say how many other Americans were doing the same thing in the privacy of their own homes, but in the lineage of modern pot smokers, Foster was something of an oddity. Most people who smoke pot do so for recreational purposes, as a means of relaxing, socializing, and de-stressing, in the same way that others pour a martini after a hard day's work. Most marijuana growers assume the enormous risk of doing so in order to make money. Foster was rare in that he fit into neither category—he grew for himself and smoked for pain relief.

But in the eyes of the law, that didn't matter. Growing even one plant, no matter what it's used for, is a federal felony. Foster had been lucky that he had such a perfect place to raise his plants. Due to the bomb shelter's sturdy underground construction and thick walls, it was completely clandestine, impossible to be noticed by casual visitors. Foster had to do little more than hang a high-wattage metal halide light from the ceiling and sprout some seeds under it.

But the otherwise perfect cultivation room had one glaring, fatal drawback: It was located in Oklahoma, a state largely regarded as among the worst places in North America to indulge in or supply the marijuana lifestyle, whether for medical or recreational purposes. Pot laws in Oklahoma are extraordinarily harsh. This is the state that sentenced Jimmy Montgomery, a wheelchair-bound paraplegic, to life in prison (later reduced to ten years) for intent to distribute two ounces of marijuana. The pot was his personal stash, which he used to keep his legs from trembling so violently that they often bounced him right out of his chair if he wasn't strapped in. Montgomery nearly died twice due to inadequate medical treatment in prison and was finally released in 1995 on an emergency medical parole, but he still lost a leg due to an infection that began in prison.[4] Oklahoma is where Larry Jackson, a frequent offender with a string of nonviolent crimes on his record, was given life in prison for felony marijuana possession after he was arrested at a friend's house sitting next to a burned roach containing 0.16 grams of marijuana.[5] It's the state that sentenced James Geddes to 150 years and two days for growing five marijuana plants.[6] On appeal, the sentence was reduced to ninety years, but it hardly mattered—Oklahoma still comes to mind only behind the likes of China, Singapore, and Thailand, which are among the countries that execute drug traffickers, when thinking about the worst places to get caught with any amount of pot in any form. You could hijack an airplane in Oklahoma and expect only a maximum of twenty-five years; if you grow a particular plant for your own use, however, the possibility that you could die behind bars is quite real. Legislators there are more threatened by the cannabis plant than most anything you can imagine—if you are caught with it in any form, you are doomed.

Foster was clueless about Oklahoma's reputation for giving pot growers more time than murders and rapists. Had he known what he risked, he says, "I wouldn't have been in Oklahoma."

On December 28, 1995, police officers acting on a tip from a confidential informant raided his home on the suspicion that he was cooking methamphetamine. He later came to believe that the "confidential informant" was a police ploy to search his house for pot; there was no meth—Foster says he'd never touched it—but his little garden was just as damning.[7] Foster was offered a deal in which he could plead guilty and serve twenty years; his girlfriend was offered ten years.[8] He refused, opting to take his chances in front of a jury.

"I felt at some stage that this is enough, that these people can't be doing this stuff," Foster says. "At some stage, somebody's going to have to challenge them and I figure that, you know, I might as well be the one to challenge them."

Foster defended his marijuana operation on the grounds that he needed cannabis to cope with his arthritis, but it was a tough sell. At the time, the concept of "medical marijuana" had the same credibility in the public eye as "medical glue sniffing." Prosecutors barely needed to do more than point to the government's classification of marijuana as a Schedule I narcotic under the 1970 Controlled Substances Act. It's the most restrictive category of drugs, defined as having no medical benefit and a lack of accepted safety even under medical supervision. Foster would have had better luck using a medical defense if he'd been caught with cocaine; that drug is in Schedule II, meaning it can be used by doctors for certain medical procedures, most commonly as an anesthetic during nose jobs. Marijuana cannot be used by anyone for any reason.

In January 1997, Foster was found guilty of marijuana cultivation with intent to distribute. He was sentenced to ninety-three years in the state penitentiary.

It was his first offense for anything.[9]

BEFORE I EVER heard of Will Foster, or even knew very much about the ordeals that he and countless others like him had gone through in their pursuit of relief from chronic pain, I bought a few grams of

Strawberry Cough and Purple Kush, two pot-laced brownies, and a jar of cannabis-based salve—$42 worth of stop-and-shop pot—from a place called Medicinal Gardens in November 2009. The choices were made mainly by the "budtender" behind the counter; there were too many different strains for me to decide, all arranged fat and skunky in half-gallon glass jars in the display case and on a wooden shelf on the wall. He was one of three employees behind the counter, dressed smartly in a black lab coat with his name stitched on the pocket, and he seemed happy to spend as much time with me as I liked. Wearing latex gloves, he pulled buds out of different jars with long metal tongs and held them under a large lighted magnifying glass so I could see their little forests of resinous trichomes loaded with psychoactive delta-9-tetrahydrocannabinol (known the world over as THC, the active ingredient in pot), explaining the different strains' various effects and how they worked best to alleviate different pain.

It was my first time in this place, located not in Amsterdam but sleepy little Fort Collins, Colorado, just a block or two from Colorado State University in a smart stone building with an address that's convenient for stoners to remember: 420 Howes Street. The number 420 is code that has come to encompass all things marijuana—"I need a 420 break" or "Do you know a plumber who's 420-friendly?"—and I imagine the proprietors were happy to have found a location with the perfect street number.

You can't just walk inside Medicinal Gardens. First you ring the doorbell and follow the instructions on a hand-printed sign to remove your hat and sunglasses so you can be clearly photographed by a surveillance camera. When the door is buzzed open, the loamy fragrance of fresh pot grabs you in an embrace as you enter the dark wood-paneled waiting room. Show your state-issued medical marijuana license to the receptionist and take a seat with the other customers, who, on my first visit, were a blend of hairy hobos and perky college students. There's a bulletin board with marijuana news, a half-dozen marijuana coffee table books, and a TV in the corner tuned to a VH1 reality show.

When it's your turn, a door opens and one of the budtenders calls your name from a list. A budtender is like a coffee barista and somme- lier combined, usually a lifelong stoner who's just as amazed to be making a quasi-legitimate living with his unique knowledge as his customers are to be making quasi-legitimate pot purchases.

I paid with a credit card and was told by the spacey young cashier to try the cannabis fudge next time.

"I just had a little sliver myself," she giggled, handing me a paper sack with my drugs in it.

I didn't need to know of Foster's ordeal to be well aware that my transaction was just as illegal as his activities under federal laws. I half expected to walk into the arms of a sting operation when I left the building, but there was nothing there but the mailman, whistling up the block. It being my first reconnaissance mission into the realm of medical marijuana, I wasn't thinking of the fundamental disparity wherein a perfectly healthy man can buy marijuana with a traceable credit card and not worry very much about getting busted, but in a bordering state, someone living in chronic pain is literally taking their life in their hands by nurturing a certain plant in some dark corner of his home. All I was thinking about was making it to my car without attracting attention.

The United States has always been deeply schizophrenic about marijuana, but never so much as it is today. Since 1970, the govern- ment has spent $1 trillion in the War on Drugs trying to get Ameri- cans to stop smoking pot and using other hard drugs, spending that money on a combination of propaganda, like the "This is your brain on drugs" commercials of the 1980s[10]; paramilitary operations, in which heavily armed drug task force troopers break down doors across the country sniffing out weed; and incarceration, wherein more than half of all drug arrests in 2009 were for marijuana. Of those, 45.6

percent were for possession alone, a total of three-quarters of a million people.[11]

The War on Drugs has been, by every measure, a complete failure, especially as it relates to marijuana. More than 40 percent of the U.S. population over the age of twelve has at least tried the illegal weed, 26 million have smoked in the previous twelve months, and 15 million admit to being regular users.[12] Those numbers have remained largely unchanged in recent years despite the serious consequences imposed by law. Millions of cannabis plants grow clandestinely in suburban homes, on hillsides in national forest land, and between rows of corn in the farm belt. Millions of tons more are smuggled from Mexico—seizures at the border are on the rise, with agents intercepting 1,500 metric tons in 2009, but so is Mexican production. The Justice Department estimates Mexican suppliers harvested more than 21,000 metric tons of weed the same year, a record high.[13] It's often easier for high school students to get their hands on a few joints than on a twelve-pack of beer.

Throughout the War on Drugs, demand for pot has fed an underground economy worth billions, all of it circulating untaxed on the black market. As a cash crop, marijuana is America's most valuable, worth an estimated $35 billion, more than hay, soybeans, and corn.[14] American pot smokers might be outnumbered, outgunned, and with no legal maneuvering room, but they've proven remarkably resilient to the forces arrayed against them. Despite the odds, outlaw botanists, many of them in California, have developed strains that are unmatched in the world, and they've perfected indoor growing methods that were inconceivable decades ago. Looking at it in terms of an actual war, the marijuana insurgency has steadily gained ground, helped immensely in recent years by pot's newly rediscovered medicinal wonders.

These therapeutic benefits, well known for thousands of years, have been obscured by nearly a century of unfounded hokum about marijuana's supposed deleterious effects. Rumor once had it that pot would make men grow breasts and wantonly murder their whole families. Knowledge about marijuana's uses as a medicine was kept alive through personal anecdotes, accidental discoveries, long-forgotten reports, foreign research studies, and vibrant counterculture publications like *High Times* magazine since its prohibition in the United States in 1937. Even the U.S. government unwittingly helped bolster the medical-benefits argument despite its every effort to insist that none exist. The Food and Drug Administration ran a little-known program from 1976 to 1992 that, at its peak, provided thirty seriously ill patients with pot from the government's personal stash at the University of Mississippi, the only legal cannabis farm in the United States, operated for research and testing purposes. Paradoxically, the marijuana program stopped accepting new applications because it seemed to be helping the patients who were enrolled in it, which of course made more people interested in participating. President George H. W. Bush suspended it in 1992 just as AIDS patients were learning that pot could help them stop vomiting and gain weight. The party line—"There is no such thing as *medical* marijuana"—has dominated official U.S. policy ever since.

But if there's one thing the marijuana crowd has perfected, it's spreading information, even if it's incomplete or half-formed. While most Americans during the past twenty years still considered weed to be good for nothing other than inducing moronic stupor in its users, it was becoming more widely known among die-hards that pot could ease nausea, dull pain, and reduce potentially blinding orbital pressure in glaucoma patients. Research lagged behind the rumors, but it's catching up. And people are catching on. Every non-recreational marijuana smoker who benefits from smoking a joint on his or her deathbed leaves behind friends and loved ones who have been compelled to rethink what they've been told about this "devil's weed." That's why for years national polls have shown an increasing number of people who believe pot should be legal for medical purposes, reaching a record high of 73 percent in 2010. Supporters span all demographics and political groups. Support for legalizing it outright lags behind, but is on the rise; in 1969, the year of Woodstock, only 12 percent of Americans favored legalizing marijuana, but in 2010, 41 percent were in favor.[15]

As more and more states adopt more permissive laws regarding pot use—which were almost always initiated by citizens rather than politicians—it becomes much clearer that the government's war against marijuana is unsustainable. The question isn't *if* the nation will one day confront the differences between what its laws say about the subject and what science, common sense, and social culture say, but *when*.

And that's where my interests laid. I have no debilitating illness, no medical need to have gone into Medicinal Gardens and legally bought the same substance that initially condemned Will Foster to ninety-three years behind bars (Foster was eventually paroled in 2001 and is free in California, but still under state supervision as of this writing). When marijuana burst into the mainstream national consciousness like never before, as a Colorado resident, I found myself living in the epicenter of the national debate over marijuana's medicinal merits and its perceived dangers. I enrolled myself in its medical marijuana program to investigate the issue first-hand so that I could grow and sell cannabis as part of a vibrant and all-but-unregulated legal market that existed for nearly a year. Naturally, I was curious to see if the rumors I'd heard of incalculable wealth were true, like someone lured to pan for gold during the Western migration—but I also wanted to learn about what was at its core: a pitched debate about whether or not medical marijuana was real or a ruse.

I entered into this project undecided and, frankly, with little personal investment in where the knowledge would take me, at least at the outset. I don't even smoke pot recreationally. All I knew was that my eyes were wide open when, in the spring of 2010, I flipped the switch in a humid little room in my basement and was momentarily blinded by a pair of grow lights hanging over my very own cannabis plants. At that moment, it didn't matter if I lived in the most permissive state or the least, if I was a medical patient or a chronic pothead—I'd joined a community that had existed in the shadows for more than half a century, an invisible army of millions of suburban outlaws whose crime was horticulture.

Like Bartkowicz, I was living the dream.

· 1 ·

Pot Street, USA

"The case is made difficult by respondents' strong arguments that they will suffer irreparable harm because, despite a congressional finding to the contrary, marijuana does have valid therapeutic purposes."

—Justice John Paul Stevens, *Raich v. Gonzales*, June 6, 2005

Broadway is a main thoroughfare as it passes through the heart of Denver, with four wide lanes taking traffic south of downtown past miles of office buildings and busy retail locations—but once it crosses under the I-25 overpass, the pavement crumbles, traffic slows to two lanes in each direction, and the neighborhood goes to seed. The one- and two-story buildings fronting South Broadway were built in the 1950s and '60s, around the same time their upkeep seems to have ended. They're home to an assortment of lonesome greasy spoons, used-car dealerships, shady-looking taverns, and tattoo parlors. But those stores aren't what visitors notice—it's the neon or painted pot leaves on nearly every block that draw the most attention.

Within a mile, commuters pass Broadway Wellness, Back to the Garden, Evergreen Apothecary, Wellspring Collective, Ganja Gourmet, Little Green Pharmacy, Little Brown House, Herbal Alternatives, The Kind Room, THC/The Herbal Center, A Cut Above, Walking Raven, Green Depot, Patients Choice Colorado, Delta 9 Caretakers, and Colorado Alternative Medicine. Pedestrians weave around crudely stenciled sandwich boards on the sidewalks, most with the requisite seven-fingered pot leaf, advertising the deals of the day: "$10 any gram," "All 8ths $40 Top Shelf." Even the most sheltered teetotaler knows what's up: the marijuana once available on South Broadway only in its alleys from street dealers is now openly for sale from storefront dispensaries, each of them angling for customers with the same vigor as carnival barkers. This stretch of road has become so infamous for its dense collection of pot shops that it's known throughout the weed world as "Broadsterdam."

Dispensaries are hardly confined to just here. There are hundreds in Denver and throughout Colorado. In the summer and fall of 2009, marijuana stores proliferated so quickly that they easily outnumbered Starbucks, Burger King restaurants, and even public middle and high schools statewide. A store called Dr. Reefer, complete with as much garish neon as the owner could afford, is situated on one of the more picturesque locations of The Hill neighborhood in Boulder, across the street from the stately University of Colorado. In the city of Loveland, famous for remailing Valentine's Day cards just because of the postmark, some dudes converted an old gas station into the Smiths Tonian Cannabis Club and Wellness Center. In the tiny bedroom community of Windsor, population eighteen thousand, a dispensary opened just off the I-25 off-ramp. In my very own gym in Fort Collins, I noticed a few guys eyeballing the dimensions of an infrequently used stretching room while I was doing crunches on an exercise mat. Sure enough, when I asked at the front desk if the management was thinking of parsing off a section of the workout area to rent as a separate business, I was told it would be converted into a medical marijuana dispensary, one of scores that were opening in my city of 140,000 people.

In fact, in those heady, freewheeling days around Thanksgiving 2009, when there were almost no regulations to prevent them, more than a hundred such places were putting down roots, quite literally, in Fort Collins alone. When the boom caused by the Justice Department memo occurred, the only law on the books was the 2000 amendment to the state constitution, which said nothing about the legality of such operations but which also didn't prohibit them. Until the state legislature could convene in January 2010, there would be no other state laws that cities and towns could look to for guidance. So the citizen politicians—the businesspeople and working parents who decide such mundane matters as flood plain regulations and local municipal codes—had to take up the matter themselves. These poor devils unexpectedly found themselves at the very center of a debate over marijuana's potential impact on society that has been argued for decades, and they were besieged on one side by potheads, hippies, and the disabled and on the other by drug abuse counselors, cops, and fretful parents. Watching these two sides clash in local chambers of government was enough to make you either laugh or cry.

THE FIRST GUY who took the microphone could have walked straight out of any one of the Fort Collins City Council members' nightmares. He's big, with a shaved head and a crooked nose, dressed that night in November 2009 in baggy NBA garb and wearing a flat-rimmed ball cap cocked to the side. He was unlike the usual scrum of political gadflies who attend city council meetings, the perpetually irritated geriatric contingent and eccentric wing nuts with nothing better to do on Tuesday nights than bring their complaints about recycling or energy rates or potholes to this paneled old chamber week after week. In fact, no one in the crowd was typical of those who would normally line up to harangue the council for three minutes at a time during "citizen participation." The place was standing room only, and because the pro-pot contingent outnumbered the anti-pot faction by at least two to one, it smelled vaguely like a barn; many attendees were smart enough to anticipate the tedium of a city council meeting and medicated heavily enough to produce a contact high in those who hadn't. When it came time for the citizens to speak, the young guy in the NBA jersey grabbed the sides of the podium as if to shake it down for lunch money, scanning each of Fort Collins's elected officials sitting at a long elevated desk as if trying to decide which of them was this "mayor" he'd heard about.

"Ah'm representin' out of Fort Collins," he began, pronouncing it *repra-ZEH-in*. Several people in the audience groaned under their breath. Even though many of them had never participated in the trappings of local government before, they were in tune enough to know that now was not the time to come off like a street thug. Here, as in practically everywhere else in Colorado, the Great Green Rush was suddenly a crisis for the local politicos—where there were maybe four medical marijuana dispensaries operating quietly in Fort Collins's shadows in the summer of 2009, within a month of the Justice Department memo, there were plans in the works to open at least a hundred, maybe more. The city council had declared the proliferation of marijuana dispensaries worthy of an emergency moratorium that would halt them in their tracks precisely because they assumed the city was being overrun by a horde of criminal barbarians.

The dispensary owners and their supporters came together to convince them otherwise, itself a minor miracle considering that most seemed stoned and included at least a few shady businessmen I recognized from my time as a local reporter and editor in this community. Despite their common cause, I had noticed in the weeks before the meeting a rift among them that I'd later also find among advocates on the state and national level. Half of the dispensary owners in town didn't even know one another, and those who did often didn't get along too well. They were as good at spreading rumors as any knitting circle. One dispensary owner's product was said to come from Mexico rather than his own cultivation operation, which is strictly taboo under the constitutional amendment. Another was supposedly a serial spammer who anonymously trashed the competition on the pot blogs. Fledgling industries with a low price of entry that don't require hard-to-master skills tend to engender cutthroat competition, and medical marijuana is a good example. Any half-bright fool with enough money to buy lights and rent a warehouse can learn in just a few harvest cycles to grow marijuana properly, and now that the risk of arrest was lower than at any other point in the previous seventy-two years, the underground cultivators who had kept the pot flowing through the dark days were among the first to emerge into the daylight. And more often than not, they were chaffed by all the opportunistic newbies with dollar signs in their eyes stepping on their turf.

But this was the time for a unified front, and the dispensary owners had rallied some persuasive witnesses to speak on their behalf, including botanists, chronically ill patients, lawyers, and lifelong cultivators. The goal here—as it was in every community in every medical marijuana state experiencing such a burst of ganjapreneurialism—was to convince the council that they were businesspeople who were as legitimate as any of the city's stockbrokers and real estate agents. No one wanted to come off like an illiterate pothead.

Then this guy, *reprazehin* his homies, who were sprawled across a row of seats looking like The Beastie Boys, took the podium.

"I agree that there should be a lot of limitations or whatever about school zones and things like that," he said. "We don't, as dispensary owners, we don't, um, want it to end up in our kids' hands or anything like that. By *far*. That's not our drive or anything. Our drive is to get the wellness for everybody that they deserve, you know? It's like saying '*nay*.'"

My friend Mike, a local photojournalist, was in the audience. Mike smokes a quarter ounce of weed a week, and not for medical reasons. He's the sort of guy who buys artificial urine to pass drug tests, and he's usually oblivious to social blunders. But even he couldn't keep from squirming.

"I just put my head in my hands," he said later. "This guy was singlehandedly ruining everything. I almost left."

But the guy gamely plowed ahead, oblivious.

"It's not like we're all sitting out there and just trying to sell drugs to everybody. It's not an illegal issue anymore. It's not like a game anymore. This is serious, you know? A lot of us have health issues and everything, but just because we don't look like we have it, maybe we have it. You know? And we're just trying to get the best medication out there without having to do OxyContins and things like that that destroy our kidneys and everything else too, you know? We're not here just to say we want to sell marijuana to everybody in your city. You know what I'm saying?"

Things didn't immediately improve. The next speaker was an old ganja veteran who sounded like Dennis Hopper's character in *Apocalypse Now*. He was clearly medicated on the best of whatever the dispensaries were offering.

"We want to weed out the bad actors," he began carefully, before immediately losing his train of thought. "I'm not objecting, and I didn't study up to give you an answer to anything, but I wanted to make that point. I'll leave it simple. I think that's the issue. And I'll just see if I can quickly share my experience, give you the, ah . . ."

He grasped in the air, snapping his fingers, at a loss for words. For a brief moment, hope flared that he would give up and sit down. But he found a thread of thought and clamped down on it with renewed spirit.

"From what I've seen, and I don't pay attention to everything all the time, I'm a regular person. We're not genetically designed yet to be information absorbers. We're just people, and you can study the species. The scientists will show you that. But I will tell you my experience. Took me awhile to figure it out and go through the system and was hugely, totally underground in the beginning."

The mood of the audience was dour. The first two speakers were not delivering the first impression they hoped the council would have of them. With every tick of the clock counting down the guy's 210 seconds, they could feel the cause being lost. People sitting behind the podium batted their wide eyeballs left and right without moving their heads. *Is this really it?* you could almost hear them thinking. *Does it all end here?*

I gave the council credit for not grappling for the gavel to declare that they'd heard enough to ban dispensaries forever. As much as some of them may have wanted to, the truth is that they had little choice but to listen to what became hours of testimony over several meetings. Some of it was spaced out, some of it was eloquent, some of it was rubbish, but all of it was aired in the council chambers over the course of the following weeks. Unlike in other cities where elected officials voted to ban the offending businesses with little more than a cursory hearing (bans that, incidentally, no one was certain were constitutional), Fort Collins's elected officials seemed to realize that medical marijuana—and all of its attendant miracles and freak shows, the good and bad side by side—was not going away. The least they could do was try to figure out a way to make it work without damaging anyone's psyche or getting sued.

FEW PEOPLE WILL argue that the medical marijuana laws in effect around the country by the summer of 2009 have since created a tangled mess of conflicting rules in the city- and county-level jurisdictions of every state that has adopted them. California's passage of Proposition 215 in 1996, the Compassionate Use Act, set off the chain reaction that is still unfolding today. The law was extraordinarily simple, stating only that medical patients have a "right to obtain and use marijuana for medical purposes," as long as a doctor recommends it.[1] Prop 215 put the matter of what a marijuana distribution system would look like in the hands of the state legislators, but the General Assembly wouldn't pass any regulations until 2003. Until that time, it was up to local governments to set the rules, and they varied wildly. The counties of Fresno and San Bernardino, for instance, adopted "zero tolerance" policies for pot cultivation, while Sonoma County allowed patients and caregivers (the term generally applied to those who grow marijuana on behalf of patients if the patients opt not to grow for themselves) to grow as many as ninety-nine plants and possess as much as three pounds of manicured marijuana. Northern California, already widely known for its illicit pot farms, soon became the national epicenter of marijuana horticulture. Humboldt, Trinity, and Mendocino counties became known as the "Emerald Triangle" even outside the world of recreational smokers, who had known it as such for the past thirty years. It was soon hard to find anyone living in the area who wasn't involved in the pot industry, or who at least knew someone who was. The cannabis plant became the lifeblood of the region; it was estimated that by 2008, pot accounted for two-thirds of Mendocino County's economy and that growers there were turning over $1 billion or more per year in sales.[2]

With nothing but the vague Compassionate Use Act to rely on, cops had no idea who was a medical patient and who wasn't; to this day, there is no mandatory registration system for patients and their caregivers, and initially, there were no rules at all about the legality of cannabis clubs and retail dispensaries. The implications for law enforcement were obvious—criminals had virtually free reign.

"The DEA and its local and state counterparts routinely report that large-scale drug traffickers hide behind and invoke Proposition 215, even when there is no evidence of any medical claim," reads a notice on the DEA Web site that points out many of the law's short-comings from the cops' point of view. "In fact, many large-scale marijuana cultivators and traffickers escape state prosecution because of bogus medical marijuana claims. Prosecutors are reluctant to charge these individuals because of the state of confusion that exists in California. Therefore, high-level traffickers posing as 'caregivers' are able to sell illegal drugs with impunity."

The enactment of California's Senate Bill 420 in 2003—whose wink-and-a-nudge title is a conscious nod toward marijuana culture, not a coincidental gaffe—attempted to impose some parameters on the situation, which inevitably led to more confusion. It outlawed for-profit dispensaries but allowed patients and caregivers to form not-for-profit collectives and co-ops to grow and distribute marijuana.[3] Those businesses could collect payment to offset the cost of growing. The bill established limits on the amount of pot that could be possessed or grown—six mature or twelve immature plants and up to a half pound of harvested pot per patient—and allowed jurisdictions to increase, but not lower, that amount. Therefore, Fresno and San Bernardino had to at least allow patients to grow or possess marijuana up to the statewide limit. And SB 420 also established a voluntary registration system to be administered by county health departments so that patients and caregivers who wished to have them could be issued ID cards to help prevent their arrest. Some counties refused, leading to lengthy and costly legal battles.

That the California law resulted mostly in chaos is putting it mildly. From the time the Compassionate Use Act was adopted in 1996, local cops and federal drug agents went on a multiyear blitz-krieg, raiding farms, busting collectives, and arresting patients. They were egged on by outrage from Washington, D.C., where President Bill Clinton threatened to revoke the ability to write prescriptions for any drug for doctors who recommended marijuana to their patients, and to throw them in jail. Clinton, who famously admitted to smoking pot in England "a time or two" but not inhaling the smoke, has long frustrated marijuana legalizers. During his eight years in office, more than 4.1 million Americans were arrested on pot charges, the most in history. Yet two weeks before handing the reins of power to George W. Bush, he told *Rolling Stone* that he supported decriminalizing possession of small amounts of marijuana. Allen St. Pierre, the executive director of the National Organization for the Reform of Marijuana Laws (NORML), called Clinton's eleventh-hour claim of solidarity with the cause "bittersweet," because at that point in his presidency it was practically meaningless.[4]

The only bright side for the California growers was that there was safety in numbers. In the Humboldt County city of Arcata, for instance, it's estimated that one in seven homes is used exclusively to grow marijuana, an epidemic that has people who aren't in the drug trade living in fear or being priced out of their community. There's no telling if those living across the street are growing for sick people or if they're connected to a Mexican cartel, and there's very little that law enforcement can do about it. There simply aren't enough cops.

"I never thought that I'd ever be carrying a gun, never ever," one resident told the producers of an A&E documentary called *Pot City USA* in 2009. "I've never felt threatened before. But things just seem like they're out of control here."

Landlords have found that they can demand up to three times the rent from a pot grower than they can from a working family, but often at the cost of trashed houses. Growers in Arcata don't always bother to clean up after themselves; if the mildew or spider mites get too bad, they just move to another rental, often in the same neighborhood.

Because California's law was the first of its kind, no one knew how the courts would enforce it, and California became the "laboratory" for "novel social and economic experiments" that Supreme Court Justice Louis Brandeis envisioned in 1932. It was an experiment that required that many people be arrested and prosecuted.

What developed, gradually and painfully for those directly involved, was a tense and unstable draw that still leaves much uncertainty and conflict. Prosecutors have become warier of taking cases to trial than in the past, after having seen cases lost or overturned. In some cases, defendants who've been acquitted or had the charges dropped have successfully argued to have their seized pot returned to them. A trend emerged wherein cops would raid pot farms and destroy the plants, but make no arrests. Even successful prosecutions have sometimes resulted in perfunctorily short sentences that have hardly been worth the time and expense.

Consider the case of Ed Rosenthal, the prolific author of numerous marijuana cultivation books and the former author of a *High Times* advice column. DEA agents arrested the self-described "guru of ganja" in 2002 for possession of hundreds of marijuana clones, small starter plants grown from clippings taken from mature mother plants. They were for distribution to Bay Area medical marijuana clubs, but his defense team was not allowed to raise any arguments about their medical purpose or that Rosenthal was in compliance with state and local ordinances. He was found guilty, but as soon as the jurors learned that the plants' purpose was medical, nine of the twelve held a press conference denouncing their own verdict. Because of the outcry, Rosenthal was sentenced to one day in jail, which he'd already served when he was arrested. (The case dragged on for years; Rosenthal's conviction was overturned on appeal, but he was retried and reconvicted in 2007. The one-day sentence still stood, and Rosenthal saw no extra jail time. He appealed yet again in an effort to clear his name, calling himself a "soldier in the movement to change marijuana laws." The Ninth U.S. Circuit Court of Appeals upheld the conviction, saying that the intended use of the marijuana plants was "irrelevant" since pot is illegal under federal laws no matter what the use.)

Rosenthal's case won't be the last of its kind because the U.S. Supreme Court has ruled twice that federal agents have the legal jurisdiction and authority to bust people in permissive states, an authority that they've used with great zeal. These raids happen with or without the cooperation of local authorities; in fact, sometimes they happen despite the local authorities' disinterest in a case. One such raid led to one of the Supreme Court decisions.

When a mixed agency task force hit the Butte County, California, home of Angel Raich and Diane Monson in 2002, they discovered six marijuana plants. Raich suffered from a wide array of serious illnesses, including chronic pain and debilitating nausea, the root causes of which were a mystery to her doctors (she would later be diagnosed with brain cancer). She couldn't eat or drink without becoming nauseous, and smoking pot was the only thing that enabled her to keep food down and maintain her weight; without it, her doctors feared she would starve to death. Monson grew the plants and provided Raich with pot for free.[5] It was a perfect illustration of everything the Compassionate Use Act was meant to accomplish.

The sheriff's deputies on the scene considered the women's modest home-grow operation to be legal under California law. But the federal agents on the scene were determined to seize and destroy the plants under federal jurisdiction, which they did. The women's subsequent lawsuit against DEA administrator Asa Hutchinson and U.S. Attorney General John Ashcroft (changed to Alberto Gonzales when Gonzales succeeded Ashcroft) went all the way to the U.S. Supreme Court. In it, the women claimed that it was unconstitutional for federal agents to interfere with a state's sovereign right to enact and enforce its own laws; enforcing the federal Controlled Substances Act, they claimed, violated the U.S. Constitution's Commerce Clause; the Fifth, Ninth, and Tenth Amendments; and the doctrine of medical necessity.

The DEA had long justified such raids under the Commerce Clause, which allows the federal government to regulate interstate commerce and which has generally been interpreted narrowly by the Supreme Court to preserve states' rights. In the case of marijuana, regulating interstate commerce means eradicating it. Raich and Monson argued that, by definition, marijuana grown at home for use in that home, involving no actual commerce, could not contribute to the illicit interstate market in marijuana—meaning, in other words, that the feds would have no jurisdiction to "regulate" their marijuana by destroying it because their personal stash is outside the commercial, albeit illegal, market. [6]

The case was unique in that several parties filed amicus briefs in support of the plaintiffs who were strange bedfellows indeed. In addition to those parties that might be expected to side against the government on the matter of medical marijuana, such as NORML and the lobbying group Marijuana Policy Project, was a brief filed on behalf of Raich by the states of Alabama, Louisiana, and Mississippi, anti-pot strongholds with little intention of following California's lead. The opening statement makes clear that these states don't condone or support the "so-called" Compassionate Use Act; quite the contrary, it boasts that Alabama "routinely" maintains laws to throw people in jail for up to ten years for a first-time possession-with-intent-to-distribute offense and from fifteen years to life for three possession convictions. "It is not a reputation of which Alabama is embarrassed or ashamed," the brief reads, noting as well that it has a history of not allowing a medical defense for pot cases, proudly citing a case in which the defendant suffered a crippling illness leading from paraplegia to quadriplegia. He wasn't allowed to mention before the jury that marijuana was the only thing that eased his pain and suffering. Alabama, Louisiana, and Mississippi were defending California's sovereign right to enact and enforce what laws it chooses without federal interference through the Commerce Clause, not because they in any way supported the use of marijuana for medical purposes.

The split court sided with the government, clearing the way for the DEA to bust anyone it liked, sick or healthy, small-timer or kingpin, and regardless of whether they were complying with local laws. Six months after the Supreme Court ruling, in December 2005, the DEA raided Hopenet Cooperative, a San Francisco cooperative that served about a thousand patients, including a hundred indigent patients who were given marijuana for free. First they raided the home of Steve and Catherine Smith, Hopenet's owners, bringing them outside to stand handcuffed in their underwear while their house was searched. Agents later used a battering ram to break down the co-op's door. They took about $20,000 in assets, including cash, and more than a hundred pot plants, but didn't arrest anyone.[7]

"I can tell you that it is a clear violation of federal law to cultivate, possess, and distribute marijuana," DEA spokeswoman Casey McEnry told a reporter when asked why the feds were raiding a business operating within the parameters of California law. "Today, as the DEA, we enforced federal drug laws and conducted a lawful search of these four locations and we seized marijuana."[8]

In 2006, following a raid in Modesto, she issued a warning to pot cultivators: "The magic plant count number is zero, the distribution number is zero if you want to be safe from us possibly knocking at your door. Anyone who cultivates or distributes marijuana is at risk."[9]

The DEA conducted nineteen raids on medical marijuana providers in California in 2005, including thirteen in one day in San Diego. The number rose to fifty-three raids by 2007, an average of more than one per week.[10]

Cynics could argue that the Compassionate Use Act actually made it easier for the DEA to arrest pot providers. Thinking they were covered under the law, growers were less cautious about their activities than they were in the past, and commercial operations like cooperatives and collectives were easy enough to find. Arresting sick people and their caregivers and tearing up their cannabis proved much easier than investigating organized crime and hard-drug rings.

They don't advertise in the local newspapers.

WITH CONSTERNATION OVER legalizing pot for medicinal purposes running at a high pitch by 2009, it was quite easy to lose sight of the fact that not every state hewed to the federal example when it came to heavy-handed enforcement of marijuana laws. Long before the current anxiety over medical marijuana, thirteen states had decriminalized marijuana possession since 1973 down to a mere petty offense.[11] Colorado is one of those. If you're caught with an ounce or less of pot, the most punishment you'll face is a fine on par with a speeding ticket.

For this reason and others, Colorado has long been a relatively comfortable place for those who like to get stoned. Its unparalleled natural beauty includes the towering peaks of the Rocky Mountains and endless expanses of high-plains prairies, the landscape etched with the winding courses of wild rivers that carry melting snow down through the foothills and across a checkerboard of irrigated farmland.

The scenery has long attracted those who prefer to enhance the view through the kaleidoscopic effect of a strong joint, whether it's from a chairlift taking you to the back bowls of Vail Ski Resort or from a remote mountain switchback sprawled out in the hot summer grass next to your mountain bike. John Denver knew this, and his iconic folk hit "Rocky Mountain High" was very nearly adopted as the state's official song until someone explained to the politicians considering the idea that the refrain had nothing to do with the state's altitude.

For an area of the country in which history is dominated by no-nonsense pioneers and rugged individualists—folks whose descendants would form the backbone of Colorado's philosophical disposition as a generally conservative state with strong libertarian ideals—its reputation as a relatively safe harbor for marijuana users (at least when compared to places like Oklahoma or Alabama) might sound contradictory. But liberals, pacifists, and progressives began establishing outposts in the 1950s and 1960s in Denver, Boulder, Aspen, and other enclaves. They were hippies and musicians and Beat poets lured to the state for its clean air and its expansive open spaces that serve as refuge from urban sprawl and the trappings of city life. They were no less pioneers than the people who came before them, and the resulting mixture is an odd combination of left-wing zealots and hard-core conservatives, with enough influence from both extremes to imbue the majority of middle-grounders with characteristics of both. It's not at all unusual to see gun racks and NRA stickers in Boulder, for instance. With an electorate almost equally divided among Democrats, Republicans, and unaffiliated voters, Coloradans tend to prefer small government and fiscally conservative policies, but also have wide latitude for tolerance and progressivism. It's home to both the sex-change capital of the country in small-town Trinidad as well as former three-term Republican Congresswoman Marilynn Musgrave, who once tried to anoint the year 2007 as the "National Year of the Bible" and who sponsored legislation to outlaw same-sex marriages. In Colorado, you can find both the ultraconservative Focus on the

Family in Colorado Springs and the Allen Ginsberg–founded Jack Kerouac School of Disembodied Poetics at the Naropa Institute in Boulder. It's a place where hippies own firearms and where preachers can be forgiven for buying meth and sex from male prostitutes. This is the land of Hunter S. Thompson and Ted Haggard, and neither belongs here more than the other.

Colorado is therefore uniquely suited to serve as a test case for exactly how much latitude the country's nascent medical marijuana industry can expect. The push and pull between liberal ideals and conservative values is at a near equilibrium, and an innate sense of libertarian ethics that looks with suspicion on government overregulation tends to temper overreaching policy decisions better than in many other areas of the country.

Prior to the Green Rush, pot was literally the least of the state's worries. Possession was decriminalized in 1975 with the maximum penalty for possessing up to an ounce of pot being a meager $100 fine. By 2009, voters outright legalized simple possession in the capital city of Denver, the ski town of Breckenridge, and the high-altitude mountain village of Nederland, meaning they struck down local laws under which to charge those caught with marijuana. Of course, cops can still cite users under the state law.

Colorado even had a medical marijuana statute on its books from 1979 to 1995, although it was apparently never used. At various times, other states had as well, including Alabama and New Mexico, demonstrating that not only was the concept of medical marijuana not new, but neither were statutes that sought to investigate its use. Colorado's effort was a research program that directed the University of Colorado Health Sciences Center to investigate the effects of pot on cancer and glaucoma patients. The chancellor was to report back annually to the state legislature. It seems, however, that no reports were filed in the sixteen years the law was on the books. When the small mountain town of Frisco asked its state senator, Sally Hopper, to revive the law, Hopper moved quickly—she scrubbed it entirely.

Each year, the legislature passes a bill to remove from the books obsolete laws, and Hopper slipped the medical marijuana research law into that bill in 1995, just a year before California voters passed its landmark Compassionate Use Act.

LIKE COLORADO, CALIFORNIA is one of twenty-four U.S. states that allows its citizens to initiate new laws, first by collecting a certain number of signatures on a petition that is submitted to the Secretary of State and then, once those signatures are validated, to vote on the proposed law in a general election. The Compassionate Use Act began as Proposition 215, written by, among others, Dennis Peron, a San Francisco marijuana- and gay-rights activist who earlier had authored that city's Prop P, a nonbinding resolution passed by 79 percent of voters in 1991 that voiced support for medical marijuana laws. Peron was drawn to the cause by his late partner, Jonathan West, who found relief from his AIDS symptoms by smoking pot. Peron's lobbying resulted in the California legislature passing statewide medical marijuana bills, but Gov. Pete Wilson vetoed them. Peron and a tight group of supporters and fellow activists then turned their backs on the politicians and went to the voters through the initiative process. But as is common with citizen initiatives, Peron and his inner circle of activists couldn't afford the often-formidable costs of employing signature gatherers, and as the deadline approached, it seemed they were doomed for failure.

But their effort caught the attention of a group of powerful rich men who would come to bankroll the pro-pot efforts in California and elsewhere, including billionaire philanthropist George Soros; George Zimmer, the founder of Men's Wearhouse; John Sperling, the founder of the University of Phoenix; and Peter Lewis, the retired CEO of Progressive Insurance. A 2002 *Time* magazine article explained at least some of these men's motivations—Sperling told the magazine that he smoked pot to deal with the pain of cancer he suffered in the 1960s, and Lewis said colleagues had described him as a "functional pothead."

"The absurdity of its illegality has been clear to me for some time," Lewis told the magazine. "I learned about pot from my kids and realized it was a lot better than Scotch, and I loved the Scotch. Then I went to my doctor, and he said, 'I'm thrilled. You're drinking too much. You're much better off doing pot than drinking.'"[12]

With their help, Prop 215 passed with 55 percent of the vote.

Inspired by the success, the group funded by these men, Americans for Medical Rights, looked to other states where the polling numbers on reforming marijuana laws were strong and where there were also initiative processes in place so that they could duplicate their success in California. Their sights were set on Colorado, Nevada, Alaska, Oregon, Maine, and Washington, D.C., for the 1998 election.

But rather than roll into Colorado to open arms, bolstered by their historic success in California, AMR encountered resistance, at least from one of the principle indigenous reform groups, the Colorado Hemp Initiative Project, or CoHIP. The organization was formed in the early 1990s to agitate for the legalization of hemp, which is a perfectly harmless and quite useful plant whose only sin in the eyes of mankind is that it is in the same *Cannabis* genus as marijuana. Therefore, it's just as illegal.

The continued criminality of hemp is one of the more ridiculous realities of the prohibition on marijuana. Not only does hemp contains almost no THC—the high-producing cannabinoid—but it has a high concentration of another cannabinoid that counteracts the effect of THC, leading some to call it "anti-marijuana." You could smoke a hemp cigar the size of a telephone pole and never get high. To date, the United States is the only industrial country without an agricultural hemp program, yet it's used here in certain industries. Its usefulness providing fiber for rope and clothing is perhaps its most well-known application, but hemp fibers can also be used in composite plastic panels in automobile manufacturing and to reinforce concrete, among numerous other uses. All hemp products sold in the United States, with an estimated retail value of $70 million in 2006,[13] are imported or made from imported hemp from Canada and France. Meanwhile, law enforcement officers uproot the plants wherever they're found growing wild. DEA statistics note that 98 percent of all "marijuana" plants reported as destroyed by the DEA and local law enforcement each year are in fact "ditchweed": feral hemp plants.[14] Technically, a farmer could apply to grow hemp, but it would require a special DEA permit, which wouldn't be issued unless the applicant agreed to install costly security measures around the farm, such as fences and security cameras. This is presumably to keep anyone stupid enough to try to smoke it from getting a terrible headache.

CoHIP had been trying to do away with this nonsense, partly because it's crazy to continue banning hemp, but also in the hope that, if hemp were to be embraced, marijuana might be one step closer to general acceptance as well. But two separate efforts by CoHIP to petition onto the Colorado ballot a measure that would legalize hemp farming failed to gather the required number of signatures, and attempts to shepherd similar bills through the state legislature also fizzled.

Considering CoHIP's complete lack of success, you'd think it would be a natural partner for a medical marijuana effort. Theoretically, CoHIP was. But Laura Kriho, one of the group's most active and hardest-working activists, said AMR never sought the help of the locals, not only in Colorado but also in the other states they'd targeted for medical marijuana campaigns.

"In three of those states [Alaska, Maine, and Washington, D.C.], the activists already had their own initiatives [for approving the use of medical marijuana] that they were circulating and collecting signatures on," she said. "Then this out-of-state group came in with the big money and just totally stomped all over what they were doing. They didn't ask for their help, didn't ask for their input, didn't want them involved at all. They kept saying 'we'll only work with professionals,' so it was like OK, we're not professionals, I guess. We had to make a lot of noise to get heard."

In the world of pot activists, there is a deeply entrenched sensitivity about one's own turf, a congenital sense of vain propriety that leads everyone to believe that they know best. Cooperation can often be a precious commodity. Very active states can produce dozens of ad hoc organizations with similar names, all jockeying for a meeting with the same politicians and lobbying for new laws that *they* have written, which are always better that what those other guys have come up with, even if they're largely identical. Alliances can be as fragile as on *Survivor*, and conflicts just as petty. Thick skin is a prerequisite to becoming a marijuana activist, and not so much to survive the attacks from anti-pot forces. With so many people vying to save the day for cannabis, there is never a shortage of gadflies in the wings willing to tell you how badly you screwed everything up.

It would be easy to think of Kriho as one of them. We talked over a lunch of tacos and burritos in a strip-mall restaurant in Boulder in the spring of 2010, and even though the closest marijuana retail store was no more than a few blocks in any direction, a reality that was still unbelievable even for many die-hard pot advocates, she sounded as if the marijuana movement had been set back by decades due to recent events rather than moved forward by leaps. But she was worried that an unregulated free-for-all, which had introduced all sorts of ignorant riffraff to the general population as the new faces of medical marijuana—that is, people like Chris Bartkowicz, who didn't have the sense to understand that most people weren't ready to accept a neighbor who bragged about growing hundreds of pot plants next door to their kids' elementary school—would spur a regulatory backlash that would effectively eliminate the gains that had been made. It would later be proved that she had reason to worry.

Kriho is a typical Colorado mountain woman who is not afraid to make noise. In her mid-forties, she has the presence of Mama Cass

Elliot and the strength of conviction of Rosa Parks, for better or worse. Although willing to work with her opponents, compromise is not her default position. I first met her in 1996, when she went on trial in Gilpin County accused of jury nullification—somehow, the longtime marijuana activist who was busily working to change drug laws made it onto a jury in a drug trial. She refused to convict the defendant in an otherwise open-and-shut case of methamphetamine possession, arguing with her fellow jurors that the sentences were too harsh and that rehab was a better solution than jail time for the defendant. No one agreed with her, but Kriho refused to change her vote.

The hung jury resulted in a mistrial and angered the judge enough that Kriho herself was charged, with perjury for allegedly lying during jury selection—she didn't volunteer to the court that she had a deferred sentence for possessing LSD in 1984 and that she was opposed to drug laws—and contempt of court for ignoring the judge's instructions that the jurors not weigh the possible sentence during their deliberations. She was convicted, but the conviction was later overturned on appeal.

The members of CoHIP were at first excited that the Prop 215 moneymen came to Colorado in 1998. But they quickly learned that the language of the amendment they proposed would differ significantly from California's law. For one thing, California allowed patients with *any* medical condition to qualify for marijuana use as long as a physician signed off on it. That meant you could smoke pot for PMS or depression or ringing ears or anything else that bothered you as long as your doctor agreed it would be helpful. The Colorado law restricted the list of qualifying ailments to eight: cancer, HIV/AIDS, cachexia (a form of wasting disease), glaucoma, muscle spasms, seizures, severe pain, and severe nausea. The authors originally specified that marijuana patients could possess up to an ounce of weed before the locals informed them that possession of an ounce was merely a petty offense for everyone, medical patient or not.[15] They upped the amount to two ounces.

But the biggest flaw in the proposed amendment, as Kriho saw it, was that it didn't specifically address distribution—legalizing marijuana use for sick people was significant, but without a system in place through which they could obtain it, it would be almost meaningless. The free-for-all in California served as a good example of why it's smart to outline a distribution scheme—by defining "dispensaries," outlining profit models, and the like—to avoid confusion later. Many of the various medical marijuana laws adopted since 1996 suffer this same problem, leading to all sorts of headaches, creative interpretations, political interference, and wild contortions by suppliers to stay within the letter of the laws, or at least try to, while still getting away with things that aren't specified in them.

Kriho and others hoped to avoid such a mess in Colorado by including clear language in the amendment that specifically addressed distribution—legalizing dispensaries, in other words. But the amendment's authors were worried about explicitly laying out for voters that marijuana would be openly sold for profit in their communities. Protecting wheelchair-bound patients from arrest was one thing, but setting up a new industry based on the sale of an illegal drug that had been branded for decades as particularly dangerous and addictive was another.

"They didn't think it could pass if they put in a distribution system," she said. "What they said to us over and over again was 'Don't worry, [the measure] is symbolic. It doesn't mean anything, so don't worry about the words so much.' We were like, 'It's an amendment to our constitution, it's not symbolic.' We fought with them quite a bit. There are still people who don't like me because of how vocal we were against the language of that law."

Still, when the measure came up for a vote in November 2000, Kriho voted for it along with 53.8 percent of the electorate.[16] Without any specific mention of how medical patients can get their medicine and from whom, Kriho was wary.

"This thing is poorly written," she remembers saying at the time. "There's no distribution system. It's going to cause a lot of problems."

NEARLY TEN YEARS after the law was passed, I encountered what many people in my community might consider to be one such problem—the medical marijuana dispensary that had opened right in the middle of my gym. It was just the sort of thing that had panicked the city council into calling for an emergency ban. These things were popping up everywhere—above yoga studios, across the street from the post office, ringing the campus, and now here, right in the middle of the space where I used to do sit-ups and crunches. There was no escaping them, and it was easy to understand why people who were terrified of marijuana were having fits. Anyone who'd gone on vacation during the month of November would have returned to think Rastafarians had staged a coup.

Technically, the dispensary was next door, a separate business that had subleased what had been an underused fitness room from the gym management. They built walls so that you couldn't access it from inside the gym, and the entrance was from the street. But before they perfected their odor control system, the other members and I lifted weights and ran on the treadmill to the loamy scent of fresh marijuana. I didn't mind if only because it was fun to watch those who weren't familiar with the smell secretly whiffing their armpits trying to figure out what it was and where it came from.

While the dispensary was being built, I hadn't yet fully formed my plans to get into this industry myself and didn't have any idea that I would soon be personally familiar with the challenges of disguising the smell of blooming marijuana, which, incidentally, would come from that very dispensary.

Like the vast majority of such businesses, it was under construction just a few weeks after the Justice Department memo. It was called

Abundant Healing, and the three principal owners were gym rats themselves, which in the early days led to some tense conversations by the bench presses.

"Yeah, I had one guy tell me medical marijuana was a bunch of bullshit, that we were all a bunch of stoners just out here getting wasted," said Drew Brown. "It's a pain. You gotta talk to people like that, though. Most of them have no idea what they're talking about."

In his late thirties, Brown looks like an old-school Irish boxer, a muscular fireplug of a man with short brown hair and a thin beard trimmed to frame the lines of his square jaw. When I mentioned this, he laughed—as it turns out, he's been around boxers his whole life. Brown's father was boxing champ Joe Frazier's sparring partner when Frazier beat Muhammad Ali in the 1971 "Fight of the Century," one of the bouts in Ali's famous comeback circuit after his reinstatement to boxing.

The three owners of Abundant Healing are as unlikely a trio as one can find among business partners, but they are pretty standard in terms of being drawn to the medical marijuana industry from eclectic backgrounds. Brown had bummed around the East Coast doing odd jobs from helping his dad promote boxing in Key West, Florida, to selling diamond rings in a jewelry store in Maryland, "everything I could do to pay the rent." He'd spent a few years in community college when he made his way to Colorado but never completely committed to it. "I was always pulled away by some dream," he said.

In recent years, his dream had been to make enough money to move to Costa Rica and be a surf bum, maybe open up a beachfront board rental kiosk and spend the day teaching tourists to ride the waves. So far, the dream hadn't gotten off the ground—he'd never been to Costa Rica and doesn't know how to surf, but more important, he wasn't making any money. For a while, he made a decent living in construction and as a roughneck on oil rigs up in Garfield County, but it was brutal, taxing work and he quit in frustration after crushing his hand between a pipe and a rock. Finally, his friend Joey

Simental lured him back to Fort Collins and convinced him to trade in his hard hat to make a living with a substance he'd known intimately since he was seventeen.

"I love marijuana," Brown said. "I've always loved it. Marijuana lightens the room."

Compared to Brown, forty-five-year-old Simental is the one who looks like a surfer freshly minted from the beaches of the North Shore, with the deep coconut skin of a native Hawaiian and a laid-back "hey, dude" inflection, but he's actually of Hispanic descent and hails from the Emerald Triangle. He comes from a long line of pot cultivators who run a few illegal acres near Ukiah in Mendocino County. His dad and uncles, all former Marines and Vietnam vets, bought about twenty acres in 1972 so that their families would have a nice spread of land to use for camping and to get away from the hustle of living in Oakland. They soon found that the land was good for something else as well. During harvest season, Simental's aunts would spend the day trimming pot while the men would pull security and guard the forest. Simental played in the woods with his younger brother and sister and a smattering of cousins.

"To us, they were just trees," he said of the towering pot plants that, when grown outdoors, can reach well beyond Christmas tree height. But as he got older, he began paying more attention. He grew up knowing pot the way an Iowa farm boy knows corn, but he didn't move directly into the family business. Simental went on to study energy physics at Colorado State University in Fort Collins and later got a degree in finance. He plans to get a law degree in the future.

Simental and Brown met at the gym and became fast friends, pumping iron and smoking weed. When the Green Rush began, deciding to go into business was natural. "Between me and Drew, I don't know anyone who knows pot as well as we do," Simental said. "It was a no-brainer."

At that time, dispensaries in Colorado could be as lit-up as an ESPN Zone or as sketchy as an underground gambling den. Some operators sunk hundreds of thousands of dollars into their operations, while others invested no more than a few hundred, and it showed. Brown and Simental wanted to do it right and open a respectable shop that would appeal not only to their patients, but also to the skeptics. For that, they needed money, and they couldn't have found a more amenable source of it than Dave Schwaab.

Whereas the other two provide the street cred, Schwaab provides the business cred. A former employee of computer giant Hewlett-Packard, Schwaab made enough money to retire early when he branched out to develop his own data storage system, a slim, lightning-quick external hard drive not much bigger than an iPod. Like the others, he was a gym member and a lifelong casual smoker who was more than happy to come out of early retirement to get into a fast-growing, embryonic industry. Schwaab is mild-mannered, with a strong resemblance to a bespectacled Christopher Lloyd in *Back to the Future*, often found sporting Hawaiian shirts and jeans behind the counter.

Abundant Healing opened for business in January 2010, within weeks of its inception. Except for the words *medical marijuana* embossed on the front window, it would be difficult to tell what sort of business it is. It's a small space, barely eight hundred square feet, and it's hard to remember that it was once a sweaty fitness room. Smart leather sofas and chairs are scattered in the corners facing a long wooden bar top fronted with high stools. Behind the counter is a decorative display of jars containing non-psychoactive herbs, old-fashioned mortars and pestles, and containers of salves and creams. To one side is a giant aquarium filled with tropical fish, which has proven on more than one occasion to be a hysterical distraction to some of the dispensary's patients, and numerous ferns droop down from the tops of walls that come short of the open ceiling that's criss-crossed with ductwork and piping. It's like a modern interpretation of an old-time apothecary, one that's observed by unobtrusive security cameras in the corners.

The pharmacy, as they call it, is in an adjoining room secured with an electronic lock. Only one patient at a time is allowed inside with one of the owners. It's a small room done up in handsome dark colors and dominated by an L-shaped glass display case. If the fragrance doesn't tip you off as to what this business is all about, then the contents of the display case certainly will. Row after row of round gallon-size glass jars display about twenty or thirty different strains of marijuana, all filled with fat little round buds, each labeled with such names as Purple Kush, Mother's Finest, DJ Shorts Blueberry, Sour Diesel, Banana Bread, and so on. One shelf is devoted to "edibles," marijuana-infused food products for people who don't like to smoke, but which pack just as much punch, if not more. There are brownies, Rice Krispies treats, lollipops, shortbread and chocolate chip cookies, and other creations. In one corner is a cooler filled with pot ice cream, and in another, a cooler filled with cannabis soda. Yet another section offers prerolled joints, tiny bottles of cannabis oil and cannabis ointments, and small packets of hash, concentrated powdered resin rich in THC. There is a laptop computer on the counter connected to a lighted electronic magnifier; curious customers can ask to look more closely at one of the buds in the display case, and one of the owners will snap on blue plastic gloves, extract a sample with long metal tongs, and hold it up to the end of the device. What appears on the computer screen is a microscopic forest of clear and milky little protrusions that look like Dr. Seuss trees. These are the trichomes that are filled with cannabinoids, primarily psychoactive THC.

I became a regular at Abundant Healing, stopping in before or after my workouts to chat with the staff and customers and to glean what tips I could as I planned my own modest operation. The proprietors were happy to help, and in fact offered to sell me what I needed most: marijuana plants.

For that, though, I would have to be escorted to another location. Plants aren't grown on site—that operation is far too big to fit into the confines of the small retail space.

Rocky Mountain High

*"Medical marijuana is nothing more than a smokescreen,
an excuse for lifelong pot smokers to get high."*

—Colorado Attorney General John Suthers in a statement
made when he was U.S. Attorney

*"I think people need to be educated to the fact that marijuana
is not a drug. Marijuana is an herb and a flower. God put it here.
If He put it here and He wants it to grow, what gives the
government the right to say that God is wrong?"*

—Willie Nelson

In the summer of 2009, I was quietly living a typical suburban American life. I had a house on a peaceful tree-lined street in a quiet part of Fort Collins, two SUVs in the garage, a smart and beautiful wife, and a twelve-year-old son I loved spending time with. My days as a war correspondent, which could find me negotiating my well-being with Sierra Leonean warlords or talking my way through an embattled checkpoint in Kosovo, were mostly in the past, and I was making a living as a freelance journalist and author. The economy was in shambles and my profession—journalism—was in even more of a free-fall than usual. As I drove by the pot dispensaries that began cropping up on College Avenue, the main drag through Fort Collins,

I gave no real thought to the fact that I was living at what was quickly becoming ground zero in America's latest and most robust debate about the legalization of pot. After all, I had no medical need that required me to smoke pot, and not since my days as a college dropout in North Carolina had I felt the desire to light up for fun. In fact, I had never given a single serious thought to Colorado's medical marijuana law since the day I voted to include it as part of the state constitution nine years before, in 2000.

But that changed one day as I sat in a Denver cafe with some media friends and we were all griping morosely about the state of our industry. Just as selling real estate or manufacturing cars, making a buck as a writer or photographer was proving to be tougher than usual.

The benefits of being a journalist have rarely ever been financial, but 2009 proved especially brutal. Newspapers from coast to coast were collapsing under their own weight. The immediacy and low overhead of the Internet had rendered the old broadsheets nearly obsolete and the landscape of my profession was filled with their former employees wandering, unemployed, from door to door looking for work, just like my friends at the café that day.

When I stepped out of newspapers to pursue a career as a freelance writer, there was still some romance in it, sort of like deciding to give up your nine-to-five office job to move to the Caribbean to hunt for sunken treasure. It was a risky endeavor, in other words, trading the security of a regular paycheck for the uncertainty of being a scribe for hire. The payoff, of course, was freedom and adventure and the license to investigate and write about whatever I wanted, and over the years I'd managed to cobble together enough work to maintain it. Now, however, I faced competition from people who'd had the freelance lifestyle thrust on them because their newspapers went out of business. When I began my career as a writer in 1993, there were some 430,000 newspaper employees across the country; by the time I sat down with my coffee to survey the landscape in 2009, there were about 275,000 and the number was dwindling.[1] Most of the losses had come in the previous twelve months, including the almost 150-year-old *Rocky Mountain News*, which closed earlier that year. Overnight, it seemed, identifying yourself as a "freelance writer" was like admitting that you couldn't find a real job.

If there was any consolation, it was that I was far from alone. From July 2008 to July 2009, 5.5 million Americans lost their jobs and 9 million more faced foreclosure. In Colorado, unemployment doubled over three years to 7 percent and the governor had to cut a billion dollars out of the 2010–2011 budget. Across the state, potholes grew to axle-crushing depth, commercial vacancies gathered dust, and universities hiked tuition in response to funding shortfalls. Local communities tightened their belts by closing parks, cutting library hours, and turning off public fountains to save on the water bill. Cities from Bangor to Barstow were in the same boat; there wasn't a politician in the country that didn't have job creation and economic stimulation at the top of his or her to-do list. There was barely enough money to tip the waitresses, as a former photographer discovered while rooting around in his wallet for spare change that fateful day in the Denver café. What fluttered out instead was a folded red card with the words *medical marijuana* printed across the top.

"What's this?" I asked. "You're a medical marijuana patient?"

"Yup," he said. "Well, no. I mean, it's not like I'm sick or anything, but I was doing a story last year about this guy who grows marijuana for some dispensaries around here and I decided that I smoke enough pot that I might as well get the card. Now I get all my weed from a dispensary."

He explained that the guy kept a warehouse not far from where we sat, filled with "forty or fifty pot plants *this high*," and that he bragged about making several hundred thousand dollars a year.

"*That's* the business we ought to be in," he said, tucking the card back into his wallet.

A little bell dinged in the back of my head. Indeed, why not?

"So that's legal, what that guy does?" I asked.

"Yeah, I think so."

"And what did you have to do to get that card?"

He explained the process and it sounded simple. There are eight qualifying illnesses in the law, including a few that are easy to fake and hard to disprove. Like "pain" and "nausea." I've had both, I thought. Reading the fine print on the license, I saw that it declared the holder to have "a debilitating medical condition that the patient may address with the medical use of marijuana." I wondered if there was any hope of faking my way through a doctor's appointment with a straight face while trying to convince him that any one of my getting-older aches and pains—random back spasms, cricked neck—were "debilitating." If so, I knew I could find a pot doctor in the back pages of the local alternative newspaper and be legal the same day. The doctor's recommendation granted me the right to buy pot, but my interest was in that it also allowed me to grow it. Just by signing the approval, he would bestow upon me the constitutional right to grow as many as six cannabis plants, three of which could be flowering at once. Since I wouldn't be tempted to smoke any myself, it would be a 100 percent profitable operation once I recouped whatever overhead was involved. I almost regretted that I'd given up pot so long ago, back during the fateful summer in 1991 when no amount of trying could make me overcome what Hunter S. Thompson called The Fear, a gripping, paranoid paralysis of mind and body that was totally unlike everyone else's experience of getting stoned. I hated it for myself but always harbored a secret jealousy of those who enjoyed it.

But the truth is, I hadn't given pot much thought at all in the previous twenty years. Since the summer of my experimentation, I'd developed an almost perfectly balanced ambiguity about the topic. I didn't care if it was legal or illegal for recreational use. I didn't use it, so I didn't really dwell on it. I happily voted in favor of the medical marijuana law in 2000 because it seemed like a no-brainer—if I didn't object to recreational smoking, why would I object to medicinal smoking?

I also voted yes knowing full well that people would try to exploit it for nonmedical reasons, although I had no idea at the time that I would be one of them. I simply assumed it to be true since all the people pushing for its passage were the same usual suspects who supported hemp farming and decriminalization and outright legalization. You can't be a reporter in a community for very long before you're able to identify the cannabis activists no matter how hard they try to cover their real agenda with a clever ploy. *Good for them*, I remember thinking when I marked my ballot; *maybe they can get a win for a change*.

Naturally, I had no idea how much of a win it would turn out to be. Voters passed a simple law, but one that contained a massive but well-concealed loophole that would play a significant role nearly a decade later: The law makes no mention of *how* medical marijuana patients are expected to actually obtain their marijuana.

Here's how it's been creatively interpreted by dispensary owners: According to the law, if a patient either can't grow marijuana for himself or just doesn't want to, he can designate someone else to do it for him, a person called a caregiver. A caregiver can be anyone eighteen or older who lives in Colorado, and he or she is transferred the patient's "right" to grow up to six plants.

The loophole is that it doesn't limit the number of patients a single caregiver can care for, meaning that a caregiver could theoretically "care for" a hundred patients and have the legal cover to grow six hundred plants. And since there's nothing in the law preventing the caregiver from selling it to legal patients, he or she stands to become a millionaire, especially since the law doesn't specify a requirement to pay taxes on the revenue—another huge loophole.[2] In 2004, the Colorado Department of Public Health and Environment, the state agency that runs the medical marijuana registry that issues the red cards, tried to close the "unlimited patients" loophole by limiting caregivers to no more than five. It was a completely arbitrary number, picked during a closed-door meeting, which should have been open to public input. The number five came at the prodding of the DEA, which likely foresaw the possibility of marijuana Walmarts on the horizon.

In 2007, a few years after the closed-door meeting that established this limit, a medical marijuana advocacy organization called Sensible Colorado sued the state to overturn the rule on behalf of patient Damien LaGoy, a Denver man suffering from HIV and hepatitis C. He argued that the limit was unconstitutional since none is mentioned in the state law and that any new rules are required to be open to public debate. LaGoy argued that under the five-patient limit he couldn't use his caregiver of choice, a person he trusted to have a reliable supply of quality medicine, because the caregiver already had too many patients. A judge agreed, blasting the agency for being "very unfair" to the state's medical patients, considering no one at the health department evaluated any scientific evidence when setting what he called a "capricious" limit.[3]

As I sat in the café that day in the summer of 2009, drowning out the chatter at the table to turn over this nugget of a plan in my head, I had no idea how perfect the timing was. In less than a week, the health department would officially abandon the idea of imposing a patient cap on caregivers, which they continued to weigh even after the 2007 lawsuit. Officially, their decision not to act removed statewide barriers that stood in the way of an entirely new industry unique in the history of the United States—for-profit retail sales of marijuana.

The only thing obstructing my path—and those of thousands others in the state—would be the feds. But with the timing of the marijuana gods, President Obama's Justice Department took care of that roadblock just three months later.

FUTURE HISTORIANS LOOKING to pinpoint the exact moment when marijuana and its attendant horde of flamboyant enthusiasts burst from the shadows and into the mainstream of the American conscience will circle the date October 19, 2009.

That's when Deputy Attorney General David W. Ogden delivered that now-famous memo to the Justice Department's ninety-three U.S. Attorneys, the federal prosecutors who are assigned to every judicial district in the country and the U.S. territories.

The memo advised federal prosecutors to reconsider using their limited resources chasing and prosecuting pot smokers who were "in clear and unambiguous compliance with existing state laws providing for the medical use of marijuana.

"For example," it read, "prosecution of individuals with cancer or other serious illnesses who use marijuana as part of a recommended treatment regimen consistent with applicable state law, or those care-givers in clear and unambiguous compliance with existing state law who provide such individuals with marijuana, is unlikely to be an efficient use of limited federal resources."

There was much more to it, but many people stopped reading right there once the memo was posted on the Internet and e-mailed to every pothead in the world. Their interpretation was simple: Obama just legalized pot.

Of course, he did no such thing, but that was the essence of what many people took the memo to mean. And once the notion was fixed in the brains of those who had been underground for so long, there was no turning back. Not since George Washington grew hemp at Mount Vernon did the nation's estimated 25 million annual pot smokers hold a president in such high esteem. "Yes We Cannabis" became the new rallying cry.

Even when the memo was read correctly as merely a suggestion for federal prosecutors (not as a new official policy, and certainly not as a law), it was momentous news—at that point thirteen states had laws on their books allowing seriously ill people to obtain and use pot for relief from their symptoms (New Jersey would join the club in January 2010). But because none of the state laws affected federal law, they did nothing to relieve a suffering patient's biggest symptom of all—fear of a raid by the DEA. The country's top cops seemed to feel that voters had given Washington, D.C., the finger by enacting laws that completely contradict its stance, which is that marijuana is not only extremely dangerous and addictive, but also that it has no accepted medical use. Ever since California passed its law in 1996, the White House and the DEA had stepped up the War on Drugs against users of this particular narcotic for this specific reason. After all, marijuana remained in the same category of controlled substances as heroin and LSD, drugs that are deemed simply irreconcilable with civilized life. The feds weren't about to reverse course on marijuana, even though many read the Ogden memo to mean just that.

Others, like Denver's DEA Special Agent in Charge Jeff Sweetin, read it completely differently, paying particular attention to a section that was skipped over by many people on first reading—the part that reads, "This guidance regarding resource allocation does not 'legalize' marijuana or provide a legal defense to a violation of federal law."

"It says in there, this creates no defense," Sweetin said. "We do what we want, we prosecute what we want, based on guidance, the law, and discretion."

Still, there was no denying that the memo was a crack in the government's defenses, one that the marijuana movement took full advantage of. If nothing else, the hordes of ganjapreneurs who suddenly sank their life's savings into grow lights and hydroponic gardens provided safety in numbers. Medical marijuana might not be used as a defense in a federal case, but it could at least be used as a shield on the battlefield. Smart investors realized they just had to keep a lower profile than their more flamboyant competitors to increase their odds of staying off Sweetin's radar. As long as there was some dimwit willing to go on TV to show off his crop and practically give his address, you could hope that the DEA would be busy with someone other than you.

In that first headlong rush, it was easy to lose sight of something important: If given enough breathing room, Colorado had the chance to prove to the world that it could implement a sensible and responsible system for providing relief to people suffering terrible illnesses with a natural, renewable, nonlethal, and nonaddictive substance without destroying the fabric of society, as critics fear. We could create jobs, economic growth, and badly needed tax revenue for those parks and universities. We could lead the way to overturning senseless rules that keep it from those who need it. It was easy to forget that in more than half the states, those who grew marijuana to relieve their pain or someone else's didn't have even a semblance of legal maneuvering room. There are no confused cops in those states, no conflicting laws to make them question right from wrong when it comes to any use of marijuana. The laws in the permissive states might mean nothing in light of federal law, but they at least provide some hope to cling to—anyone busted outside those borders has none.

MOST DRUG RAIDS go something like this: Early in the morning, when the suspects are as groggy as possible—or, better yet, still asleep—ten or fifteen cops dressed in black body armor and armed with specialized assault rifles, shotguns, and stun grenades trot silently across the lawn and through the flower bed. Sometimes they'll knock and shout, "Police!" but when they expect a confrontation or suspect that evidence could be destroyed, they'll bash in the door with a metal battering ram. With the door open, they stampede through the house, guns at the ready, flooding inside like water through a breached dam. The supervisors with the search warrant usually hang back until the target building is secured, generally after much shouting and chaos. The idea is to move swiftly and to cause as much fear and disorientation as possible, something that's not hard to achieve with suspects who are usually paranoid to begin with and who, just moments earlier, were snoozing peacefully before snapping awake to the sight of a masked soldier screaming "Police!" from behind the barrel of an automatic weapon. Done right, a raid can jangle everyone in the house so thoroughly that they're immobilized with dread. They're in handcuffs before they can even think about flushing any drugs or grabbing a pistol to shoot it out with the invaders.

Bernie Ellis avoided a scene like that because his house is remote and it's not easy for an army of men to sneak up on quietly, but also because it's hard to beat him out of bed. With 187 acres of Tennessee farmland to tend, the fifty-two-year-old is usually among the first people in his county to wake up in the mornings. And on one unlucky morning in the summer of 2002, it was no different. For most of the thirty-plus years he's lived at Trace View, as he named his spread, he bathed in the creek because his farmhouse didn't have running water. He'd be up with the dawn, boiling water on the wood stove for a warm creekside shower before rinsing off in the icy waters that flowed past the house. It wasn't so bad in the summer, but in the winter, his wet hair would often freeze before he got back inside. After a breakfast that usually included toast and jam he'd made himself from the abundant berries growing on his land, he was off to tackle the farm's myriad and never-ending chores.

And on August 28, 2002, seven years before the Ogden memo would be drafted, there was work to do. Brambles and weeds were choking the berry bushes and needed to be cleared. Ellis was riding a tractor first thing in the morning, towing a Bush Hog mower chewing up the underbrush, when he saw a pair of helicopters painted in the distinct black and gold of the Tennessee Highway Patrol flying fast and low over the treetops, headed for his farmhouse.

Ellis knew what was happening as soon as he saw the helicopters— the Tennessee Marijuana Eradication Force was raiding him. And he suspected he knew why. A few days before, some stoner showed up at the farm asking to buy pot. "Have you ever known me to sell pot to anyone?" he asked the man before turning him away empty-handed.[4]

It was true. Ellis did not sell pot. But he grew it and gave it away for free to some select people, a handful of terminally ill cancer and AIDS patients. And he certainly used it himself. Smoking a joint, he found, eased the pain of his degenerative joint disorder and his fibro-myalgia. Without pot, he could barely sleep for an hour at night, constantly awakened by pain in his bones and muscles. Scattered here and there, about twenty or twenty-five maturing marijuana plants grew hidden among the farm's trees and other foliage. Some were nearly six feet tall. And scattered around the house and garden— where he also grew roses, carnations, lettuce, and tomatoes—were about a hundred immature marijuana plants, little ten-inch seedlings cut from the mother plants that would grow into genetically identical specimens. "Cloning" marijuana in this way is a means of replicating a particularly good or high-yielding plant without having to start from seed; Ellis had only recently begun experimenting with cloning, and his mistake was in rooting them in plain sight around the house, where they would be obvious to anyone who knew what they looked like. Ellis assumed the stoner had been peeved that he hadn't sold him any weed and tipped off the cops that they were growing right next to the begonias. If so, it's another way in which the raid deviated from what's typical; generally, the cops are alerted to a suspected drug dealer when he sells pot to someone, not when he refuses to.

There were other major differences between Ellis and others who've been raided throughout the past forty years of the War on Drugs. The graying man with a beard and a slight potbelly farmed mainly as a hobby; he made his living as a consultant epidemiologist specializing in public health programs. His resume includes research management stints at the National Institutes of Health and the Centers for Disease Control and Prevention, and he's worked for the state governments of Tennessee, New Mexico, and Wyoming.

Working with the National Cancer Institute, he developed smoking cessation programs used by many doctors to wean their patients off tobacco, and he was the principal consultant for public education around the release of Nicorette, a nicotine gum used to help people quit smoking. His research for the previous twenty years has focused on substance abuse (Ellis himself is a recovering alcoholic), and he helped develop and manage treatment and monitoring programs in Wyoming, Alabama, and New Mexico. Officers searching his house even found documents from the Republican governor of New Mexico, Gary Johnson,[5] asking for Ellis's help in setting up a state-run marijuana production facility, in anticipation of a new law that would allow marijuana to be used by medical patients for certain serious illnesses, a law Johnson supported.

A few of Ellis's professional colleagues across the country knew that he both used marijuana and provided it for grievously ill patients, a calling that grew from his experience as the former program director for the Tennessee AIDS Project. For years, Ellis supplied dying people with marijuana to ease their end-of-life suffering just as it eased the symptoms of his illnesses.

By doing so, he risked everything. Tennessee does not have a medical marijuana law.

For some of his patients, it helped with the side effects of treatment—pot is particular good at quelling nausea, which is important for people who must take oral medications—and for others, it provided a spiritual preparation for transition into the afterlife, one of marijuana's uses that Ellis learned from Native American friends in New Mexico. He never accepted payment, even if someone were to offer it. At the time, Ellis was helping four terminally ill patients, three of whom died within months of the raid on his farm.

Ellis was cooperative with the state and federal agents that day. Men on ATVs found and uprooted the mature plants while others dug up what he called the "embarrassing midget plants" around the garden. They found manicured marijuana in the house and, as they would in any farmhouse in America, a few guns. They confiscated those, along with his computers and some paperwork.

But Ellis wasn't arrested, at least not that day. Part of the reason could be that the agents weren't sure exactly how to charge him. He admitted to cultivating marijuana, which was obvious, but without any evidence that he sold the product of his harvests, it was hard to label him a "drug dealer." The only deals Ellis appears to have made were karmic.

It would be some time, however, before he would see any returns on that investment. Three months after the raid, Ellis was charged in federal court with manufacturing more than one hundred marijuana plants, a felony that carried a mandatory minimum sentence of five years in prison. The presence of weapons added another possible five years. It didn't matter that most of the plants seized from the farm were immature and incapable of producing any intoxicating effect; in the eyes of the law, marijuana is marijuana. A seedling is just as illegal as a brick of manicured pot. The charges also qualified his beloved farm for seizure under federal civil asset forfeiture laws, meaning he would be evicted and the land sold. Proceeds would go to the U.S. Department of Justice and distributed to the DEA and the local task force that assisted in the raid.

While Ellis hired a lawyer and attempted to work out a deal that would save his farm and keep him out of jail, word of the bust spread to corners of the country that Ellis didn't even know he'd touched. Hundreds of letters of support flooded the chambers of the judge who would hear his case. They came from patients and their family members, scientists, university professors, physicians, and even politicians. One even came from the White House. Gregory L. Dixon, the former administrator of a program called Drug-Free Communities within the George W. Bush Administration's Office of National Drug Control Policy, was a friend of Ellis's, and his request for leniency was his last official correspondence before he retired from his position.

Other letters were no less impactful despite their writers' more modest pedigrees. Ellis's neighbor of thirty-four years, Ellen Humphrey, wrote on behalf of her late husband, Junior, who died from lung cancer: "When a man like Junior is in pain, he needs whatever it takes to help him stop hurting. The marijuana that Bernie Ellis provided to Junior helped make him more comfortable during the last months of his life [and] made it possible for Junior to rest and to sleep, and it helped him keep his appetite up. Before he died, Junior said that he was thankful that his neighbor had been able to give him some marijuana. As Junior's widow, I also want to say that I appreciated the gesture, and the help that Bernie Ellis was able to provide to my husband before he died."

Some credit Ellis with helping save their lives, such as Maggie Aderhold, who survived ovarian cancer with his help.

"There were a number of nights when I wasn't sure I would pull through my cancer," she wrote in a letter to the court. "But the marijuana that Bernie provided helped me deal with the awful nausea that came with the cancer treatments, and it also helped me sleep when I was uncomfortable and in pain. With the love, the prayers and the help from people like Bernie, I was able to survive my cancer and to be here today."[6]

Those letters, and scores like them, had an impact. During sentencing, U.S. District Court Judge William Haynes qualified Ellis for special sentencing consideration under what's called a "safety valve," allowing the judge to consider extenuating circumstances under certain guidelines.[7] Rather than five to ten years in prison, Ellis was sentenced to four years of probation (later reduced to two), eighteen months of which were required to be served in a Nashville halfway house. The matter of his farm forfeiture would take years more to resolve; finally in December 2009, the government agreed to settle with Ellis for a twenty-five-acre parcel of his land, worth about $150,000 to $200,000.

After years of courtroom battles, Ellis, now sixty, is "flat broke" from nearly $100,000 in legal fees and an estimated $600,000 in lost work, but he kept most of his land and stayed out of jail. In terms of outcomes for the target of a drug-enforcement raid, few go better—many are handed mind-blowing sentences for far less than Ellis was charged with. Consider Will Foster in Oklahoma, the man sentenced to ninety-three years in prison for growing roughly the same number of mature plants as Ellis; Foster didn't sell his pot either, but used it to alleviate the pain of chronic arthritis.[8] Foster was eventually paroled, but not after years of suffering behind bars and in court.

When Ellis was arrested, he joined a not-so-exclusive club, one whose annual enrollment (or reenrollment in many cases) has more than doubled since 1980. In 2006, when pot arrests set a record of 847,864, smokers were being locked up or cited at a rate of nearly two per minute. Since President Nixon officially declared the War on Drugs in 1971, the United States has spent $1 trillion waging it and arrested some 17 million marijuana users. So as disheartened as he may be at losing his life's savings and a portion of his land to the government—to say nothing of his ability to ease the pain of those with life-threatening illnesses—Ellis could consider himself quite lucky. Compared to Jimmy Montgomery, the paraplegic who lost a leg in prison serving his life sentence for possession of two ounces of pot, Ellis got off easy.

At least his ordeal hadn't cost him any body parts.

"I'M A LITTLE nervous," my friend Nick said, leaning toward me on the secondhand sofa where we sat with someone's bulldog sprawled out asleep on the floor between our feet. "He just rejected someone. I was going to go with 'anxiety,' but I think I should come up with another story."

Anxiety wouldn't do it, I agreed, eavesdropping on a conversation between a teenage girl and an old man sitting on folding chairs nearby. She was telling him that she was born without cartilage in her spine and had developed scoliosis. His problem was a blood disease I'd never heard of. Both cases seemed serious. Nick needed more than a worried mind if he was going to convince the pot doctor that he was debilitated.

"Yeah, I think you at least have to be in pain," I said, scanning a sheet of paper in my hand with a short list of ailments printed on it. Most are pretty grievous and hard to fake. Cancer and AIDS, for instance, and something called cachexia, which I learned later is a wasting disease. Neither of us wanted to pretend to have it if only because we weren't sure how to pronounce it. The one providing the most leeway was "severe pain." Nick is a rock climber who makes adventure films for a living, so I suggested that perhaps a life of mountaineering has left him with achy joints.

"What should I say about this?" he said, holding up an empty bottle of Restoril, a sleeping aid he was prescribed a few years ago for insomnia. We both brought similar props to back up our stories for when it came time to make our cases; mine was an empty bottle of Ambien.

"Tell him your joints are so bad you need it to sleep, but you want to try something natural."

He weighed the idea, then gave a satisfied nod and got up to see the doctor. I waited with the bulldog, eyeing the roomful of patients toting personal medical files, X-rays, or empty pill bottles of their own. Most of them looked like I did: a little disheveled but in need of nothing more medicinal than a cup of coffee. For a clinic filled with people claiming to be in constant pain and discomfort, they were a remarkably peppy bunch, nursing their Starbucks and chatting amiably with one another. If all went as planned, we'd have entered the clinic as shiftless criminals in the eyes of the law and exit as freshly minted medical marijuana patients.

Actually, the place wasn't yet a "clinic" but an empty old home on the outskirts of Boulder that had until recently been a thrift store. On that day, Candy's Vintage Clothing & Costumes was still undergoing its transformation into a medical marijuana dispensary to be called The Med Shed, but right then, it was just an unnamed, unfinished business filled with people waiting to see a doctor who—they hoped—would recommend they smoke pot to alleviate their illnesses. Handymen worked around us, painting the walls and installing the water fountains. There weren't enough folding chairs or thrift-store sofa space to accommodate everyone, so late arrivals made do sitting cross-legged on the floor. More people arrived by the minute.

Navigating the throng was a bearded man named Pony in jeans, a T-shirt, and a ball cap; he was one of the owners who showed up that Saturday morning to find more of a crowd than he could handle. Dozens of people had responded to an e-mail blast or Facebook alert or whatever means he'd employed to announce The Med Shed's grand opening that day. Trouble was, The Med Shed wasn't ready to open. The copier for processing paperwork was out of ink and there weren't enough pens for more than two patients to fill out their forms at a time. The most obvious shortcoming was the lack of pot; there was none in evidence, making many of us wonder why they bothered to hold a grand opening if there was nothing to sell.

But pot wasn't necessarily the main attraction—the doctor was. At that particular moment in history—the week before Thanksgiving 2009, a mere month after the Ogden memo—there were so many marijuana stores opening on so many different street corners in so many cities throughout Colorado that it could be hard to muster fresh enthusiasm for yet another, even among die-hard ganja freaks, of which Boulder has no shortage.

No, the reason for the crowd was because Pony had arranged for a mass house call by a physician to churn out medical evaluations and turn the rooms full of illegal drug users into legal patients with the stroke of a pen. The Med Shed was picking up the tab, and *that* was something to get excited about, even if we had to go elsewhere to take advantage of our new status. Such a visit can cost anywhere from $150 to $250 for a three-minute consultation, and getting it for free was a big deal.

The dispensary wasn't doing this just to drum up goodwill; in exchange, patients agreed to designate The Med Shed as their caregiver, in order for the owners to legally cover the marijuana they grew and offered for sale. No one who was offered a free doctor's appointment seemed to balk. All we wanted was the ability to get legal, and going to the pot doctor, whether in Colorado or in any of the other medical marijuana states, is the necessary first step. He or she listens to complaints, checks out any supporting material one might have, and, as long as the symptoms are covered by one of the qualifying illnesses allowed by the law, signs a simple sheet of paper.

That paper becomes the golden ticket to legally buy, use, grow, and possess the substance that has landed millions of Americans in court and behind bars over the decades. The paper is notarized, copied, and mailed along with a check for $90 to the health department, where your name is entered on the official medical marijuana registry. Theoretically, in a few weeks, someone at the health department will issue you an official license about the size of a paycheck with your name on it, just like the one my friend showed me at the coffee shop. It's scored in two places so you can fold it into thirds down to the size of a business card and keep it in your wallet. This document, called a "red card," is what you show to cops, caregivers, dispensary clerks, and bemused friends to prove that you are qualified to do something that most Americans haven't been able to do in their lifetimes without risking their freedom and property: buy and cultivate pot.

In practice, though, the clerks at the health department in charge of the paperwork were so buried under new applications that it could take up to nine months to get the red card in the mail. Just as you can easily identify the date when marijuana laws got turned upside down, you can also pinpoint when the health department got flooded with paperwork; nearly a year later, the agency's Web site that tracks monthly medical marijuana statistics was still frozen in time on November 2009, as if marking the exact moment of some cataclysm. Five years before the big boom, there were only 512 patients on the registry, a small enough amount to easily keep track of; by the summer of 2010, 110,000 people had sent in their checks and their paperwork, the majority of them within the previous nine months.[9]

Until the license arrives sometime in the distant future, the notarized paper with the doctor's signature is good enough to buy pot. And so tens of thousands of Coloradans carry these creased and dog-eared papers in their purses or billfolds like some sort of raggedy Third World proof of citizenship. Less flashy than an official license, for sure, but it gets the job done.

GETTING THE DOCTOR to agree to recommend marijuana was more than just a rubber-stamp formality. A prospective patient had to at least follow the script dictated by the state of Colorado itself and claim to suffer one of the eight qualifying illnesses, which were listed right there on the form that awaited the physician's signature. The woman who was denied a recommendation, and who caused Nick to rethink which illness he suffered from the most, had tried to argue that smoking pot helped her cope with stress. While that may have been the case, and might have been approved had she been in California, where the law gives doctors greater leeway to recommend pot for anything they feel it might help, stress is not on the list in Colorado. The doctor had no choice but to turn her down, and she left The Med Shed in tears.

I was confident that Nick would succeed with the achy-joints idea we'd agreed upon because my own appointment a few minutes before had gone perfectly, even though no one had provided the physician with so much as a semiprivate space to interview his patients. I sat next to him on a folding chair in the middle of the room, surrounded by eavesdroppers. Our medical complaints would be aired communally. Luckily, there was no physical exam or taking of vital signs. It wasn't that sort of appointment.

I'd rehearsed my story all morning: I suffered from a painful back as a result of an extremely uncomfortable transatlantic flight in 2001. The backrest was broken, the flight was crowded, and I slept for about six hours jammed into an awkward position, forced into a cramped little space by the heavy woman next to me who overflowed her seat. Halfway through the flight, I also managed to crack a molar on a peanut, which led me to favor one side of my jaw when I chewed. A dentist told me the screaming headaches I suffered were probably caused by temporomandibular joint disorder caused by the broken tooth. I hobbled off the plane with a swollen face, looking like I'd had to be subdued by the flight attendants. My jaw fixed itself, but my back has never been the same.

Because it was entirely true, the story seemed very reasonable as I ran through it in my head, but saying it out loud in front of this doctor, I realized how ridiculous it sounded. Yet there was no denying that for several years, sitting, standing, or lying in any one position for too long could be agonizing. I went to a general practitioner, who prescribed the Ambien to help me sleep through the night, and she referred me to a specialist, since the injury reoccurred on my way back from several weeks in Africa. She was worried I'd developed some exotic disease. The specialist ran bone scans and blood tests and took X-rays, but could find nothing wrong. He suggested exercise and yoga.

"Did any of that help?" The Med Shed doctor asked.

"Not really," I replied. "Sometimes it helps for a little while, but sometimes it makes it worse."

I also described a brief trip to Amsterdam during which I took a few puffs of a friend's joint and then slept like a baby.

"Oh, so you've used marijuana for this," he said.

"Only that once," I answered. "Since I was in Amsterdam, I thought it would be a good time to try it without getting into trouble."

That last bit was an especially clever flourish, I thought; despite how suspicious my tale sounded, I didn't want to give the doctor any reason to suspect that he was giving some stoner a legal pass, even though three Advil and a glass of wine are all I need to sleep through the night. If I didn't spend six or ten hours a day typing cross-legged and hunched over my laptop like an orangutan, I'm sure I could cure my back pain for good.

He checked the box for "severe pain" and signed his name at the bottom. It was the only way I ended up knowing his name because he never introduced himself. The appointment took four and a half minutes.[10]

"Good luck," he said as the next patient took my seat.

With that, I was legal. Or at least I thought I was. Truthfully, I wasn't 100 percent sure. It still seemed unlikely that the ratty paper I folded up and put in my pocket would be enough to keep me out of prison if I were caught growing marijuana in my home, which was shaping up to be my plan. I wasn't asked about any other drugs I might be taking, or asked to detail my medical history, or required to sit before a panel of psychiatrists to prove my sanity.

I knew my challenges weren't over, though. There *was* one group of people I had to convince I wasn't crazy: my family.

⋆ 3 ⋆

Reefer Madness, Pot Peddlers, and Dope Fiends:
How Pot Became Poison

"The fear of Marihuana must be hammered deeply into the hearts of our people, and the country must be galvanized into action to prevent further spread of this new form of mental slavery —Marihuana smoking."

—Harry J. Anslinger, the country's first drug czar[1]

There's a scene in the 2008 movie *Pineapple Express* where Dale and Saul, two chronic stoners on the run from a gang of thugs, get themselves some much needed cash by selling ultra-high-grade pot to a trio of kids who look to be about twelve years old. They take the kids to an alley behind a liquor store and toke up out of a gallon-size Ziploc bag full of Pineapple Express—a strain that Saul describes as "the dopest dope I've ever smoked"—instructing the kids, once they're good and stoned, to empty their pockets of cash in exchange for as much pot as they can grab with one hand. Depending on your viewpoint, either the scene is a funny bit of proof that potheads *can* creatively problem solve while simultaneously spreading the love, or it's a perfect encapsulation of the sort of family-wrecking threat that marijuana "pushers" pose to the very foundations of our society.

Marijuana is a plant with many mysterious properties, but one of the most intriguing is its ability to elicit reactions in people that range from outright loathing to religious ecstasy. Some think it leads to moral depravity and are convinced it will cause the downfall of society. Others consider it nothing short of a heavenly sacrament, or at the very least an evolutionary blessing from Mother Nature, put here to ease our pain, cure our diseases, and tune us in to the spiritual realm, much like a powerful antenna that can pick up radio waves from around the globe. At its least mythologized, it's a symbol of community—putting a pot leaf sticker on your car is a signal to those in the counterculture that you're part of the 420 kinship.

For most of the past century, pot smokers have been portrayed as either a bunch of nutcases who surround themselves with crystals and Indian dream catchers or as a caste of losers who'd rather get baked and freeload on the backs of the hard workers in society than contribute meaningfully to their communities. Never mind that their ranks include some of the greatest and most inspiring people of our generations, including entrepreneur Sir Richard Branson, Olympic gold medalist Michael Phelps, media mogul Ted Turner, author Stephen King, performer and breast cancer survivor Melissa Etheridge, and President Barack Obama. Regardless, those who've outlawed marijuana and fought to eradicate it are against them and others of lesser accomplishment. Opponents believe pot is a dangerous poison that renders us intellectually defenseless and developmentally stunted, one with a latent power to enslave both body and brain, and one that has no medically redeemable attributes at all. In short: Pot makes you stupid and endangers your health. Without constant vigilance and rigorous eradication efforts, they believe, marijuana use would spread geometrically and threaten not only individuals, but also families and entire communities. It's a message that was borne in the anti-drug temperance-driven hysteria of the 1930s but that is still largely echoed to this very day, despite decades of scientific advancement and quantum leaps in medical knowledge.

The rhetoric against marijuana was given its first nationwide public forum during several hearings before the U.S. House of

Representatives in April 1937. That's when Rep. Robert L. Doughton of North Carolina introduced the Marihuana Tax Act. The country's first drug czar, Harry J. Anslinger—who from 1930 to 1961 was the commissioner of the Federal Narcotics Bureau, a predecessor to the Drug Enforcement Administration—wrote the legislation.

Anslinger, who seemed to sincerely believe that pot was from the devil, makes today's anti-pot activists look like amateurs, and he clearly took his mission to sober up America quite seriously. He had been preparing the tax act for years, amassing a damning body of voluminous evidence against cannabis and its users that a journalist later nicknamed the "Gore Files," which consisted mostly of newspaper clippings, magazine articles, and pulp crime accounts. ("Stop This Murderous Smoke" was a typical headline of the age, appearing over an editorial in *The Tampa Morning Tribune* in 1933.) Anslinger's testimony before the House Ways and Means Committee remains one of the most histrionic condemnations of marijuana on record, blaming it for everything from rape and murder to insanity and suicide. He opened his statements to the committee with the warning that marijuana trafficking had become a cause for the "greatest national concern."

"In medical schools, the physician-to-be is taught that without opium he would be like a one-armed man. That is true, because you cannot get along without opium," he said. "But here we have a drug that is not like opium. Opium has all of the good of Dr. Jekyll and all the evil of Mr. Hyde. This drug is entirely the monster Hyde, the harmful effect of which cannot be measured."

For proof, he turned to the Gore Files and paraded before the committee members one horrible—and supposedly marijuana-induced—act of violence and depravity after another. He told of "seven young men" who terrorized central Ohio with a string of thirty-eight stickups: "They all boast they did those crimes while under the influence of marihuana," he said. Another story from Ohio was of a crook who held up a hotel clerk before killing him: "[H]is defense was that he had been affected by the use of marihuana."

Anslinger counted off the instances, painting a picture of a nation of criminals in the clutches of an insidiously evil drug: In Chicago, two potheads killed a policeman; elsewhere a fifteen-year-old boy was going insane because of his habit; in Baltimore, a man was hanged for a rape committed while he was high; in Colorado, a county sheriff was shot dead by a stoned assailant. The worst mention was of a Florida ax murderer, who brutally killed his entire family—mother, father, two brothers, and sister, leaving only the family dog alive but wounded. "The evidence showed that he had smoke[d] marihuana," Anslinger said.

He testified that pot smokers experience feelings of euphoria and invincibility, of increased strength and stamina. "Some people will fly into a delirious rage, and they are temporarily irresponsible and may commit violent crimes," he said. "Other people will laugh uncontrollably. It is impossible to say what the effect will be on any individual."[2]

Anslinger—whose bald and beefy appearance many modern marijuana advocates have been happy to compare to Benito Mussolini—was actually tempering his comments for an audience of politicians. He was also an avid writer on this topic, and in the summer of 1937 he coauthored an article titled "Marijuana: Assassin of Youth" for *The American Magazine*. It's there where he really took the gloves off, opening his long evisceration of cannabis with a scene in which a young girl, worried about her studies and stoned out of her gourd, leaps to her death from an apartment window. "Thus can marijuana 'solve' one's difficulties," he wrote.

"America now faces a condition in which a new, although ancient, narcotic has come to live next door to us, a narcotic that does not have to be smuggled into the country," he wrote. "This means a job of unceasing watchfulness by every police department and by every public-spirited civic organization. It calls for campaigns of education in every school, so that children will not be deceived by the wiles of peddlers, but will know of the insanity, the disgrace, the horror which marijuana can bring to its victim. And, above all, every citizen should keep constantly before him the real picture of the 'reefer man'— not some funny fellow who, should he take the notion, could walk across the ocean, but—"

The sentence cuts off there for dramatic effect before the article wraps up with a long anecdote about a drug-crazed "reefer man" murdering an innocent shoe-shiner for no reason other than the voices in his head. "That's marijuana!" Anslinger concluded.[3]

Anslinger was not the only one railing against the demonic properties of cannabis, although he was undoubtedly among the most influential. Equally so was William Randolph Hearst, the newspaper baron, who was an avid Anslinger supporter and anti-marijuana zealot. His hatred of pot was probably nurtured by his hatred of Spaniards, Mexicans, and anyone of Latino descent; Hearst's chain of sensational tabloids (as well as those of Joseph Pulitzer and others) were instrumental in fostering hysterical prejudice against Spain and Spanish-speakers during the 1898 Spanish-American war. Later, Hearst turned his ire toward Pancho Villa, the prominent rebel general in the 1910–1920 Mexican Revolution, whose soldiers seized some 800,000 acres of Hearst-owned timberland. (As unlikely as it sounds, there is a pot connection to this: Villa's supporters rewrote the lyrics to the age-old Mexican ditty "La Cucaracha" to slander their enemy, President Victoriano Huerta, a notorious drunk and pothead known as "the cockroach." The new verses sung by Villa's troops included the lines, "The cockroach, the cockroach/cannot walk . . . because he hasn't got any marijuana to smoke.")[4]

Mexicans helped introduce marijuana into the United States when more than a million came to the southwest in the first three decades of the 1900s; since they were regularly depicted as lazy job-stealers in the pages of Hearst's newspapers, it made sense that he would also go after their preferred recreational substance and those who used it. Mexicans weren't the only "drug fiends" Hearst ran down in his pages; "negroes" were just as much of a menace to him, particularly how they supposedly behaved toward whites when they were drunk, high on coke, or stoned, and "heathen Chinese" smoking opium were also no strangers to the Hearst yellow sheets. He ran so many lurid, breathless tales about "dope fiends" that a California judge lauded him on a radio show in 1934 as "the person personally responsible for the greatest service to mankind in exposing the dope menace and educating the public of its evils."[5] A typical Hearst headline ran in the *San Francisco Examiner* in 1923: "Marijuana makes fiends of boys in 30 days: Hasheesh [*sic*] goads users to blood-lust," a story which contained the warning that "marijuana is a shortcut to the insane asylum."[6]

Such sensationalism might have worked well in the newspapers, but it didn't quite translate to film. A year before Anslinger took the stand to testify on behalf of the Marihuana Tax Act, a propaganda film called *Reefer Madness* made its premier. Although he had nothing to do with production of the film, it was essentially Anslinger's hysteria on celluloid. The movie tells the story of Jack and Mae, two pot peddlers who lure high school kids to their apartment for reefer parties. Participants laugh maniacally, go crazy dancing to wild piano music, and grope each other with abandon. The fun times don't last long. They end with Jack murdered at the hands of a stoner who beats him to death with a fireplace poker; innocent, virginal Mary shot and killed while fending off an attempted rape by drug-addled Ralph; once-wholesome teen Jimmy, too high to drive, running a red light and flattening an upstanding citizen with his car; and sexy siren Blanche, whose role in this degenerate enterprise is as a sort of temptress who plies the local jitterbug joints for a new crop of future addicts, leaping to her death from the upper floor of a police station.[7]

Reefer Madness doesn't seem to have been very popular because it wasn't in circulation long, but today, it's the Holy Grail of cult classics among potheads. From the psychotic-looking jazz pianist early in the film, who smokes a joint like an alcoholic slurping spilled bourbon off the bar top to psychotic Ralph telling Blanche to play the piano "faster, *faster!*" until she reaches Bugs Bunny velocity, *Reefer Madness* is now considered to be one of the campiest movies ever made.

But while poorly filmed and grievously overacted, the film dutifully captures the zeitgeist toward weed at a time when the country was coming to grips with all sorts of intoxicants and their effects on citizens, notably opium, cocaine, heroin, and alcohol. The movie even makes reference to Anslinger's later invocation before Congress of the marijuana-crazed ax murderer from Florida, probably his most horrific example of reefer madness leading to wanton killings.

The massacre did happen—a man named Victor Licata killed everyone in his family with an ax on October 17, 1933. And according to most reports, Licata did smoke marijuana. But what Anslinger failed to mention was that Licata was found to be clinically insane, suffering from dementia praecox (which would later be reframed as schizophrenia) with homicidal tendencies.[8] Anslinger's assertion that Licata killed because he smoked pot was baseless.

Yet many historians believe that the conflation of this story and others—most of which could never be proved or disproved because Anslinger's references to them were vague and anecdotal at best—helped win passage of the Marihuana Tax Act, which essentially banned cannabis, a common ingredient in medicinal tonics and other pharmaceutical preparations, by saddling it with a hefty tax and complex red tape. It's worth remembering that in the time before bloggers, there were no checks and balances on the media; newspapers like Hearst's held enormous sway over public opinion and public policy. However, that Anslinger's "evidence" consisted mainly of garish and imprecise news clippings didn't escape the notice of one person who testified in opposition to the bill on the last day of hearings. Dr. William Woodward, a physician and lawyer who represented the American Medical Association, told the committee members that he thought there was "probably" a trend of marijuana abuse in the country, but that Anslinger had produced no hard evidence to say for sure.

"That there is a certain amount of narcotic addiction of an objectionable character no one will deny," Woodward said. "The newspapers have called attention to it so prominently that there must be some grounds for their statements. It has surprised me, however, that the facts on which these statements have been based have not been brought before this committee by competent primary evidence. We are referred to newspaper publications concerning the prevalence of marihuana addiction."

He noted that representatives of the Bureau of Prisons, the Children's Bureau, the Office of Education, and the Public Health Service—all of whom would be able to testify about evidence of a marijuana menace, if one existed—were notably absent from the hearings. In fact, he added that the AMA barely made it to testify because Anslinger's bill, even though it had been in the works for nearly two years, was called the "Marihuana" Tax Act; doctors didn't know cannabis by its then-obscure street name and didn't realize until the last moment that the bill concerned a medicinal substance.

"No medical man would identify this bill with medicine until he read it through, because 'marihuana' is not a drug," Woodward said. "It is a popular term to indicate cannabis, like 'coke' is used to indicate cocaine, and as 'dope' is used to indicate opium."

Woodward was a man before his time, suggesting to the congressmen that, rather than adopt a new law that he deemed to be unenforceable and unnecessary, they amend an existing law that regulated the distribution and use of other narcotics, the Harrison Narcotics Act, to include marijuana. Moreover, he reminded them that the statute that created the Bureau of Narcotics in the first place, adopted in 1930, required the Secretary of the Treasury to assist the states in controlling drug abuse, a state-based solution that Woodward preferred over new broad federal powers. This was a foreshadowing of later arguments used by medical marijuana advocates to protest DEA raids in permissive states.

Finally, he argued that to whatever extent there was a marijuana abuse problem in the United States, it had nothing to do with any medical use; dealing with the problem by effectively outlawing it, even for doctors, was shortsighted, he argued.

"To say . . . that the use of the drug should be prevented by a prohibitive tax, loses sight of the fact that future investigation may show that there are substantial medical uses for cannabis," Woodward said.

That the congressmen were unmoved by the doctor's arguments is an understatement. In fact, he was browbeaten as a sourpuss who was simply "peeved" that the AMA wasn't involved in drafting the legislation. At one point, the chairman accused him of "throwing obstacles in the way" and proposing "nothing whatever to correct the evil that exists."

Woodward wasn't cowed: "You may absolutely forbid the use of cannabis by any physician, or the disposition of cannabis by any pharmacist in the country, and you would not have touched your cannabis addiction as it stands today, because there is no relation between it and the practice of medicine or pharmacy."

In the end, Woodward wasn't even thanked for his testimony.

The Marihuana Tax Act passed easily, and it didn't outlaw pot so much as burden anyone hoping to touch it with an onerous tax and a complicated system of requirements that made it so difficult to comply that it was effectively banned in the United States. Possible penalties included a $2,000 fine, a relative fortune in those days, and five years in prison.

The new law went into effect on October 1, 1937, and within days, the first two of an estimated 20 million Americans since then were busted and jailed on marijuana charges. Twenty-three-year-old Moses Baca was found to have had about a quarter ounce of pot in his house after he was arrested for drunkenly beating his wife—he was sentenced to eighteen months in Leavenworth Prison, a length of time the judge hoped would "cure" him.[9] The day after Baca's arrest, police in the same city busted Samuel Caldwell, who was caught trying to sell three reefers on a street corner. The cops found four more pounds of marijuana in his hotel room. He got four years in Leavenworth.

"I consider marijuana the worst of all narcotics—far worse than the use of morphine or cocaine," the judge is quoted as saying in one newspaper account after the verdicts were handed down. "Under its influence men become beasts, just as was the case with Baca. Marijuana destroys life itself. I have no sympathy with those who sell this weed. In [the] future I will impose the heaviest penalties. The government is going to enforce this new law to the letter."[10]

Baca and Caldwell were arrested in Denver, which, seventy-two years later, would become the undisputed gravitational center of marijuana's reemergence from the underground.

MORE BRAIN CELLS have been destroyed trying to reach back into history searching for a motive for marijuana's outlaw status than actually smoking marijuana ever could. In 1985, pot activists were given what was presumed to be an answer by the late Jack Herer, the equivalent of a cannabis evangelist who believed that hemp—a maligned plant that is related to marijuana, but distinct in that it has almost no psychoactive THC—could "save the world." He wrote *The Emperor Wears No Clothes*, an almanac of information about hemp and marijuana that is often called the bible of the marijuana legalization movement. It's currently in its twelfth printing, and it has done more than any other book on the topic to show that cannabis has far more uses than just getting stoned.

Although *The Emperor Wears No Clothes* hasn't always stood up to scrutiny—it claims in one entry that hempseed is the most "desirable and nutritious food" for fish, which is ridiculous, and also claims that the Continental Army would have "frozen to death" at Valley Forge if it weren't for the hemp clothes they wore, which overlooks that the soldiers presumably would have worn other fabrics if hemp weren't available—Herer nonetheless managed to unearth and publicize valuable historical documents and artifacts. One was a film called *Hemp for Victory*, which was produced by the U.S. government during World War II and encouraged farmers to plant hemp to produce ropes and cordage once its sources of imported hemp were blockaded during the war. Later, the government insisted the film never existed, but a VHS copy made its way into Herer's hands in 1984. He also dug up an old bulletin of the U.S. Department of Agriculture from 1916 that predicted that hemp farming would become America's largest agricultural industry once a machine was developed to quickly harvest the plants' extremely useful fibers.

This is key because the harmless hemp plant was outlawed along with intoxicating marijuana as a result of the 1937 tax act—in its effort to stamp out illicit use, the act also erased a burgeoning industry that promised to be worth billions to the country's farmers. According to the theory laid out in *The Emperor Wears No Clothes*, marijuana was criminalized as part of a secret plot orchestrated by Anslinger, Hearst, chemical conglomerate DuPont, and Pittsburgh banking tycoon Andrew Mellon to rid the land of hemp so that it wouldn't supplant timber as a source of paper. Thus, pot became political.

The theory goes like this: In 1937, DuPont had patented a technology to make paper from wood pulp. Hearst owned timber farms and numerous paper mills. Mellon, who served as the Secretary of the Treasury from 1921 to 1932, invested in DuPont and financed the company through his bank. The theory is that Mellon helped appoint Anslinger, his nephew-in-law, as the Commissioner of Narcotics so that Anslinger, with the help of Hearst's anti-pot print campaign, could spook the country so badly with fears of "reefer men" murdering and raping anything in their paths that Congress would ban all forms of the hemp plant, clearing the way for Hearst and DuPont (and Mellon, as a DuPont investor and financier) to make millions.

This conspiracy theory is custom-tailored for the marijuana crowd to believe without question—it represents oppression by The Man at its most insidious, a scheme by business tycoons, government stooges, and media barons to enrich themselves and their companies at the expense of an innocent plant and the people who enjoy smoking it. Although the theory has become so widespread so as to be accepted as truth by Herer's "hemp can save the world" disciples, it couldn't survive a close inspection. The dismantling of the Anslinger/Hearst/DuPont conspiracy fell to Steven Wishnia, who, as the author of *The Cannabis Companion* and a former editor of *High Times* magazine, is probably the only person with a chance of being taken seriously by the pot zealots, who are predisposed to look on anyone challenging their conspiratorial beliefs as part of the conspiracy themselves. *High Times* is to pot people what *Sports Illustrated* is to season-ticket holders.

Relying on respected historians, autobiographers, and financial experts, Wishnia wrote in a 2008 article that Herer was "completely wrong on this issue." Hearst, one of the biggest purchasers of newsprint, was deeply in debt to North American paper suppliers and should have welcomed a low-cost substitute. His vituperative attacks on "dope fiends" were no more biased and outrageous than his attacks on pinkos and commie subversives, casting doubt on the idea that he had a hidden agenda; most of Hearst's agendas were overt. There's also no evidence of a connection between Mellon and DuPont. Another researcher, Mike Gibbons of Denver, who has conducted select but thorough investigations into certain aspects of marijuana history, can't even find evidence that Anslinger was related by marriage to Mellon.

The more plausible motive, espoused by Wishnia and many others, is that racism drove the anti-marijuana legislation. For evidence, he points to the country's long and shameful history of racial prejudice, which is readily obvious in the justice system as a whole and drug laws in particular. This legacy stretches from the very first drug laws in the country, which were aimed at Chinese opium users, to the very latest—one introduced in 2010 to finally even out the steep penalties for people arrested on crack cocaine charges, who are usually black, with the less severe penalties for people who are arrested with powdered cocaine, who are usually white.[11]

In the late 1800s, opium-based "patent medicines"—cure-all elixirs meant to treat everything from gunshot wounds to labor pains to general malaise—were sold throughout the country in pharmacies and by traveling salesmen roaming the frontier settlements and cowboy towns. Opium was just one ingredient in a mixture that could also contain alcohol, heroin, cocaine, cannabis, and other ingredients. They were wildly popular, and it's not hard to understand why—frontier medicine left a lot to be desired, and opiates stood head and shoulders above anything else in terms of symptom relief. They quelled nausea and diarrhea, eased pain, and soothed muscle spasms. They also knocked you out cold if you needed to sleep and induced a feeling of euphoria if you had to escape your backbreaking existence as a silver miner or cattle rancher. That they could also kill you with an overdose and make you physically dependent upon them was seen in those days as an unfortunate trade-off that had to be made in exchange for at least some medicinal salve for the difficulties of pioneer life.

There's no question that the reliance on opium-based cure-alls created addicts among both the working class and the upper crust, but as long as they were white, no one called them "dope fiends" or "wretches."

Those slurs were reserved for the Chinese, especially in Colorado, which had a high population of Chinese migrants working in mountain mining encampments and on the railroad along the Front Range of the Rockies. According to their traditions, they enjoyed their opium in a pipe smoked at one of the numerous opium dens in Denver's Chinatown district. Drug abuse via elixir was rarely mentioned in the press because that tended to mostly affect white people, but smoking dope by the Chinese—especially in a locale that could be frequented by white people—was an outrage. An article in the *Central City Register* was topped with the screaming headline "The Opium Pipe: The Heathen Chinese and the Narcotic of Death; How John Smokes His Pipe." The *Rocky Mountain News* applauded a plan by the high-altitude mining town of Leadville to eliminate opium there by kicking out the Chinese.

As with cannabis in the following decades, hyperanxious headlines led to action—but as was the case in the Wild West, it didn't involve committee meetings and congressional testimony. Instead, a crazed mob burned down the Denver opium dens, evicted hundreds of residents, and beat an elderly Chinese man to death. The *News* defended the ransacking as civic progress.[12]

Opium and cocaine were the main targets of the uniform federal drug law, the Harrison Narcotics Act of 1914, which required their controlled distribution from pharmacies. Many bigots encouraged the passage of the law using blatantly racist rhetoric. "It has been authoritatively stated that cocaine is often the direct incentive to the crime of rape by the negroes of the South and other sections of the country," Congress was told by Hamilton Wright, the U.S. Opium Commissioner and a U.S. delegate to the first international drug control treaty, the International Opium Convention of 1912.[13] Alcohol prohibition, while rooted in temperance, found momentum in anti-immigrant sentiments aimed at Poles, Jews, Germans, Irish, and Italians in the urban centers and blacks in the south.

Prior to the passage of the Marihuana Tax Act, state-level pot laws were spurred by fear and dislike of Mexicans in California, Texas, and Colorado. In fact, one Colorado newspaper editor wrote Anslinger a letter as the narcotics commissioner was preparing the federal law, complaining about what "one small marihuana cigarette can do to one of our degenerate Spanish-speaking residents. That's why our problem is so great; the greatest percentage of our population is composed of Spanish-speaking persons, most of whom are low mentally, because of social and racial conditions."[14]

It wasn't just discriminatory forces that worked to seal marijuana's fate, but economic and international pressures as well. When he was first appointed to head the Federal Narcotics Bureau in 1930, Anslinger was initially dismissive of a federal ban on marijuana, recognizing that the perceived "menace" was just so much media hype. A 1932 bureau report makes it clear that the agency didn't consider the matter very pressing.

"A great deal of public interest had been aroused by newspaper articles appearing from time to time on the evils of the abuse of marijuana, or Indian hemp, and more attention had been focused upon specific cases reported on the abuses of the drug than would otherwise have been the case," the report read. "This publicity tends to magnify the extent of the evil and lends color to the inference that there is an alarming spread of the improper use of the drug, whereas the actual increase in such use may not have been inordinately large."

A few years later, the policy had obviously changed and Anslinger used the magnifying ability of the press to make his case. Some historians think Anslinger turned marijuana into the great monster he depicted before Congress because he was facing massive budget cuts as a result of the Great Depression: he needed a drug menace to justify a funding increase.[15]

Last, there was the matter of a multinational drug control treaty, the 1912 International Opium Convention, the first in history. By the time Anslinger made his case to Congress, the United States was the only country among the signatories without a federal law addressing cannabis. Considering that halting importation of opium into the United States from China was one of the driving forces behind the Opium Convention, it was a source of embarrassment that the United States did not have laws outlawing cannabis.

"Canada made some seizures over here last year and they pointed the finger of scorn at us and said, 'Why do you not do something about this?' We had to admit that we did not have any legislation," Anslinger testified. "There is some evidence that this drug is being smuggled to China today. We have always pointed the finger of scorn at China, and now marihuana is being smuggled out to China, by sailors."[16]

In whatever ways these motivations combined, the result was that the "finger of scorn" turned its knotty condemnation toward the cannabis plant and it hasn't moved since.

FAST-FORWARD THREE DECADES. While it was the administration of Franklin Roosevelt that presided over marijuana's denigration in the court of public opinion, it was that of Richard Nixon that sealed its fate as the most illegal plant in the world. Nixon hated pot and the people who used it.

"My attitude toward penalties on marijuana is very powerful," he told staffers in a meeting at the White House in September 1971.

One year into Nixon's first term, in 1970, Congress passed the Comprehensive Drug Abuse Prevention and Control Act, a sweeping piece of legislation that consolidated all existing federal drug laws under one umbrella. It set the federal drug policy that is still in place today and greatly expanded federal police power to enforce it. In the streets of America, meanwhile, it was the height of flower power, *Hair*, and Woodstock. Hippies were smoking pot and dropping acid, soldiers were returning from Vietnam hooked on heroin, and Nixon felt surrounded by "pushers" and "dopers" on all sides, with nothing less than the fate of the country in the balance.

"An awful lot of nations have been destroyed by drugs," Nixon mused once with radio and TV personality Art Linkletter, who visited the president in the Oval Office, where Nixon's network of secret tape recorders captured their conversation.[17] "I have seen the countries of Asia and the Middle East, portions of Latin America, and I have seen what drugs have done to those countries. Everybody knows what it's done to the Chinese, the Indians are hopeless anyway, the Burmese. They have different forms of drugs. . . . Why the hell are those Communists so hard on drugs? Well, why they're so hard on drugs is because they love to booze. I mean, the Russians, they drink pretty good. But they don't allow any drugs. And look at the north countries. The Swedes drink too much, the Finns drink too much, the British have always been heavy boozers and. . . . the Irish of course the most. But on the other hand, they survive as strong races. . . . And your drug societies inevitably come apart."

Nixon was determined not to let the same fate befall the United States.

Title II of the new law was the Controlled Substances Act, which classifies narcotics into five categories, or schedules, based on several criteria, including a drug's potential for abuse, its potential for addiction, and its medical efficacy. Marijuana is classified as a Schedule I narcotic, meaning it is considered to be among the most dangerous, addictive, and medically useless drugs known to man. Pot shares the same official disrepute as heroin; GHB, the "date-rape drug"; MDMA, or ecstasy; psilocybin, the active ingredient in psychedelic mushrooms; LSD; and other hard drugs.

By including pot in this dubious crowd, the U.S. government sent a clear message to a nation of potheads at a time when the White House was feeling besieged by them: Marijuana is sinister and evil with no redeeming qualities whatsoever. Those who use it run the risk of becoming hopelessly hooked, reduced to scrapping ashtrays for loose shake or wayward resin as they chase a high that threatens to lead them to worse substances. Putting a drug in the Schedule I classification is like putting an inmate in the high-security solitary-confinement wing of the federal penitentiary, a place to sock away from society the most incorrigible creatures humankind or nature has cursed us with. From the federal government's point of view, cocaine and opium are less harmful than marijuana—they are Schedule II drugs, defined as having "a currently accepted medical use in treatment in the United States."

Possessing any amount of marijuana for any reason anywhere in the United States is a federal crime that carries a possible one-year prison term and a $1,000 fine for the first offense. Get caught three times with a joint in your pocket and you could potentially spend three years in jail and pay $5,000 in fines. If you're busted growing or selling any amount of pot up to fifty kilograms—even a single plant— you will face felony charges, a possible maximum five-year sentence, and a $250,000 fine for the first conviction. Federal sentencing guidelines ratchet up the possible jail time and fines in increments of fifty, one hundred, and one thousand kilograms; the more pot you are busted with, the longer your possible sentence, all the way up to life in prison. Punishments can be enhanced if firearms are involved, if you deal within one thousand feet of an elementary school, or if you have previous drug felony convictions on your record. Federal law even allows for the death penalty in cases tied to organized crime where the amounts of marijuana equal or exceed sixty thousand kilograms, sixty thousand plants, or $20 million in revenue during any twelve-month period of the crime syndicate's existence. As has been noted, state laws are often harsher than these baseline penalties; in places where they're less harsh, as in the medical marijuana states, DEA or local law enforcement can turn cases over to federal courts for prosecution under these guidelines.

What's often just as bad as possible jail time is the even higher probability of losing your property. Cops need only probable cause to seize your car, your cash, and even your home if it's suspected they were used in the commission of a drug crime. This was originally designed as part of the Racketeer Influenced and Corrupt Organizations (RICO) Act of 1970 to deny drug kingpins and organized crime bosses the spoils of their ill-gotten gains. It was expanded in 1984 as part of the Comprehensive Crime Control Act, which divided the spoils among the Justice Department, the Treasury Department, and the local cops who aided in the seizure in the first place. Critics of the law say cops and prosecutors have a built-in incentive to drum up charges or overblow their sense of "probable cause" to initiate a search if there's cash and property to be had.

Twenty-two-year-old college student Anthony Smelley fell prey to this racket when he was pulled over in Indiana for a traffic infraction in 2009. A police K-9 unit indicated the presence of drugs in the car, but all police found after a thorough search was a clean and empty glass pipe in his girlfriend's purse. No drugs. Not even any residue. Yet the police confiscated $17,500 in cash that Smelley had in his pocket from a recent settlement in an auto accident claim. Prosecutors attempted to keep it with the explanation that they suspected Smelley *would* use the money in a drug transaction. Even though the argument that an American could be punished for a crime that had yet to be committed sometime in the future—if, in fact, he were planning to commit a crime at all—is unprecedented and unconstitutional, it took thirteen months and numerous court appearances to have the cash returned.[18]

These laws create a hierarchy of punishments and a nation filled with drug users for whom the worst-case scenario might be loss of freedom, but a close second is the loss of a car or home and a person's life's savings.

One aspect of the Controlled Substances Act that's often lost to history is that marijuana's fate as a societal scourge wasn't without at least some hope for redemption. Part F of the act called for a national commission to study the drug from all angles—medically, culturally, and legally. The point was to analyze where marijuana fit within federal drug laws and to see if the commission's findings justified such harsh penalties.

Nixon appointed former Pennsylvania Gov. Raymond Shafer to lead the commission, and the president made no secret to his staff at the White House about the conclusion he expected it to reach.

"Now, this is one thing I want," Nixon said in May 1971, just a month before he first used the phrase *War on Drugs* in public. He was speaking to his chief of staff, H.R. "Bob" Haldeman, and again the men were being recorded on the Oval Office's network of secret microphones. "I want a goddamn strong statement on marijuana.

Can I get that out of this sonofabitching, uh, Domestic Council?"

"Sure," Haldeman reassured him, even though Nixon couldn't remember the name of the group he expected to deliver such a statement.

"I mean one on marijuana that just tears the ass out of them," Nixon said. "You know it's a funny thing. Every one of the bastards that are out for legalizing marijuana is Jewish. What the Christ is the matter with the Jews, Bob, what is the matter with them? I suppose it's because most of them are psychiatrists, you know. There's so many. All the greatest psychiatrists are Jewish."

Nixon's bigotry has since become legendary, but wasn't limited to Jews, Catholics, homosexuals, and others who were easily identified by race, creed, or sexual preference. He also hated "druggers" and "pushers," whom he saw as morally corrupt. Nixon's great fear was that pot would soon become a "white problem," leading users to heroin and LSD and eventually sending America the way of ancient Rome, to the dustbin.

"Do you think the Russians allow dope? Hell no," he once railed at Haldeman and John Ehrlichman, his domestic policy advisor. They were discussing an episode of *All in the Family* that had really gotten under Nixon's skin. No less an American icon than Archie Bunker himself learned to tolerate gay men, right there on prime-time TV. For Nixon, it was yet another example of how America was rotting from within.

"You see, homosexuality, dope, immorality in general: These are the enemies of strong societies," he said. "That's why the Communists and the left-wingers are pushing the stuff, they're trying to destroy us. . . . Goddamn it, we have got to stand up to these people."

Nixon wanted Shafer's report to "hit the marijuana thing . . . right square in the puss," he said. "I want to hit it, against legalizing and all that sort of thing."

The boss's opposition to relaxing pot laws, repeated not just in the privacy of the Oval Office but at press conferences while the commission's work was still under way, put poor Shafer in a serious jam. Nixon already disliked him because Shafer gave the nominating speech for New York Gov. Nelson Rockefeller at the 1968 Republican National Convention. Nixon, of course, had won the nomination and the election. The president wasn't someone who easily forgot political slights. Heading the National Commission on Marijuana and Drug Abuse presented a means of getting back into Nixon's favor, which didn't escape either Shafer or the press; Shafer, a lawyer, was angling for a seat on the federal bench. The commission was composed of thirteen members, including Shafer, two senators, two representatives, three physicians, two doctors of law, a psychiatrist, a higher-education specialist, and a cofounder of *Sesame Street*.[19,20] Newspapers openly suspected that these old futzes would simply kowtow to the president.

So Shafer felt pressure from both directions—to reach a foregone conclusion on one hand with the reward being a federal judgeship, and to preserve his public reputation on the other by following the evidence. And the evidence wasn't turning out to be the ass-ripper Nixon expected it to be.

The commission's research involved more than fifty studies conducted around the country, a national survey of trends and opinions, public hearings, and a review of law enforcement priorities in six metropolitan areas. The commission's members even traveled to Greece, the Netherlands, North Africa, Jamaica, and Afghanistan in order to put American pot culture into context with others around the world. It spent nearly $4 million in its effort to take the pulse of marijuana in the country. It was—and still is—the largest and most thorough government study of marijuana in American history.

When Shafer announced the findings in March 1972 in a report tellingly titled "Marijuana: A Signal of Misunderstanding," he suggested a course of action that was completely counter to what the president wanted to hear: The Shafer commission recommended decriminalizing personal possession of marijuana, finding that the punishment of arrest simply didn't fit the crime of getting high.

"With possession and use of marihuana, we are dealing with a form of behavior which occurs generally in private where a person possesses the drug for his own use," the report states. "On the basis of this evaluation, we believe that the criminal law is too harsh a tool to apply to personal possession even in the effort to discourage use. It implies an overwhelming indictment of the behavior, which we believe is not appropriate. The actual and potential harm of use of the drug is not great enough to justify intrusion by the criminal law into private behavior, a step which our society takes only with the greatest reluctance."

The document is unusually eloquent for a government report. It's also quite thoughtful in its approach to the topic, aptly nailing the cause for concern about marijuana throughout the decades preceding the commission's investigation:

> Although marihuana is taken by most users for curiosity or pleasure, the non-using public still feels seriously affected by use of the drug. Several decades ago it was popularly asserted that the drug brought about a large variety of social and individual ills, including crime and insanity. As a result, it was prohibited by federal law in 1937. The marihuana explosion of the mid-sixties occurred within the context of 30 years of instilled fear. Although based much more on fantasy than on proven fact, the marihuana "evils" took root in the public mind, and now continue to color the public reaction to the marihuana phenomenon. Even beyond the violation of law, the widespread use of marihuana is seen as a threat to society in other ways. And the threats grow proportionately as the controversy swells.

It has been astutely observed that any statement frequently repeated in public assumes the status of fact. With so many people continually arguing about marihuana, the public has understandably become alarmed and confused. . . . The threat which marihuana use is thought to present to the dominant social order is a major undercurrent of the marihuana problem. Use of the drug is linked with idleness, lack of motivation, hedonism and sexual promiscuity. Many see the drug as fostering a counterculture which conflicts with basic moral precepts as well as with the operating functions of our society. The "dropping out" or rejection of the established value system is viewed with alarm. Marihuana becomes more than a drug; it becomes a symbol of the rejection of cherished values.

The Shafer commission suggested, presciently, that marijuana shows promise for medical applications. The report includes a long chapter summarizing marijuana's historical uses as a medicine as well as more contemporary studies that showed its potential as an anti-emetic (suppressing nausea), as a treatment for muscle spasticity, as an appetite stimulant, as a treatment for depression, and even as a possible aid for overcoming alcoholism and drug addiction. Continued criminalization would not only hinder future studies, the report argued, but would unnecessarily criminalize those who sought to use it for treatment of their symptoms.

"The possibility of criminal prosecution deters users who are experiencing medical problems from seeking assistance for fear of bringing attention to themselves," the report said.

In the end, a year's worth of work costing taxpayers nearly $4 million, conducted by a Republican politician handpicked by a president who exerted an enormous amount of public and private pressure to deliver a specific conclusion—and who held the keys to a prized federal judgeship—had this to say about the "marijuana problem" plaguing America: "Recognizing the extensive degree of misinformation about marihuana as a drug, we have tried to demythologize it. Viewing the use of marihuana in its wider social context, we have tried to desymbolize it. Considering the range of social concerns in contemporary America, marihuana does not, in our considered judgment, rank very high. We would deemphasize marihuana as a problem."[21]

Nixon was beyond pissed. On March 21, 1972, he fumed in the Oval Office to Haldeman.

"They put in as a quote from the President, on the front of the pamphlet with a picture . . . that said that the problem of drugs is our number one and must be dealt with in a 'variety of ways,'" he said. "When I saw 'variety of ways,' I goddamned near puked. I thought, for pity's sake, we need . . . all-out war, on all fronts."

Three predictable things happened as a result of the Shafer commission. The first was that Nixon refused to adopt the commission's suggestions, and the report was quickly forgotten. A few activists managed to grab copies before it went down the memory hole, but there was no national mainstream media interest in bringing it to wider attention; it wasn't until the advent of the Internet that it could be read by anyone who sought it out, if they knew it existed.

The second was that the "extensive degree of misinformation about marihuana as a drug" decried by the report was allowed to further solidify as truth in the American consciousness with each year that it remained a Schedule I drug, classified next to heroin as very dangerous, highly addictive, and with no use as a medicine.

The third was that Shafer never got his judgeship.

While all this was happening, I was twenty-one months old and living in the state that Shafer had represented as governor, Pennsylvania. I would be nearly twenty-one *years* old before I literally crashed into one of his report's findings, albeit one that was buried deep inside and given scant consideration at the time—that marijuana can relieve pain.

· 4 ·

One Toke Over the Line: Summer of 1991

"As a rule the addict passes into a dreamy state in which judgment is lost and imagination runs riot. Fantasies arise which are limitless and extravagant. Scenes pass before the mind's eye in kaleidoscopic confusion and there is no sense of the passing of time."

—Dr. Irving S. Cutter in "A Dangerous Intoxicant," the title of his "Daily Health Talk" column in *The Washington Post*, November 23, 1936

"Everybody must get stoned."

—Bob Dylan, 1966

Joe slept with a bong on his night table, a knuckle of marijuana jammed into its metal bowl, so that all he had to do in the morning was reach for the plastic butane lighter the same way most other people reach for the snooze button on the alarm clock. Groggy with sleep, he would take a long, deep hit and fill his disheveled bedroom with musky exhaust before kicking off the sheets and stumbling out of bed. He'd watch the news while the coffee brewed and take another big hit before getting in the shower.

The ritual marked the milestones of his day, announcing that it was time for lunch or dinner, or that he was heading out soon for a night of barhopping. When his bedroom door was closed at night, the final few flicks and coughs of the day were followed by the sounds of rummaging through the closet and the crinkle of a plastic bag as he pinched off another wad to load in preparation for the morning.

Our apartment reeked of marijuana. There were days when, if there wasn't much on the agenda, an electric blue haze crept along the ceiling from room to room. If you raked your foot over the carpet nap, you could loosen seeds lost in the fiber and make them spring up like gravel tracked in from the yard. Even if no one was home, you could press your nose to the screen on the storm door and picture the near-endless cloud that wafted through it in the summer of 1991.

All I knew about Joe before he became my roommate was that he served drinks at a fern bar near the university, the sort of upscale tavern where parents took their kids for Cobb salads and Bloody Marys when they graduated. Like me, his pastime was rock climbing, a sport we both pursued with near-religious zeal. I knew his name from the circle of longhaired cliff-bums I hung out with that year, skinny guys with forearms like teakwood who held odd jobs to afford new ropes and gas to get to the crags. Joe moved in with a chalk-dusty backpack of climbing gear; a little suitcase of shorts, T-shirts, and Teva sandals; and a thirteen-gallon Hefty bag that smelled like a freshly mown lawn. The pot that went into the bong like coal into a furnace came from that bag, as did the stashes of half the stoners in Greensboro. Joe kept the bag of pot in his bedroom closet. Where it came from before it arrived at our house, and how often it was replenished, I never asked.

I was remarkably uninquisitive in those days, which was probably the most important virtue Joe wanted out of a roommate. The day he moved in, he told me his only rule was that I not go into the closet. I was happy to oblige.

Marijuana culture and all that it entailed had arrived on my doorstep the summer I turned twenty-one, and I invited it to live in the bedroom across the hall.

WERE YOU ASKED to pick the pothead out of a lineup during that time, you would point at me no matter whom I was standing with. Stuck between sophomore and junior years at the University of North Carolina in Greensboro, I dropped out of college for a semester to try to figure out what I wanted to do with my life. Like many of my fellow climbers, I sold it to my parents as a time of reflection, a few months to escape from the pressure of studying to gain perspective on where my life might go so that I could channel my educational efforts accordingly. Not surprisingly, I ended up doing nothing very worthwhile. I grew my hair long and matted it into dreadlocks, got some tattoos, and pierced my nose, a far cry from the clean-cut suburb-dwelling family man I was to become. I worked in the kitchen at a chain restaurant in the mall called Spinakers, running the deep fryer and the sauté station. A restaurant job was good in that it provided flexibility for climbing. At least once a week, I went with Joe or one of a half-dozen friends to cliffs in the nearby Piedmont foothills or up to the vast stone canyons of the New River Gorge in West Virginia. I bought a blue 1975 VW camper van for $800 and christened it by following the Grateful Dead for three shows, selling grilled cheese sandwiches and Heinekens in the parking lot to afford gas home. I was one of those damned hippies.

I forgave a lot of people for assuming that I smoked acres of pot, especially once the local pot dealer became my roommate. But I didn't. With my twenty-first birthday still a few months off, all of my energy was focused on cultivating a mental database of bartenders, state liquor stores, and roadhouses within a pedestrian-level radius of my apartment where I wouldn't be asked for ID until I could legally produce one. This was probably the only useful knowledge I accumulated during my educational hiatus. I knew that on Mondays and Wednesdays, a big plastic cup of Busch draft was $1 at College Hill Sundries, and the place was usually so packed that the overwhelmed bartenders never bothered carding anyone. On Tuesdays and Thursdays, the place to be was New York Pizza, where you practically only needed spare change for a pitcher of Bud. Between the two was a convenience store on Tate Street—Greensboro's psychic and cultural equivalent of San Francisco's Haight-Asbury district—that hired college kids to work the graveyard shift, meaning the odds were about even that you could stroll in for a twelve-pack around midnight and bluff your way into walking out with it, especially if you had dread-locks and a hoop in your nose. Most clerks assumed I was a veteran street hobo, of which there were no shortages on Tate Street.

Although we were on the cusp of the Clinton years and the Inter-net age, the old-timers would attest that not much on Tate Street was any different than in the 1970s; most of the people I knew were either stoned or tripping on acid at any given moment. There was a powerful anything-goes peace-and-love ethos among the drugged-out freaks and the street drunks and the hippie students. Most people you ran across were happy to lend you a buck for a coffee or a beer, and it wasn't unlikely at all to wake up in the morning to find a well-known panhandler or bartender had come home with a roommate to crash on your sofa after a night of partying. That eventually happened at my house with a friend of Joe's, a homeless guy who was a climber of some note back in the day but who'd fallen on hard times. He was also a talented artist who earned a little money sketching mansions in the rich neighborhoods and selling them to the homeowners. He kept the fridge stocked with beer, and in return, he had dibs on the Hefty bag in the closet. For about a month, he crashed in his sleeping bag on the floor under our kitchen table, an arrangement that never struck me as odd. It was just part of the bohemian zeitgeist that had made the Tate Street neighborhood friendly and appealing for decades.

Although drugs were everywhere, there was no particular concern about getting caught. Unless you gave the police no choice but to hassle you—by openly smoking on the sidewalk, for example—there seemed to be a respectful détente in place between the potheads and the law. Watching the police break up a fight across the street from a friend's house once, I saw one officer pick a three-foot-long glass bong off the neighbor's lawn, admire its craftsmanship for a moment, and then place it carefully in a safe spot on the porch so it wouldn't get crushed in the fracas. It's funny to reflect on how casual everyone was indulging in this recreational crime when twenty years later, people utilizing quasi-*legal* marijuana for medical needs live in a state of perpetual fear of arrest and prosecution.

It surprised many people in this well-lubricated social orbit to learn that I never even picked up a bong until the drug dealer became my roommate. Part of this is because I was the precise target demographic of a near-evangelical antidrug campaign that began in the early 1980s, just as I was entering adolescence. Surely it had some subliminal effect. When then–First Lady Nancy Reagan implored the nation's youngsters to "just say no," she was speaking directly to kids in my age group, the so-called Generation X. Marijuana was lumped in with cocaine, heroin, and crack as deadly narcotics, cancers that are "threatening our values and undercutting our institutions," in the words of the president. "They're killing our children."

Ronald Reagan was a great orator, and his and Nancy's September 14, 1986, speech kicking off their antidrug campaign was impregnated with every patriotic flourish his speechwriters could muster. He invoked Lincoln, the beaches of Normandy, immigrants fleeing Soviet gulags, and even "divine providence" in inspiring Americans to rid the land of narcotics. In turn, he addressed business owners, union bosses, members of the clergy, the media, and each individual watching to join the fight, likening it at one point to the unifying effect of the Pearl Harbor attack that drew the country into World War II.

"The war was not just fought by the fellows flying the planes or driving the tanks," Reagan said. "It was fought at home by a mobilized nation—men and women alike—building planes and ships, clothing sailors and soldiers, feeding marines and airmen; and it was fought by children planting victory gardens and collecting cans. Well, now we're in another war for our freedom, and it's time for all of us to pull together again."

He also took the occasion to announce massive amounts of new spending on antidrug law enforcement efforts totaling $3 billion and involving thirty-seven federal agencies. But it was Nancy who summed up the lengthy speech by imploring Americans to make "a final commitment not to tolerate drugs by anyone, anytime, anyplace."[1]

I didn't pay much attention to this call to arms, because I was sixteen at the time and too busy trying to get a fake ID. Still, I formed an impression of marijuana smokers that wasn't very flattering—in my mind, they were bombed-out zombies with reddened craters for eyes, dimwitted oafs and misfits who could barely remember their names. This had less to do with Ronnie and Nancy than with their polar opposites, Cheech Marin and Tommy Chong.

I'm sure the president and his wife considered the stoner comedians to be Public Enemy Nos. 1 and 2, responsible for making battalions of teens think that smoking pot was a bunch of fun and games, but to me Cheech and Chong were just a couple of dorks who made the stupidest movies of all time. In one film, they unwittingly drove a van made of marijuana from Mexico to L.A., and in another, Chong smokes an actual cockroach to get high.[2] I didn't get it at all. *If that's what potheads are like*, I remember thinking, *I'll pass*. The Reagans should have hired Cheech and Chong to go on the road demonstrating what they were talking about.

Still, I had no particular opposition to getting stoned to see for myself what it was like; I just never had the chance. I was one of those rare students who managed to navigate junior high and high school on a course that coincidentally never included being in close proximity to weed. It was purely by chance, I'm sure. I was always at least one or two degrees removed from wherever marijuana was actually making the rounds, the point where I would inevitably be the next guy in line in a toking circle. To be sure, I had plenty of other drugs offered to me in my teenage years—including lots of booze and cigarettes, but also LSD, mushrooms, and crack—but marijuana was never a part of my high school world.

Therefore, when Joe handed me his bong, I had only the most rudimentary idea of what to do with it, or what it would do to me. Had it been anyone else passing the smoke, I might indeed have just said no. Most of the stoners whose paths I crossed did nothing to make me rethink the Cheech and Chong stereotype. The grill cook at the restaurant, for instance—a hairy, wiry guy who could have popped off the page of a Fabulous Furry Freak Brothers comic book—was usually too stoned to tell a medium-rare steak from well done, resulting in all sorts of waste and chaos. One of my stoner climbing buddies decided to sell hash, but ended up smoking the whole stash himself, winding up in worrisome debt to his supplier.

Joe was different, easily the most motivated person I knew that summer. He was tall and handsome, with the wild hair of a Viking and perfectly defined muscles honed by a relentless physical fitness regime that included not only hard-core rock climbing, but mountain biking and regular circuits at the gym. He worked full-time serving drinks at the tavern, maintained respectable grades in a raft of classes at the university, juggled a few girlfriends, and kept a hectic schedule of nightly barhopping. And he did all of it while stoned around the clock. Maybe he'd figured out some secret the others hadn't.

So I took the bong and flicked the Bic. The little knot of marijuana in the bowl popped and glowed orange, the water in the tube burbling soothingly as it filtered the smoke. The green plastic went opaque as I sucked air into my mouth but not my lungs. When it seemed like the bong was full of enough smoke to do the job, I took my thumb off the hole in the side of the tube like I'd seen my roommate do. Sealing the hole creates a vacuum inside the bong, and uncovering it when you inhale draws the smoke smoothly down your throat. My first attempt, however, was inelegant—I inhaled like I was siphoning gas. Air shot into the tube and a smoky fist went straight down my trachea and punched me in the lungs. It was like taking a direct hit off the VW's tailpipe with the engine revving. I exploded in a fit of violent coughing that blew a mushroom cloud from between my lips. Unfortunately, it went right back into the bong with enough force to eject the bowl and fire the weed across the room on a vile jet of bong water. My mouth tasted like battery acid, and I fought the convulsive need to throw up.

"Dude," Joe remarked while I doubled over coughing. "Are you OK? Jesus Christ."

"Sorry," I croaked.

Had it been me, I doubt I would have wasted another hit on such a person, but Joe had the bong reassembled and refilled before I even caught my breath. That was my moment to wave him off with a humble smile and go about my life as a nonsmoker, but I felt like I had to save face. I repeated the process much more cautiously while he pawed with his toe at the wet brown stain on the rug where the marijuana projectile had singed some fibers. This time I managed to hold the smoke in for a few seconds before sending it streaming toward the ceiling. My mouth tasted horrible and my tongue felt like it was wearing old socks.

It's telling that I can't remember Joe's last name, but I remember every sensation of that first huge toke as if I'm still under its influence. The first thing was my feet going numb, followed by the awareness that I suddenly had a canine's sense of hearing. There was a lawn-mower going somewhere, and the traffic several blocks away sounded like it was just outside the door. Mostly, I was distracted by the acidic taste in my mouth.

I thought about getting up for a glass of water, but the TV was on. A story about great white sharks that was nothing but background noise a few moments ago was suddenly quite important and had me riveted. Plus, I felt like I was sinking into the sofa, the fibers of the cushions intertwining with the fibers of my jeans and gently pulling me tight.

I could see the kitchen faucet dripping from where I sat. My mouth cried out for a glass of cold water, but I decided to wait until the commercial. Then I noticed the front door was wide open, sunlight streaming through in lancing shafts that cut the pot smoke hanging in the room into crystals. Maybe I ought to close the door before I got some water. What time does the mailman come?

"You good?"

Joe was pointing at the still-smoking bong in my hands, his voice startling in its clarity. All of my other senses had me floating in a thick serum, but his voice had the quality of church bells at daybreak. I looked at the bong as if for the first time. My hands were prosthetic limbs. How long have I been holding this? It felt like a half hour had passed since my coughing fit. I stretched my arm toward him, smiling at the sensation, and wondering how far I could reach without breaking the fibers holding me to the couch. It was only then that I noticed my heart pounding. Oh boy. What if the mailman comes and sees us like this? I should shut the door.

I could feel myself staring at Joe with heavily lidded eyes and a sagging jaw as he pulled another tube, but I was incapable of changing my expression. Suddenly, I could see my face as clearly as if I were looking in a mirror, a perfect out-of-body vision of just what a drooling moron I looked like. Giggling unleashed a flock of butterflies in my gut that tickled my ribcage. I was fixated on how the sunlight oozing through the screen door fractured like hard candy against the green plastic bong like it was a kaleidoscope. The smoke from the bowl and around Joe's lips was the steam burning off a Florida driveway after a rain. My heart wouldn't stop palpitating, flapping like the pistons in a lawnmower. Do lawnmower engines have pistons? Probably tiny ones. I could ask whoever was mowing his lawn, but I could no longer hear him. *How long had it been so quiet outside?*

I was suddenly gripped with fear that the mailman was closing in fast and silent, like some Vietcong. I felt the urge to spring to my feet to slam the door, but I was sure that no matter how fast and nimble I was, it would be too late. He'd be right there reaching for the mailbox bolted to the brick wall outside the door, his nose already turned up and hooked by tendrils of smoke that you could probably smell across town by now. That's probably why the guy stopped mowing; he smelled the weed and was calling the cops. I was welded to the sofa with dread. Maybe if we sat perfectly still, whoever was closing in on us would leave. But the sharks were on TV and the volume was too high, lots of thrashing around in a frenzy of teeth and red gums. *Dear God, when is the commercial coming? Even my eyeballs are dehydrating. Wait—can that really happen?* I blinked furiously and realized I was hyperventilating.

I no longer wanted to be high.

I SPENT THE next hour fruitlessly trying to unstone myself, which is like trying to be unborn. My clutching wet fear teetered between the pending arrival of a uniformed Authority Figure on the doorstep and embarrassing myself in front of my roommate. I settled on the tactic of simply sitting as still as possible, moving only my head to see if my pounding heart could be seen through my T-shirt. Being stone silent would ensure against humiliation, and it might also fool the mailman into thinking no one is home. Getting up for a glass of water was out of the question, so I suffered through cottonmouth, shallow breathing, and tachycardia until Joe broke the spell.

"Well," he said, taking his feet off the coffee table and standing up. "I'm off to work. Catch you later."

I'd sort of forgotten he was there, and when he got up and moved fluidly around the room, kicking into his flip-flops and stowing the bong in a backpack, it was as if a hypnotist had snapped his fingers and popped me out of a trance. I could move just fine. I stood up too, easily, as if I could have done it all along. I floated into the kitchen and drank three glasses of water in a row. Then I went to my bedroom, locked the door, and crawled under the sheets.

As generally unpleasant as the experience was, it didn't steer me away from future encounters with the green bong. In fact, the opposite was true. I was more determined than ever to figure out how to smoke weed and enjoy it. Every time I heard Joe flick the Bic, I took it as a mockery of my inability to master the habit as well as he had. So, on and off throughout the summer, I grabbed the bong with new resolve. It was never any use.

The problem, I know now, was that no one had ever told me what to expect. For some reason, I thought it would be similar to shotgunning three beers in quick succession, producing an alcohol-like buzz. Getting high was nothing like drinking a beer, but I never learned my lesson. Time slowed to a crawl and I constantly forgot what I was doing, saying, and thinking. I could usually move fine, but if I stayed still for even a moment, I felt like I weighed five hundred pounds. Since these experiences were not what I bullheadedly kept expecting, I didn't enjoy them. It was like walking into a carnival funhouse over and over and being repeatedly surprised not to find a day spa inside.

It would have helped to have been told, as I was many years later, that marijuana tends to enhance the vibe of what's already going on, both in one's surroundings and in one's head. Nervous about trying pot for the first time, my jitters blossomed into full-blown paranoia. Wary about repeating the experience, my stoned mind was constantly on red alert for any feelings of nervousness or discomfort, which invariably introduced themselves. If Joe had told me to just dig the shark show on TV and not worry about anything else, I might have become a much more successful pothead.

Much later, I learned that not only does pot tend to affect people differently—some people fall immediately to sleep, but others can stay up all night and write graduate theses—but also that the strain of marijuana has a lot to do with the sensations that are experienced. It also took me two decades to learn what most others were taught from the very beginning—start with small puffs and wait awhile to see what happens before having another toke. In my ignorance, though, I filled my lungs to capacity and rarely refused another hit, determinately plowing ahead without stopping to examine what was happening to me so that I could come to expect it and work to regulate it. Instead, I just got stoned and hated it.

Invariably, when I was high, I became intolerably paranoid, worthlessly lazy, and too stupid to be around people. Worse, I could never shake one overriding thought from my mind: *I am stoned.* The words hovered in my vision and whispered in my ear. The moment I got stoned, I became preoccupied with *not* being stoned. *When is this going to end? Why did I do this? I'm not enjoying myself.* I tried all sorts of distractions, including smoking before going to bars, smoking before bed, smoking just to read, smoking before mountain biking. The results were usually the same, and on a few occasions very nearly ended in personal disasters.

Mildly stoned at work once during the pre-Sunday-brunch prep session, the boss handed me a laminated recipe and told me to make six quiche lorraines, which were to be the special for the day. Simple enough, I thought, promptly assembling six times the amount of ingredients listed. Nine cups of milk turned into three and a half gallons. Eighteen eggs turned into 108. I quickly realized the giant pot I was mixing the ingredients in wouldn't be nearly large enough to hold all the batter, so I climbed to the top of the pot rack and wrestled down a cauldron big enough to bathe in. The boss walked by a few minutes later and stopped in his tracks at the sight of me mixing the batter with an oar, a mountain of eggshells overflowing the trash can.

"What the hell are you making?" he asked, minor panic in his eyes.

"Six quiches. Like you said."

He grabbed the recipe from the counter and pointed to the top, where it clearly said that the single recipe made six quiches. I'd mixed enough batter to make thirty-six and used every egg in the restaurant in the process, just prior to brunch, when they'd be in high demand. Not once did it occur to me that the volume of batter I'd mixed up wouldn't fit in a bathtub, much less the six tiny quiche tins lined up on the counter.

On another occasion, I got high around midnight and gathered the resolve to walk to the convenience store for some beer. Every atom of my being was focused on one thing: appearing perfectly normal for the estimated minute and a half it would take to walk in the door, grab a six-pack, conduct the transaction, and leave. I concentrated on being single-minded. No distractions. I almost made it, but this store had one of those yellow funnels that you put change in for a good cause, like muscular dystrophy or something. You put a penny in a slot and it rolls all around the inside of the funnel on its edge, slowly dropping into the narrow section, going faster and faster and faster, but always held upright by centrifugal force. *Awesome.* The whole world vanished as I dropped one coin after another into the slot, forgetting all about the beer on the counter or the clerk watching bemusedly. Time was measured only in how many coins I had left, and when they were gone I looked up as if coming out of a pleasant dream and somewhat bewildered to find myself in a 7-Eleven. Standing by the coffee machine were three police officers, stirring their cream and sugar and looking me right in the eye. The funny thing about pot paranoia is that it tends to evaporate when you're confronted with something to actually be paranoid about—like facing a gang of cops after buying a six-pack of beer while underage and high on drugs. I calmly picked up my purchase and strolled out the door.

The evidence was quickly becoming indisputable that I was no good as a stoner. I couldn't function at all under the influence of marijuana. I was the classic pothead—incoherent, too easily self-amused, and thoroughly distracted. Lobotomized.

But I was stubborn.

My willingness to experiment with marijuana ended very suddenly, with the appearance of a young sapling, maybe an Aspen, barely ten feet tall, snapping out from under the van to pop up in front of the windshield as if from a giant children's book. *That's weird,*

I thought, more curious than alarmed, even though I was the one driving and the sight of a tree emerging from under the moving vehicle should have triggered all sorts of warnings. There had been no trees a moment ago, when I had been driving forward, pushing the little VW van up a steep dirt road on the side of a mountain in the rural North Carolina foothills. But the old rig's little Porsche engine didn't have enough power to make it all the way to the top of the hill on the first try, and I had to back up for another run at it. I was familiar with this steep bumpy road, and it's not the first time I had to try more than once to navigate this section. There had never been any trees in the way before. Yet there it was, its appearance from under the van as unexpected as a unicorn. Hello, tree.

The next few moments took a lifetime to unfold, as tends to happen when you're in the grip of that first fuse-burn rush, when things get really elastic. For one thing, it occurred to me—way too late—that while I was driving backward I shouldn't be looking forward, out the front windshield, watching the terrain unspool in reverse, as if I were rewinding a movie. Then logic kicked in that trees don't just appear in the middle of roadways, meaning that I was probably no longer on the roadway and making a very big mistake. Meaning I should hit the brakes before something awful happens.

By the time that thought was fully formed, it was already over. Everything flipped to the port side. I was lying on the driver's-side door looking straight up through the passenger window at the clouds. Joe, who's a foot taller and forty pounds heavier than me, hadn't been wearing his seatbelt and was sprawled all over me. He was still holding the green plastic bong. The engine sputtered out like a wet raspberry. There must have been other noises, like the crashing avalanche of rock climbing gear and other detritus as the van went over on its side, the crush of metal on rock, the snapping of branches, but what I remember most is a few seconds of pure silence.

And then the laughter, that flock of tickling butterflies, which, try as I might to stifle it, came fluttering up out of my stomach.

"You fucking idiot," Joe said, trying to untangle himself from me.

Then he laughed too. What else could we do? We weren't hurt, and the absolutely ludicrous image of that goddamned tree popping up from nowhere as I blithely backed down a four-wheel-drive Forest Service road just watching the scenery unfold was, even at that moment, hysterical.

With our eyes tearing, we crawled through the passenger window, which was now on top of the van, and jumped down to survey the damage. It was pretty bad. The hill we'd been trying to climb was perfectly straight, but while backing down to get a full head of steam for another run, I'd veered far to the left, leaving the road, running over some trees, and ending up in a steep drainage ditch. The passenger's-side wheels spun in the air pitifully. There was no way the two of us could right it. The laughter petered out as we came to grips with our new situation. We were screwed.

Still, it could have been worse. If I'd moseyed right instead of left, we would have gone off the side of the mountain. Rather than a flat belly flop onto the side, we would have been sent on a rolling, crashing cartwheel through a couple hundred feet of pine forest before exploding into a fireball or impaling on a tree trunk.

Joe still held the bong in one hand, and he turned slowly in the road, surveying the terrain like we'd just made landfall on a new continent. I stood with my head in my hands, the gravity of it dawning on me at last. Not only had I wrecked my only vehicle high up on a remote mountainside with little hope of fixing it cheaply or quickly, but I had nearly killed us both. And there was no question whatsoever as to what caused it.

Until that moment, it had been a typical midweek trip to Moore's Wall, our local climbing venue. The sun was shining, Jane's Addiction was playing on the tape deck, and we had picked a handful of challenging routes to climb. Then, just before we turned off the rural two-lane road onto the boulder-strewn switchbacks that lead to the base of the cliff, Joe pulled out the bong. He took a few hits and then offered to steer from the passenger seat while I did likewise. Why not? We were leaving the paved roads and wouldn't present any danger to other motorists. Plus, I didn't want to disrupt the bonhomie we enjoyed during the hour-long trip and, despite voluminous evidence to the contrary, I felt I could precisely calibrate the amount of pot I ingested to artfully cope with the coming tasks at hand.

I could not.

We were remarkably lucky on numerous fronts that day. As a rule, Bible Belt Southerners who opt to live on a steep and inaccessible dirt road aren't generally pleased at the sight of mentally impaired hippie people wandering their driveways looking for help. Most every home that was tucked back among the pines and boulders featured a prominent hand-lettered "No trespassing" sign, and we didn't stop to see if they were serious. We were practically back at the paved road before an elderly woman let us in to use her phone to call a wrecker.

Extracting the van from what could have been its grave was easier than anticipated. A fellow about our age in overalls and a tobacco cap came with a heavy-duty diesel tow truck, and he didn't even ask what happened. I'm sure he considered it to be obvious. We were in no position to negotiate, but the fee to winch the VW upright and back onto the road was only $75 and he agreed to take a check. Even more surprising, the van suffered only a few cosmetic scratches and started on the first try. Not even a cracked window.

Joe wanted to make the best of it and race to the cliff for one quick climb before it got dark, but I insisted on returning to Greensboro. And I insisted that he drive.

I finally learned the lesson the ganja gods had been trying to teach me all summer—marijuana was not for me. I imagine it was like how other people feel when they finally come to terms with the fact that they will never be famous rock-and-roll guitarists or Major League Baseball players, regardless of how hard they practice or how bad they want it. I felt a great pressure lifting away—I could leave the marijuana lifestyle to those like Joe, people who are somehow genetically equipped to bike, climb, drive, serve drinks, have sex, hold a conversation, and everything else involved in daily life while under the influence of a bongful of weed.

Not me. I was at peace with it.

THE SUMMER ENDED on a bummer of a note, but one that was portentous, although I wouldn't know it for nearly twenty years. The ganja gods were not done with me yet.

Shortly before the fall semester started, I was riding my mountain bike through a stand of woods on the University of North Carolina–Greensboro campus to test whether the front tire would hold air after I had patched a hole in the inner tube back at the apartment. I had been drug-free since the van crash, but I was apparently being inattentive to the trail as I zoomed along—one moment I was flashing through the trees and bunny-hopping over little roots and rocks, and the next I was flipping over the front handlebars. I came crashing down on my left shoulder, feet still tangled in the bike's pedal clips. Unlike the other accident that summer, I knew immediately that I was injured, but I wasn't sure where or how badly. I lay in a crumpled heap for a few minutes, regaining my breath. I couldn't move my left side, so I carefully felt and probed with my right hand, checking first the ribs, then the arm. When I moved to the shoulder, I discovered the problem—my collarbone was horribly broken, tenting the skin straight up like I was wearing a pyramid-shaped shoulder pad.

The slightest movement, including head movements, sent electric pain coursing from crown to sole. I rolled onto my right side and struggled to my feet, holding my left arm in the same position as when I landed on it. A broken clavicle is as useful at holding anything up as a one-sided coat hanger, and half my torso sagged. Luckily, I crashed near the university infirmary. I left my bike in the woods and staggered pale as the undead to find help.

I obviously couldn't see my wound, but I could see how serious it was from the expression on the pop-eyed attendant when I pushed through the door. I had an obvious compound fracture and needed to be in the emergency room, she said, picking up the phone to dial someone to fetch me. Ambulance or friend? I asked her to call Joe, who would be there quicker and who wouldn't charge me several hundred dollars for a ride to the hospital. A nurse kept me from passing out while we waited.

In the early 1990s, the phrase *medical marijuana* was unheard-of in my circle of friends, except possibly as a punch line. Its history as a therapeutic painkiller, muscle relaxant, and appetite stimulant—for which there is evidence dating back thousands of years—was obscured by modern laws that deemed it to be a dangerous and addictive social ill. My friends used marijuana for one thing only—recreation. If they were aware of the historic medicinal uses of *Cannabis L.*, the genus of whichever plant species came from the Hefty bag in the bedroom closet, they probably didn't care. They were stoners, not medical patients. It wouldn't become in vogue to argue marijuana's relative medical applications compared to its perceived drawbacks for another couple of years, and on the opposite coast at that.

Yet Joe was blessed with instinct. Whether he specifically knew of marijuana's medicinal value or just felt it on a gut level, he arrived at the infirmary with his trusty bong loaded with a salad bowl of a hit. At first I was mad that he was such a pothead he couldn't even rush to my rescue without first preparing a hit, but he explained that it wasn't for him, but for me.

"They're not going to give you any painkillers until they set your bone," he said. "Trust me, you're going to want this."

We drove to the woods so he could retrieve my bike, and he propped the bong between my knees and put the lighter in my right hand. It was like marijuana triage—he took care to arrange everything so that I only had to lean my head forward and flick the lighter while he put the bike in the hatchback of his little Honda.

Up to that point in my life, it was the one time I didn't mind being high. Joe ushered me through the check-in process so I didn't have to think about or stress over forms and nurses and waiting rooms. What had been a grating, nauseating pain—which was compounded by dread at what lay ahead when the bone was to be set—faded to a dull red roar, nothing worse than a bad ache. My body was slack and my mind wandered. I was actually in a pretty good mood and able to joke with the doctor, even when he stuck a needle in my wound to kill infections. And when he told me to brace myself by wrapping my right arm around the railing on the hospital bed so that he and a nurse could yank my left shoulder outward in order to manhandle the two ends of my broken collarbone back together, I wasn't even worried.

I did not know it at the time (nor did I care), but I was suffering from acute somatic pain. When the bone broke, pain receptors called nociceptors in my bone, muscle, and skin—which were dormant before the crash—sprang wide-awake and fired signals to my brain like crazed machine-gunners. Those signals whipped along my sensory and motor nerves to the spinal cord, where they were relayed to the thalamus. The thalamus dispatched news of the injury else-where in the brain, including to the cortex and the limbic system, setting off a neural chain reaction that resulted in a lot of hurt, severe anxiety, and a high heart rate. The brain's reaction to pain is more complex than simple cause and effect; there were numerous reactions taking place simultaneously, including protective ones. Natural pain-killers, part of the endogenous opioid system, were activated to help dull the pain to sub-excruciating levels—these same receptors would be activated if I were to receive a shot of morphine.

What I also did not know at the time was that the marijuana I smoked a few minutes before introduced a chemical compound into my bloodstream called delta-9-tetrahydrocannabinol, or THC. This is the magical ingredient, called a cannabinoid, that gets you high. THC is one of at least sixty-six cannabinoids found in marijuana plants, and they quickly entered my bloodstream through my lungs and attached themselves to cannabinoid receptors in my brain. Not until I read Michael Pollan's book *The Botany of Desire* in 2010 would I fully understand what happened to me, that THC jiggered with my sensory perception in the cerebral cortex, impaired my movement through the basal ganglia, and interfered with my memory at the hippocampus and the amygdala.[3] Until just two years before my bone-breaking bike ride, scientists did not even know cannabinoid receptors existed. Even as I was being attended to in the hospital, they did not know their purpose, although they must have suspected it was for more than just allowing potheads to get stoned when they smoked a joint—especially considering that the same neural network was found in most mammals, birds, and fish. It would be another year or so before an Israeli neuroscientist—the same man who discovered THC in 1964—found the body's own naturally occurring, or endogenous, cannabinoid. He named it anandamide, after the Sanskrit word for "bliss." Scientists would later refer to it as "the brain's own marijuana."[4]

Among numerous other things, most of which are still not understood, endocannabinoids (those made by the body) interfere with the brain's memory-making function, inducing a sort of short-term forgetfulness, particularly of painful or unpleasant events. This "memory-inhibitor" function also filters out noncritical daily input from the senses so that the brain isn't overwhelmed processing the memories of every license plate passed on the way to work or the transcripts of every daily conversation. The effect of endocannabinoids is undetectable, unless you try to vividly recall the sensation of a particularly painful event, like childbirth. Such a memory is usually quite difficult to conjure, and it may be no coincidence that there are cannabinoid receptors in both male and female reproductive organs. Endocannabinoids are fragile molecules that are produced on demand and they don't last long.[5]

The THC from a loaded bong, on the other hand, is more powerful by several orders of magnitude, like the difference between a firecracker and a hand grenade. To date, no other drugs have been found to recognize the cannabinoid receptors—not cocaine, caffeine, heroin, nicotine, or opium. Only cannabinoids, of which marijuana is teeming, activate the receptors. Smoke a joint and the effects are quite noticeable almost immediately. Short-term memory loss among the stoned is remarkably acute. "Short-term" in this instance doesn't mean you can't remember what happened thirty or forty minutes ago, but thirty or forty seconds ago. As one respected study of marijuana and its effects famously put it, "The most obvious behavioral abnormality displayed by someone under the influence of marijuana is difficulty in carrying on an intelligible conversation, perhaps because of an inability to remember what was just said even a few words earlier."[6]

THC also reacts on an intermediary level with the opioid system, the body's natural painkilling network, and it interferes with the work of the nociceptors, those panicked pain-recognizers that were sending all the red alerts about the broken clavicle to the brain. The bong hits had induced acute short-term memory loss, allowing me to forget—as much as was possible—that one of my major bones was broken; it stimulated the endogenous opioid system, increasing the body's natural painkilling network; and it calmed the nociceptors.

Inner bliss is an apt description of the effect THC had on me in the hospital. I was distracted and forgetful, captivated as much by the nurse's perfume as I was aware of how she was pressing my bones back into place. I was in far more agony later, once the weed had worn off and I was roped into a sling that fit like the world's tightest shoulder holster.

Marijuana had eased my pain, but I barely thought about it at the time.

In fact, the significance of the experience wouldn't sink in for another two decades.

· 5 ·

Home Is Where the Pot Is

"Clandestine growing is as simple as the name implies. The name of the game is secrecy. Tell nobody and cause no suspicion. . . . Successful growers are good citizens and keep a low profile."

—Jorge Cervantes, *Marijuana Horticulture: The Indoor/Outdoor Medical Grower's Bible*, 2006

Before I could lay my hands on a cannabis plant, I had a lot of work to do in late 2009 and early 2010. First, I waited until the holiday season passed to avoid unexpected visits from well-wishers and to avoid ruining Christmas by attracting a DEA raid. The time was spent consuming as much information I could about growing pot, while also learning as much as possible about its tangential specialties, like the basics of home electrical wiring to handle a big boost in power usage and figuring out the relative pH level of municipal tap water. I'd spent the previous weeks preparing my growing room with sundry equipment and supplies that would never be seen together anywhere but in an outlaw suburban cultivation operation. But long before I even started on that project, I had to prepare something else: my family.

Whereas my doctor's recommendation provided me with legal cover, my wife, Rebecca, and thirteen-year-old son, Turner, provided cover of another sort. Anyone who knew me when I was twenty would never recognize the person who was approaching forty and living quietly on the outskirts of Fort Collins on a tranquil, tree-lined suburban street. Just like my neighbors, I came and went through the garage when returning from the grocery store or some other errand, on the streets only long enough for a quick wave hello or a nod in passing by the mailboxes. Occasional Saturdays saw my wife planting flowers by the front door, or me mowing the lawn—less and less, actually, as Turner grows old enough to take over that chore. We're quiet people surrounded by other quiet people; we know the names of our next-door neighbors and those across the street, but everyone else is anonymous to us. And we to them. In the years I've lived in this house, I've cultivated a rather stereotypical loner-writer persona. The few people on my street who know what I do for a living seem to have grown used to the fact that I'm not a block-party kind of person, but more of a secluded eccentric barricaded for months on end inside my house, writing some article or book or blog or God knows what. This, of course, is perfect for my current needs. I didn't have to worry about some random busybody dropping by while I'm pruning marijuana in the basement.

The basement is my sanctuary, a seven-hundred-square-foot miniature apartment, complete with a cozy bedroom for out-of-town guests and a full bathroom. I converted the majority of the space into an office, the walls painted a soothing sea green and furnished with a scrounged-up medley of sofas, tables, bookshelves, funky light fixtures, and a big old butcher-block desk of four-inch-thick oak that weighs about two hundred pounds. There's an ancient stereo that's far too powerful for the small space wired to my computer, and a flat-screen TV across the room that I tell people is for watching CNN but which, in fact, is usually tuned to *The People's Court*, possibly the top-rated show among freelance writers everywhere. The walls are covered with the bric-a-brac of my profession, including framed copies of yellowing newspaper clippings, an antique letter drawer from the days when newspapers were assembled word by word, a few writing awards, a bunch of press badges pinned to a cork bulletin board, and a collection of random photos, posters, maps, quotes, and other esoterica that makes sense only to a journalist.

Not only is it a perfect place to work, but the basement also promised to be the perfect place to grow pot. Through the bathroom, a door led to a ten-square-foot storage room, and beyond that a smaller space for the hot-water heater and the furnace. These areas were chockablock with Christmas decorations, boxes of old newspapers, and storage shelves filled with typical household flotsam that didn't quite qualify for the rubbish bin until they'd languished there for a year or two. My plan was to clean this area out, sterilize it, and fill it with marijuana.

"So," I BEGAN, sipping coffee early one morning before my wife left for work, "I was thinking about growing some marijuana."

It should be said that Rebecca is the yin to my yang, the sort of partner who is priceless to someone whose job is to dream up weird things to do and then write about them. She's everything that I'm not—ruthlessly organized, gainfully employed, and grounded in reality. She's a list maker and a goal setter. Our differences would have been obvious with a glance at our work clothes, that morning and every other. I usually wear pajamas with moose on them and will have the same bed-head hairstyle at 6 p.m. as I woke up with at 6 a.m.; Rebecca, the managing editor of a craft-book publisher, dresses like she's heading to the set of *The Devil Wears Prada*. She's driven by logic and structure; I run on instinct and whim. But neither of us is deficient in the other's primary qualities, and when I proposed a pot operation to be run from inside the house, I knew she had enough of a subversive streak to at least hear me out. It helps that I've spent our entire lives together acclimating her to hearing random, semi-harebrained ideas at the breakfast table. One doesn't live with a writer for very long before realizing that we are a unique species, capable of seeing humor, adventure, and value in experiences that most sane people spend their lives trying to avoid.

My argument that morning had an extra twist: This latest plot could make money. How much money remained to be seen, but if done right, we could turn it into an ongoing, profitable enterprise. Author Sebastian Junger has a side business in a restaurant in New York City; why couldn't my personal money mill be a secret marijuana farm? While I wrote, a small jungle of plants could grow happily under bright lights, my only duties being to keep them watered and fed while they almost literally grew money, promising at least a modicum of financial stability to my more capricious professional endeavors. Growing medical marijuana could be worth at least several thousand dollars a year. I was infused with the same enthusiasm as Drew Brown, one of the owners of Abundant Healing; I secretly nourished a plan to follow him to Costa Rica to hang out and surf once I'd made my own millions. Like many of those who leaped into the fray in late 2009 and early 2010, I fantasized about growing money, encouraged by those dispensary owners who told me that demand for their products was so high, and the medical marijuana patient rolls growing so quickly, that they doubled their revenue month over month and were constantly looking to buy fresh weed from freelance growers like me to fill the void.

Rebecca listened to all this while flipping idly through a magazine and eating a bowl of fruit and yogurt, her expression one of polite but detached curiosity. Her questions were precise and appropriate, and I had an answer for all of them: Is it legal? *Yes and no. But mostly yes.* How much will the equipment cost? *Maybe $500 or $600.* You can't grow tomatoes; what makes you think you can grow pot? *Anyone literate enough to read any of the millions of cultivation Web sites can figure out how to grow pot.* How do you know you can sell it? *Seriously? If you can't sell marijuana in* this *climate, you're too stupid to live.* Only one question stumped me, one I knew had to be answered but which I kept pushing into the background for additional consideration:

"What are you going to tell your son?"

I PUT THAT one off, at least for the time being. All I needed right away was permission to begin construction on my grow room, which Rebecca agreed to so long as I promised to discuss my plans with Turner before there was any actual pot in the house.

The importance of building a good grow room was emphasized by everything I'd read about indoor marijuana cultivation. The grower plays the role of Mother Nature, and it is of paramount importance for Mother Nature to precisely control the temperature, humidity, airflow, and light. Screwing up any one ingredient badly enough could result in anything from a crummy harvest to crop death. Experience that once or twice, after spending a few hundred dollars and stressing out over your plants for a few long weeks, and it's easy to see why many people prefer to leave the growing to others and just shop at a dispensary. A grow room has to be as clean as an operating room to prevent mold spores and pests like spider mites, tiny creatures that could infest a plant and starve it of nutrients. A grow room has to have a good source of power, preferably be close to a faucet, and be incognito.

Once I cleared out the downstairs storage rooms, I found the larger six- by four-foot space to be almost perfect. It had hard tile floors that were easy to clean and power outlets on the walls. I put a thick fresh coat of white high-gloss paint on the walls, the ceiling, and the inside of the doors and doorframes. The white walls would serve to reflect the light and maximize the power of the bulbs, which had to be as intensely bright as possible. It was a good start, but there were a few deficiencies: There was no ventilation in the room at all, incoming or outgoing, and one of the walls didn't go all the way to the ceiling—it was open at shoulder height to allow access to the crawl space under the living room, a dark, spider-filled void I'd avoided exploring since we moved in. But I had to crawl up there to find a place to put an exhaust vent, and then find a way to seal the wall.

I'd learned through my research that properly expelling the air from your grow room is one of the most important things on a marijuana grower's checklist, as much to move fresh oxygen in as to move the dank and smelly air out. According to all the warnings I'd read, blooming pot is overpoweringly and distinctively fragrant, and more than a few indoor operations have been literally sniffed out by neighbors wondering if a skunk died under their porch. Although what I was doing was legal under state laws, I wasn't willing to take any chances at being discovered. It goes without saying that I would highly prefer not to have my name and picture appear on the front page of the local newspaper, regardless of whether I later cleared my good reputation. It wasn't so much a DEA raid I was concerned about, even though it couldn't be ruled out since they would have no way of knowing whether I was growing six plants or six hundred until they knocked the door down. Considering the piddling amount of marijuana I planned to grow, arrest was a remote worry; more concerning was the cops' ability to seize your pot while they decide whether or not what you're doing is aboveboard.

According to the medical marijuana law in Colorado, officers in that situation are supposed to return your property in the same condition in which it was seized if no charges are filed or if you win a case in court. What that means in reality is that the cops are responsible for caring for your marijuana until your case is resolved, a prospect that makes most cops go bug-eyed. In fact, my local sheriff at the time, Jim Alderden—who could well have been inspiration for many a Zane Grey novel, a mustachioed Wild West throwback who keeps a bronze bust of John Wayne in his office and who wears stars-and-stripes rodeo shirts at press conferences—has openly laughed at the suggestion that he require some deputies to water seized cannabis plants when drug suspects claim a medical defense.

"This is impossible for us to comply with, especially when the claim of medical use isn't raised until after we've dismantled the operation and cut the plants," Alderden once wrote in a blog he maintained, a monthly rant that was so opinionated that the Larimer County Commissioners banned editorializing on county-run Web sites. Alderden felt so strongly about things that he circumvented the ban by taking the sheriff's office site off the county's system and paying to host it himself. "How in the world are we supposed to fertilize, water and grow thousands of plants? We don't have the personnel, space, resources or time to operate a full-blown greenhouse (even if we used inmate labor, which would be ill advised). Then if the District Attorney decides not to prosecute or can't due to some technical issue that has nothing to do with the medical use claim, we have to return the live plants, thus committing a federal crime."

He once made a point of returning dead shriveled plants that had turned nearly to dust to a couple of cultivators who'd had their criminal charges dropped when it was determined that they were bona fide patients. The only difference between them and me was that they had legitimate debilitating illnesses for which they smoked marijuana. I had none, unless you want to count that problem with my back, which I'm sure they wouldn't, and presumed that a visit by the police would be the end of my experiment.

As I crawled through the cobwebs and mouse droppings under the house with a flashlight and a paper face mask, it became clear that my options for venting from the basement were limited. I could run ducting to either the chimney or the vent for the hot-water heater, both of which expelled air from the top of the two-story house. That was the optimal scenario, to lift the skunky scent up and away from any of my neighbors' sensitive noses, but I wasn't sure I wanted to commit to cutting into either outlet. For one thing, I use the fireplace six months out of the year, and mingling the pungent odor of pot with the Yule logs wasn't an appealing prospect. The hot-water heater was closer to the grow area and would be easier to hack into, but it was newly installed and required a permit inspection by a city code enforcement officer, something I'd forgotten to have done until my project was already well under way. I could delay an inspection until after the first harvest (there was no way to get to the hot-water heater except through the grow room), but the code-violating modification would be obvious.

Just when I started considering the idea of punching holes through walls to run ducting out through one of the ground-level windows elsewhere in the basement, I found the perfect solution. Hidden in the insulation in the outer wall of the house was an unused, grated vent through the concrete foundation. It exited under the back porch, so I'd hadn't noticed it when inspecting the outside of the house. I had no idea what it was for, wondering if perhaps it was to prevent carbon-monoxide or radon buildup. Whatever its purpose, I figured we could live without it for a few weeks until a more permanent idea came to me. It wasn't in a completely ideal location—we wouldn't be having any backyard barbecues with strangers for a few weeks—but it was better than anything else that presented itself.

The next mission was a Home Depot shopping spree. I bought a recessed ventilation unit like one you'd install in your bathroom ceiling to clear out the steam from a hot shower, eight feet of flexible aluminum ducting meant for a clothes dryer, an electric timer that people use to turn lights on and off when they're on vacation, an industrial fan for air circulation, a humidifier, a space heater, a dimmer switch, a digital thermometer and humidistat, a roll of white duct tape, a six-foot length of garden hose, a watering can, four or five empty spray bottles, extension cords, a drywall knife, and a collection of hooks, chains, screws, and other fasteners. As an afterthought I also grabbed a dry-erase calendar to tack to the wall and a few markers so that I could keep track of feeding and watering schedules. On my way home, I stopped at JoAnn Fabric for an eight- by six-foot swath of white waterproof vinyl, the sort you'd use to upholster the seats of a motorboat. My wife watched the grow room evolve, no doubt wondering how I could suddenly be so motivated—and skilled, if I may say so—at basic home repair and fix-it chores when I'd never demonstrated any aptitude for them before. Usually, the most basic handyman tasks take me months to complete, due to either incompetence or disinterest, but in this case, I was a virtual Bob Vila.

Step one had me back in the crawl space installing the ventilation gear, a simple enough process that involved sawing a rectangle of drywall out of the grow room ceiling and securing the bathroom fan into place. I connected the flexible ducting and ran it along the ceiling of the crawl space to the vent I'd discovered. I screwed a power strip to the wall over the electrical outlet (considering that I would be running gallons of water through the room regularly, I didn't want any electrical cords on the floor), connected the dimmer switch, and plugged in the newly installed fan. Using the dimmer switch, I could control the fan speed to regulate the airflow.

Now I needed to get air *into* the room, and leaving the door open wasn't a solution. Flowering marijuana plants need twelve solid hours of complete and utter darkness every twenty-four hours, and I couldn't chance someone coming downstairs to do a load of laundry, flipping on the light in the middle of the night, and ruining the harvest. I solved the problem by cutting another rectangular hole near the floor into the guest bedroom and covering it with ventilation grates on both sides. I positioned a little desk fan on the bedroom side to blow air through the grate.

Next, I used the white duct tape and the heavy white vinyl sheeting to cover the opening in the wall leading to the crawl space. I chose vinyl over drywall panels because it's waterproof, easy to clean, and temporary. And it was cheap and easy to install. Finally, I brought in the standing fan, the humidifier, and the space heater, arranging them on a little ankle-high shelf made of bricks and a two-by-six plank; in case a catastrophe occurred during watering, they would stay high and dry.

I was pretty pleased with my handiwork. In a room this size, I was aiming to recirculate about two hundred cubic feet of air a minute so that my plants could get the optimal amount of fresh oxygen. With the humidifier and heater, I could keep the temperature within the prime zone of 75 to 85 degrees with a humidity of about 45 to 55 percent. I could monitor both of those levels with the digital thermometer/humidistat I'd mounted on the wall. Last, the fan would blow on the leaves to circulate the air and to stimulate strong stems and branches. The electric timer would control the lights, which were the next big purchase.

The only thing I skimped on was a carbon filter to attach to the vent, a device that can scrub the air of odiferous scent-carrying terpenes so that the exhaust from the grow room is virtually odor-free. They were pricey and I'd already spent a few hundred bucks. I figured that I could pay for one with the profits from the first harvest, if I felt it was necessary. How much odor could six little plants *really* produce? I thought.

OUT IN NATURE, the sun provides every plant on earth with the full spectrum of light in an intensity that's hard to match indoors. Different color bands of light within the full spectrum produce different reactions in plants, and the aim for indoor growers is to find just the right bulb, or combination of bulbs, to produce maximum chlorophyll production and photosynthetic response. Everything in a grow room works in concert to produce killer pot, but none is more important than the light. The goal is to mimic the sun as much as possible inside a hidden room in the basement. Growing it outdoors, under the actual sun, solves the lighting problem and produces great weed, but introduces a whole new set of headaches—finding a private place to grow outdoors, where you also can't control airflow and thus odor, is difficult. But it's also illegal to grow outdoors, at least in Colorado, even for medical purposes.

The choices in the area of indoor lighting are overwhelming. And complicated. The most common lights are high intensity discharge (HID) lamps, usually either metal halide or high-pressure sodium vapor, or a combination of the two. The rule of thumb is: more watts, more weed. There's no such thing as giving your plants too much light.

Light intensity is measured in lumens, and a thousand-watt HID bulb can produce 140,000 lumens or more. In comparison, a regular sixty-watt incandescent light bulb in a reading lamp produces about nine hundred lumens. Lumens decrease quickly the farther one is from the light. Plants two feet away from their light receive only a quarter of the light as plants just a foot away. Reflective hoods help direct the light downward onto the plants, and other reflective material, such as Mylar or even aluminum foil, can also help corral the light onto the leaves rather than all over the walls and floor.

HID lamps suck a lot of power and require heavy ballasts—essentially miniature power stations—to regulate the amount of current flowing through them so that the bulbs fire up properly, perform up to their standards, and don't burn out prematurely. These ballasts can weigh from thirty to fifty-five pounds and can be a real headache. They generate a lot of heat and a lot of noise, sometimes requiring their own cooling and ventilation systems. This has caused many a grower to rejigger his or her temperature controls and security measures. And ballasts are alive with electricity, promising a quick death if handled improperly.

Prospective growers can easily spend $500 to $600 on a single thousand-watt light bulb, a reflective hood, and a ballast. Power consumption depends on the cost of electricity in one's community but can add anywhere from $30 to $140 per month to the utility bill. Of course, it's perfectly legal to use as much electricity in my house as I'm willing to pay for, but if my consumption rates are drastically higher than my neighbors', it could raise a red flag. If I'm suspected of growing pot, the police can subpoena my utility records, which, if they show a spike in usage compared to surrounding houses, can be used to swear out a search warrant. Clandestine growers have been known to take advantage of eco-friendly appliances and power-saving practices not to save the earth, but to save their skins—installing gas stoves, washing clothes at the Laundromat, and turning off their hot-water heaters in favor of showering at the gym can allow you to install a few more six-hundred-watt grow lights without raising the electric bill.

At the same time I was building the grow room, the city of Fort Collins started a new program in which they included a little graph in your power bill to show how your electric usage compared to the average rates of others in the neighborhood. Mine was off the charts, even with nothing growing. One reason was probably because my basement office has twelve lights to keep the subterranean gloom at bay, which I usually leave burning around the clock because it's a lot of trouble to turn them on and off whenever I come and go. I also prefer to wear shorts in winter, so the electric heat is generally pegged around 70 degrees. Normally this news would be alarming, but I was relieved—since we already had a pattern of grossly irresponsible energy consumption, drawing a few more kilowatt-hours of power to grow pot probably wouldn't raise any eyebrows.

In the end, I decided to go a different route than HID, opting to try a newer technology I learned about, one that the grizzled old growers who chimed into the online chat forums tended to look upon with skepticism: red and blue LED lights. According to my research, and based on what limited testimony I could find online, properly calibrated LEDs could supply the plants with the precise light spectrums and wavelengths that are most useful to them for a fraction of the cost of HID lights. I was attracted to their many advantages— they could be plugged right into the wall with no need for a ballast, they burn cool and won't affect the ambient temperature, and, compared to HIDs, they sip electricity. Best of all, they are far more affordable. I bought two ninety-watt UFO-style lamps (so-called because of their dinner-plate shape) for a total of $360 on eBay. Once they'd been delivered and hung from the ceiling on adjustable chains, the whole room glowed pinkish-purple, making it seem like I wasn't growing cannabis by the hot-water heater, but harboring space aliens.

I may as well have been planning for visitors from another planet because I quickly began to feel like Richard Dreyfuss's character in *Close Encounters of the Third Kind*. I wasn't uprooting the shrubs and shoveling dirt through the windows, but I was certainly spotted often enough by the neighbors lugging home some peculiar items, some of which would have been hard to explain had anyone asked. One afternoon I came home with my Ford Explorer sagging under the weight of a load of cinderblocks, a three-cubic-foot block of organic soil from the plant nursery, and a four-foot-long, hundred-pound shower pan retrieved from a nearby salvage yard. The thing was filthy from sitting out in the weather, probably for years, and I had to scrub it clean with bleach and dish soap out on the driveway before I could wrestle it inside. I also had to trim off one corner with a masonry saw to achieve the proper fit. Any moment, I expected one of the dog walkers or lawn mowers to amble over—"Hiya, neighbor! Redoing your shower? Why so much soil? Whatcha doing with cinderblocks?"

The shower pan was a stroke of genius I had while wandering around the trusty Home Depot one day puzzling over what to put my potted marijuana plants in. I couldn't just sit them on the floor, because you're supposed to water them until some runoff trickles out the bottom of the pots, and there was no drain in the grow room floor. I looked in every thrift store I could find for a long, slatted table or bench that would allow the water to drain into a pan or something. Inspiration hit in the bathroom aisle—a shower pan, the fiberglass thing you stand in, with a two-inch lip around the edges and a hole cut right in the middle for drainage, was just the thing I was looking for. Brilliant. It took some shopping around at the local junkyards to find the right size (mine needed to be four feet long by two feet wide so that I could fit it in the room and still open the door), but once it was in place, atop a few strategically placed cinderblocks so that I could position a Rubbermaid tub underneath the hole to catch the overflow, it was perfect. After spending a total of about $800 in material and equipment, and three weeks of busy activity during the weekday hours when the kid was in school and the wife at work, I was done. It had been hard work. More than once, I was thankful that I wasn't disabled and growing pot for a true medical necessity. I saw the value of a medical marijuana dispensary system long before I had a single pot plant in the house.

But before I could go get any, there was that final detail I'd promised to address: I had to have a talk with my son.

FATHER-SON TALKS IN my household take place in a pair of weathered Adirondack chairs on the back lawn, over by a wild bramble of berry bushes and an equally wild grapevine, which never fail to entice a menagerie of raccoons, foxes, feral cats, and, once, even a marmot to visit our yard and enjoy a feast. It was here where we discussed the particulars of human sexuality when Turner was a third-grader, him turning his upper lip blue from Gatorade and me sipping a Jim Beam to steady the nerves. We convened there again before he entered junior high for the mandatory discussion about drugs and peer pressure. Marijuana (along with booze and cigarettes) had been a primary topic; I didn't need research to know that age twelve was plenty old enough for him to be offered a joint in the schoolyard. I gave him the same advice I'd received from my parents and from Nancy Reagan—"Just say no." Now, there we were a bit more than a year later, and my task was to explain why we were about to be growing that off-limits plant twelve feet from where he plays NBA 2K10 on the Xbox.

During that first discussion about drugs, as is the case with any parent, I struggled to frame the conversation just right by forbidding the use of any intoxicating substance while explaining the justification for adults who use the legal ones. Cigarettes were easy to condemn. I've struggled with nicotine addiction my whole life and knew firsthand how insidiously dependent a smoker could become. That Turner would be legally able to buy cigarettes from any convenience store in a mere five years was completely immaterial, I told him. They are evil and deadly and should be avoided at all costs. That Dad sometimes caves in to the desire to smoke a cigar from time to time was left unmentioned.

Alcohol required a bit more finesse; my fondness for Fort Collins's wide variety of craft beers is evident every time anyone in the household opens the refrigerator. Alcohol, I told him, was also dangerous, addictive, and deadly if it's not treated with a great deal of responsibility. Drinking requires a maturity level that teens simply don't possess, I said. In fact, I added, many adults don't possess it either, so stay away until you're old enough to make a more informed, grown-up decision.

By comparison to those two topics, discussing drugs had been simple—too simple, as it turned out. My message was only that he shouldn't touch any of them because they're illegal and dangerous. I'd lumped marijuana right in with crack and heroin, as the vast majority of parents have done in conversations with their children throughout the decades, precisely as the government had done since 1970. I'd blindly perpetrated the popular view of marijuana that the marijuana forces were slowly but surely trying to reverse.

Parents in my situation can be forgiven. Not only is unbiased information about marijuana hard to come by—anyone hoping to do so has to sift through tons of propaganda on both sides of the debate—but the truth is actively suppressed. Should the government admit that marijuana has value as a medicine, and that it's not nearly as harmful as the other narcotics it's equated to in Schedule I, would be to admit that millions of people have been needlessly denied life-changing, and even life-saving, access to it based on decades of lies and disproportionate fears. And that millions more have been fined, imprisoned, and labeled as criminals for using a substance that is irrefutably safer than either tobacco or alcohol, which are the first and third leading causes of death in the United States, respectively.[1] And moreover, that this senseless prohibition has enriched and empowered ruthless criminal organizations who grow, smuggle, and sell pot—almost always in conjunction with other harder drugs like crack, heroin, and methamphetamine—and benefit by the billions of dollars, money that could be recouped and taxed should it be legalized and regulated.

Instead, the modus operandi continues to be to pour billions of dollars per year into the budgets of local and national law enforcement to hunt down marijuana users, fund anti-pot campaigns based on misinformation and panic, and to lock away or fine nearly a million nonviolent marijuana users each year. It's estimated that the United States spends $13.7 billion per year enforcing pot laws alone, the total price of both state and federal expenditures on interdiction efforts and the cost of incarceration.[2] Even as he struggles to claim that the War on Drugs is over in favor of a new effort to focus on treatment rather than arrest, Obama's 2010 drug interdiction budget is now thirty-one times Nixon's budget in 1970—$15.5 billion, with $10 billion going to law enforcement. That's a new record in both percentage and amount of money going toward cracking down on drug users.

To avoid having to make a monumental reversal in priorities and understanding, the government actively recruits parents to help spread its message that pot is deserving of this sort of treatment. The template for doing so is a publication from the National Institute on Drug Abuse (NIDA, part of the U.S. Department of Health and Human Services) called "Marijuana: Facts Parents Should Know." It's a masterpiece of creative writing that can easily convince inattentive parents that marijuana use is just as bad and horrible as they've been told since their own childhoods, even as it acknowledges in the opening letter that many parents might know better due to personal experience with pot. Its strength comes from parents' natural desire to prevent their kids from trying any drugs, and the pamphlet feeds that tendency with carefully crafted language that is meant to be spoon-fed straight from the government to their children. Unfortunately, much of that information is woefully misleading.

Consider the answer to the question "Does using marijuana lead to other drugs?" According to NIDA:

> Long-term studies of high school students and their patterns of drug use show that very few young people use other drugs without first trying marijuana, alcohol, or tobacco. Though few young people use cocaine, for example, the risk of doing so is much greater for youth who have tried marijuana than for those who have never tried it. Although research has not fully explained this association, growing evidence suggests a combination of biological, social, and psychological factors is involved.
>
> Researchers are examining the possibility that long-term marijuana use may create changes in the brain that make a person more at risk of becoming addicted to other drugs, such as alcohol or cocaine. Although many young people who use marijuana do not go on to use other drugs, further research is needed to determine who will be at greatest risk.

The clear impression is that marijuana, alcohol, and tobacco more often than not *cause* drug users to graduate up to LSD, cocaine, and heroin, perhaps by altering their brain chemistry. This "gateway theory" has been around for decades, and it's worth noting that the only source cited by NIDA for the answer to this question is a 1975 article in *Science* magazine, even though the NIDA Web site with this information says it was updated in March 2008. If so, it overlooked a 1999 study by the California-based Institute of Medicine, which offers a sociological reason why many hard-drug users usually smoke pot first: "Because it is the most widely used illicit drug, marijuana is predictably the first illicit drug that most people encounter. Not surprisingly, most users of other illicit drugs used marijuana first. In fact, most drug users do not begin their drug use with marijuana— they begin with alcohol and nicotine, usually when they are too young to do so legally....There is no evidence that marijuana serves as a stepping-stone on the basis of its particular physiological effect." [3]

The respected Rand Corporation, a conservative think-tank that funds a number of research studies into social issues, agreed, largely debunking the "gateway theory" in a 2002 study published in the peer-reviewed *British Journal of Addiction*. "Marijuana typically comes first because it is more available," said Andrew Morral, the study's author. "If our model is right . . . it suggests that policies aimed at reducing or eliminating marijuana availability are unlikely to make any dent in the hard drug problem. When enforcement resources that could have been used against heroin and cocaine are instead used against marijuana, this could have the unintended effect of worsening heroin and cocaine use." [4]

The idea that smoking pot leads to snorting cocaine and shooting heroin is also unsupported by the government's own statistics. Each year, the Substance Abuse and Mental Health Services Administration conducts something of a census of drug users to get a picture of who is using what illegal substance and how frequently. If the gateway theory were to hold up, one would expect to see the number of monthly pot users either equal to or less than the number of cocaine and heroin users. But the opposite is true: In 2009, 15.2 million Americans were estimated to be "past-month" pot smokers, while only an estimated 1.8 million are past-month cocaine users and a mere 213,000 past-month users of heroin. Even if every heroin and cocaine user identified in the study began using those hard drugs because they smoked pot, that means that 85 percent of pot smokers haven't.

The NIDA pamphlet is filled with similar examples of selective and incomplete interpretations of available marijuana research.

On whether marijuana causes cancer: "It's hard to know for sure whether marijuana use alone causes cancer. . . . Marijuana smoke contains some of the same cancer-causing compounds as tobacco, sometimes in higher concentrations." The obvious implication is that marijuana *might* cause cancer, but that doesn't seem to be the case. Recent studies have shown that marijuana may actually fight cancer by attacking and killing cells in a tumor while leaving healthy cells alone.

"Cannabinoids are proving to be unique based on their targeted action on cancer cells and their ability to spare normal cells," reads a 2008 report by the American Association for Cancer Research called *Cannabinoids for Cancer Treatment: Progress and Promise.* "Thus, over-expression of cannabinoid receptors may be effective in killing tumors, whereas low or no expression of these receptors could lead to cell proliferation and metastasis because of the suppression of the antitumor immune response." [5]

Smoking anything, including marijuana, is not good for the lungs, but a 2006 study by the American Thoracic Society found that even heavy pot smokers, those who've smoked as many as twenty-two thousand joints in their lifetimes, show no increased risk of lung cancer compared to nonsmokers. This isn't because pot smoke doesn't contain irritants and carcinogens—it does—but because of some reason scientists haven't yet pinpointed. [6] Still, critics often try to debunk the concept that marijuana can be medicine by pointing out that no other medicine is rolled into a joint and smoked—but entrepreneurs are already rendering the argument moot. There are scores of marijuana vaporizers on the market that heat the pot, but don't burn it. THC is turned into a mist that's inhaled, not unlike cortico-steroids that are inhaled by people with asthma.

In answer to the question "Can marijuana users become addicted?" the NIDA pamphlet actually skips the answer and instead provides a statistic: "In 2004, more than 298,317 people entering drug treatment programs reported marijuana as their primary drug of abuse, showing they needed help to stop using." The number of people entering drug treatment for pot during this period is correct, but this non-answer fails to mention that 57 percent of such admissions in 2004 were court-ordered, meaning the choice was either rehab or jail.[7] Others were referred to treatment by schools, employers, and health care providers. In fact, according to the data, only 16.3 percent of people admitted themselves to treatment programs for marijuana use in 2004, a total of 46,973, or 0.00015 percent of the U.S. population.

Marijuana has indisputable "reinforcing" properties, meaning that it produces pleasurable sensations that a pot smoker would be interested in feeling again, and some users experience withdrawal symptoms when they quit altogether, including nausea, restlessness, and irritability. But pot's ability to "hook" users is very low when compared to other drugs, including legal ones.

In 1994, NIDA's Dr. Jack E. Henningfield and Dr. Neal L. Benowitz of the University of California at San Francisco were asked to rank several substances according to their addictive properties. In the categories of dependence, withdrawal, and tolerance (which is the ability of a drug to immunize a user to its intoxicating effects, so that a heavy drinker, for example, might need more alcohol to feel tipsy than an infrequent drinker), pot was ranked lowest behind every other substance to which it was compared: nicotine, heroin, cocaine, alcohol, and caffeine. A cup of coffee, in other words, was more likely to create dependence and withdrawal than marijuana. Comparatively, nicotine scored highest for dependence and alcohol was at the top for withdrawal. It hardly needs to be pointed out that these substances are not only legal but celebrated as part of our national heritage.[8]

There is perhaps no better example of NIDA doublespeak—or

halfspeak, as it were—than in its response to the question "Can marijuana be used as medicine?" The answer, in full:

> There has been much debate in the media about the possible medical use of marijuana. Under U.S. law since 1970, marijuana has been a Schedule I controlled substance. This means that the drug, at least in its smoked form, has no commonly accepted medical use.
>
> In considering possible medical uses of marijuana, it is important to distinguish between whole marijuana and pure THC or other specific chemicals derived from cannabis. Whole marijuana contains hundreds of chemicals, some of which may be harmful to health.
>
> THC, manufactured into a pill that is taken by mouth, not smoked, can be used for treating the nausea and vomiting that go along with certain cancer treatments and is available by prescription. Another chemical related to THC (nabilone) has also been approved by the Food and Drug Administration for treating cancer patients who suffer nausea. The oral THC is also used to help AIDS patients eat more to keep up their weight.
>
> Scientists are studying whether marijuana, THC, and related chemicals in marijuana (called cannabinoids) may have other medical uses. According to scientists, more research needs to be done on marijuana's side effects and potential benefits before it can be recommended for medical use. However, because of the adverse effects of smoking marijuana, research on other cannabinoids appears more promising for the development of new medications.

Technically, there is nothing inaccurate with this response, other than that it provides no context whatsoever. That marijuana has "no commonly accepted medical use" is true only under the government's definition of a Schedule I controlled substance. There are numerous commonly accepted medical uses for marijuana, including for pain relief, to quell nausea, and to stimulate the appetite, to name but a few. Since at least the late 1970s, oncology doctors and nurses have been secretly recommending and tolerating pot smoking in cancer wards across the country in order for their patients to find relief from chemo-induced vomiting, which can last for days. Synthetic drugs "taken by mouth, not smoked," have an obvious drawback that can render them useless—they must be swallowed, which can be impossible for someone suffering chronic nausea, and they must be kept down long enough to take effect. This isn't likely to work well for someone who throws up every four or five minutes for up to a week. Finally, it's true that more research needs to be done, but here, NIDA is particularly insidious in failing to mention that NIDA itself stands in the way of that research.

Any research facility interested in conducting a clinical test of marijuana's effect on medical patients requires the permission of NIDA and the DEA. NIDA controls access to the only source of government-approved marijuana grown in the United States, at a facility of the University of Mississippi. And NIDA is not interested in any research proposals that hope to show that marijuana benefits anyone. As spokeswoman Shirley Simpson told *The New York Times* as recently as 2010, "Our focus is primarily on the negative consequences of marijuana use. We generally do not fund research focused on the potential beneficial medical effects of marijuana."

The starkest example of this is the now-absurd case of Professor Lyle Craker of the University of Massachusetts at Amherst's Department of Plant and Soil Sciences, who has been trying for a decade to receive approval to grow marijuana as part of a research study to test its medicinal effects. Craker hopes the research will be the first step on the long road of drug-development research required by the U.S.

Food and Drug Administration before new drugs can be prescribed by doctors and sold in pharmacies. The research and development phase of such a trial is estimated to cost about $10 million and take about ten years. But the first step for Craker is to get NIDA/DEA approval to grow pot legally, as the agency does itself at its pot farm in Mississippi.

Craker first applied for his license in 2001. Three and a half years later, the DEA rejected it and Craker appealed to the DEA's administrative law judge. In 2007, Judge Mary Ellen Bittner overturned the DEA's decision and issued an eighty-seven-page decision saying that NIDA's monopoly on the only source of legal pot should be dismantled to allow for independent research. In 2009, the DEA overturned the judge's ruling, and in 2010, it denied Craker's motion to reconsider. Finally, in March 2011, Craker and his lawyers submitted their final motion in the case and, as of this writing, are waiting to hear back from the DEA. After ten years of denials and roadblocks, surely they aren't holding their breath.[9]

Finally, NIDA's FAQs omit what may well be a frequently asked question by parents and children alike: "Can smoking marijuana kill you?" According to the *Journal of the American Medical Society*, in 2000, tobacco killed 435,000; alcohol killed 85,000; adverse reactions to prescription drugs claimed another 32,000 lives; illicit drugs other than marijuana killed 17,000; and another 7,600 were killed by over-the-counter drugs like aspirin. In fact, 400 percent more people have died due to adverse reactions to aspirin-like painkillers than died from the H1N1 swine flu in 2009.[10]

The number of people known to have died from smoking marijuana in all of recorded history?

Zero.

In 1971, the Shafer commission reviewed studies in which scientists tried to kill monkeys and dogs by giving them massive oral doses of THC—three thousand milligrams per kilogram, which is the equivalent of a 154-pound man consuming forty-six pounds of marijuana all at once. The dose wasn't fatal. Medicinal drugs are assigned a number called LD-50, which is the dosage at which half the number of animals receiving a drug would be expected to die. Even today, scientists haven't been able to determine cannabis's LD-50 because they can't pump enough marijuana into test animals to kill them. Their best guess is that pot's LD-50 is 1:20,000 or 1:40,000, which simply means a suicidal pothead would have to ingest twenty thousand or forty thousand times the amount of marijuana found in one joint in order to overdose. Put another way, he'd have to smoke 1,500 pounds of marijuana in fifteen minutes.

Neither Cheech nor Chong could do that.

I DIDN'T HAMMER Turner with all of these details when I finally laid out my plans for him; I simply distilled it into bite-size generalities that I hoped didn't make me look like too much of a hypocrite. Luckily I was aided by the fact that the medical marijuana discussion was on everyone's lips. It was the number one story on TV and in the newspapers for weeks on end, and that provided an excuse to bring it up. I told him that I was working on a story about medical marijuana and in order to really know what I was talking about, I would be growing some in the basement. I emphasized that it wasn't for anyone's personal use in the household (especially his), and that once I'd grown and harvested the marijuana, I'd be selling it to patients or dispensaries. The catch, I told him, was that we needed to keep it secret—from the neighbors, from our friends, and most definitely from his buddies and classmates. The last thing I needed was for my little experiment to end up on his Facebook page.

"But wait," he said. "If it can help sick people, why is it illegal?"

It was the one question I didn't have a good answer to.

"I'm still working on that," I told him.

· 6 ·

Up in Smoke

"The movement is bigger than the plant. It's about freedom."

—Richard Cowan, former national director of NORML

My search for answers led me, oddly enough, to a cafeteria tucked deep in the bowels of the Los Angeles Convention Center in early 2010, where I sat in a garish plastic chair across from a giddy, disheveled little man with slightly bloodshot eyes.

Engrossed in our discussion, Bruce Perlowin was oblivious to a never-ending stream of pretty women chirping past the cafeteria, cheerful brides-to-be and their bridesmaids on their way to a wedding expo around the corner. Perlowin was talking about changing the world and just starting to pick up steam. Very little could distract him at that point.

"It's a totally, totally different economic paradigm that I call quantum economics. Or compassionate capitalism. Or marketing for the heart," he said, speaking slowly and carefully because he could see from my expression that I was having trouble following along. "Quantum physics is the underlying reality of how we understand the way the world is put together. We've built this entire world under Newtonian physics; but now, the quantum science is leaking in. You're going to see a dramatic example of an explosive growth curve that is rarely seen in the socioeconomic landscape in this company. All that is, is quantum mechanics manifesting itself in the socioeconomic realm."

He sat back and smiled, raising his eyebrows as if to ask, "*Now* you get it, don't you?"

The truth is, not really. But I was willing to give him a bit of leeway. As much as he looked like he would be the one vacuuming the carpet after the brides were gone, Perlowin is the CEO of Medical Marijuana Inc., a publicly traded company that had brought together a who's who of cannabis luminaries to speak at the inaugural Medical Marijuana Education Expo under way in a small room on the floor above the cafeteria. What he was trying to explain was his business plan, which he complained no one except him could understand.

But I was willing to try to let him educate me a bit longer because Perlowin is more than just the slightly kooky boss of a marijuana business. Known everywhere from the Northern California pot havens of Santa Cruz and Arcata to the urban smoking dens of Miami and New York as the King of Pot, he has smuggled more marijuana into the country—an estimated 250,000 tons between 1979 and 1983—than anyone else who's been caught so far. It's no stretch to say that he and the men upstairs, all of them now into their sixties and beyond, were responsible for practically every joint smoked between San Francisco and Fort Lauderdale from the late 1970s to the early 1980s. At that time, most of the pot in America was smuggled into the country rather than grown here, and men like Perlowin are considered to have been integral in keeping the supply lines open, using a sort of ganja navy and air force to keep tons of marijuana in circulation. Eventually, strong border interdiction and concerns over an herbicide sprayed on Mexican pot led to the formation of America's underground indoor-growing network, which gave the marijuana community new heroes, but the men upstairs are still considered to be royalty.

Perlowin is the self-proclaimed king of them all.

A PEACE-AND-LOVE HIPPIE from the flower-power sixties, Perlowin started as a small-time hustler selling dime bags at his Miami, Florida, high school. He was into everything from LSD to bellbottoms to The Doors, and sometimes he and his friends would head to the local park to turn complete strangers on to the consciousness-expanding qualities of pot and acid. Drugs were all part of the social fabric back then, and in 1973, when he was in his early twenties, Perlowin was happy to stow a few bales of marijuana in his house for a buddy. The friend let him sell a few extra pounds for the trouble. The next time Perlowin provided the stash house, he and his friend David Tobias (whom he'd known since the third grade and who was later nicknamed the Sultan of Shrimpers because of his preference in smuggling vessels) sold all fifty pounds and made themselves a small fortune. Drug running became a full-time occupation, and by the age of twenty-five, Perlowin was a multimillionaire.

"The nice thing about marijuana smuggling," he said, "is that you could mess up a whole bunch of times and recover, because if you didn't make $100,000 every week you weren't doing something right. You could blow all your money in a week and get $100,000 the next week to start all over again. And there was a lot of starting all over again, but each time you got more and more sophisticated and fine-tuned what you did."

By the late 1970s, with stepped-up Coast Guard patrols and law enforcement crackdowns, Florida was proving risky for drug runners. So Perlowin hired a research firm called Information on Demand, spinning them a yarn that he was writing a book about marijuana smuggling; he wanted research on every major pot bust in the United States over the previous ten years. Not surprisingly, he learned that most of the big busts happened near the borders. So he located his new headquarters where the research told him there was very little drug interdiction activity: in San Francisco Bay.

At the height of his criminal career, Perlowin commanded a flotilla of fishing boats that ran marijuana under the Golden Gate Bridge from Colombia practically around the clock, offloading pot by the ton on a private thousand-foot pier that he bought with the proceeds of the operation. From 1979 to 1983, it's estimated that Perlowin put a quarter of a million tons of pot, most of it Punta Red from Colombia and Thailand, onto the streets. The DEA and the Federal Bureau of Investigation estimated the street value to be close to a billion dollars.

It was a sophisticated operation. Colombian suppliers would grow and bale the marijuana inland, and then fly it to remote coastal areas accessible only by boat, dumping the bales out of the low-flying planes onto the beach. Perlowin hired whole villages to gather up the pot and secure it until the boats could arrive to deliver it to California. At one point, his personal fleet consisted of ninety-four marine vessels, including trawlers, tuna boats, an old tugboat, a converted mine sweeper, crabbers, shrimpers, fast-moving speedboats, and even counter-surveillance vessels heavy with radar and communications equipment used to monitor Coast Guard activity.

On land, he employed about two hundred people and owned or rented several stash houses, a surveillance outpost with a direct line of sight to the dock, VIP retreats for his Colombian connections, a motor home rigged with communications and surveillance equipment capable of tracking Coast Guard flights throughout North America, and a personal fortress for himself in Ukiah, California, the Mendocino County seat. This last property was a work of art—located on a twenty-four-acre plot, the house was outfitted with surveillance cameras with night-vision capability, a steel-lined bulletproof nerve center, a fourteen-line telephone hub, and a spiral staircase leading to the bedroom that could be electrified with the flip of a switch in case of home invasion.

Perlowin's cash circled the globe to come out clean, running through Vegas casinos, trust companies in Luxembourg, banks in the Caymans, real estate firms in Florida, and shell companies in Nevada.

He was unlike other drug barons in that he smuggled only pot and never used violence in his operation—although he added, "I wasn't a wimp, you don't get to be a marijuana kingpin by being a mild guy." He remained a hippie at heart, spending his time doing yoga and pondering the meaning of life.

"It was a training ground," Perlowin said of the old days. "I remember I was up in Ukiah at my house making millions of dollars, in this big beautiful mansion in the middle of the woods, you know, right on the creek in the mountains, and one of the guys says, 'Man, you're just rocking. You've got everything going for you.' And I said, 'Yeah, but I wish my real work would start. . . . This isn't my real work. This is my training ground with the millions, so that when the billions come in, I know how to handle it.'"

That's one way of looking at what happened in 1983, as just a cosmic extension of his training. One day, after eating breakfast at a Denny's in northern California, Perlowin paid the bill and left behind a notebook filled with his operation's every incriminating detail. It made its way eventually to the FBI's Chuck Latting, an agent who had been trying to pick up Perlowin's trail and figure out the source of all the pot flooding the streets of San Francisco, a search that had until then been fruitless.

Losing the notebook was such a boneheaded move that Latting, on a CNBC documentary about the marijuana trade, seemed embarrassed to admit that it was Perlowin's dumb mistake and not his keen detective work that finally led to the King of Pot's arrest, in Chicago while on his way to a three-day tantric yoga seminar.

"The book was the key to everything we found," Latting said. "I couldn't imagine that anybody who was somewhat competent running an organization would walk away leaving their most prized possession sitting in a booth at Denny's."

Federal prosecutors charged some thirty people in connection with Perlowin's smuggling ring, some as far afield as Ann Arbor, Michigan. The King of Pot himself served almost ten years in prison.

Perlowin might have been out of the marijuana business temporarily in the early 1990s, but he wasn't through hustling. Jerry

Rubin—the social justice radical and yippie best known as one of the Chicago Seven, who were indicted for starting an antiwar riot at the 1968 Democratic National Convention—introduced Perlowin to the concept of network marketing, also known as multilevel marketing and pyramid schemes. Drug smuggling is the ultimate pyramid scheme, with money flowing upward from the street-level dealers all the way to the kingpin and the suppliers, and Perlowin put his experience to use hawking long-distance calling cards; he and another former drug runner formed Globalcom 2000, the first calling-card company to sell corporate advertising on their faces. Their first client was 7-Eleven.

Now Perlowin had come full circle. Within weeks of Ogden's memo, Perlowin changed the name of his most recent venture, a debit-card company called Club Vivanet, to Medical Marijuana Inc. and began trading stock on the Pink Sheets board, a penny stock market that doesn't require any filings with the Securities and Exchange Commission.

Despite all the razzle-dazzle about quantum physics, MMI is simply a pyramid scheme, one that doesn't involve any actual marijuana—as Perlowin pointed out, with the company's principal officers being some of the biggest drug felons on the United States, "it wouldn't be wise." Instead, the company hopes to service all of the industry's peripheral needs, in particular information and knowledge, which at that time was in short supply. The linchpin is a series of educational seminars and brick-and-mortar "cannabis centers" that would act as local clearing houses for information on local rules, resources, and ongoing training for those in the medical marijuana business, even in locations that don't yet have such an industry; like lots of other people, Perlowin saw the Ogden memo as the long-awaited signal that legalization was on the horizon. He hoped that selling licenses to prospective franchisees for as much as $100,000 for control of a territory would parlay the "King of Pot" brand into the billions he'd been training for.

IT WAS A testament to how mainstream pot had become that the Medical Marijuana Education Expo was held not in someone's basement, but right next door to the Staples Center, home of the L.A. Lakers and about a twenty-minute drive on the 110 from the hotel I'd booked for the weekend. Despite that Perlowin had organized the affair in a matter of days, the slate of speakers was impressive. There were master cannabis growers, longtime activists, representatives of marijuana farming collectives, and legal experts. If anyone could muster such a brain trust on short notice, it was the King of Pot. Seeing as how the event was touted as an "education expo"—and knowing I could use all the education I could find—I couldn't think of a better way to spend a weekend than in L.A. rubbing elbows with drug smugglers and pot farmers.

Equally impressive was the wide diversity of those in the audience who weren't dissuaded by the steep ticket price—$420, naturally. They came from every corner of the country, including many states that had no medical marijuana laws and few hopes of getting any soon. But that was the appeal of Perlowin's business model—there's nothing risky in opening a cannabis center that has no cannabis, and many who'd flown from places like Florida, Oklahoma, and other restrictive locations felt as he did, that it was only a matter of time before medical marijuana swept the nation, with legalization not far behind. Looking around the rows of seats, I spotted a few typical stoner types in "Hemp Can Save the World" T-shirts who were snoozing in the back rows, but by and large the crowd was composed of the same sort of business-casual professional you'd expect to see at any convention of dentists or insurance agents. They were a curious mixture of grandmothers, venture capitalists, dispensary owners, entrepreneurs, and everyone in between. There were also many people like me, people who needed to fill the gaps in a knowledge base about marijuana that was rudimentary at best.

Things kicked off with a legal presentation by San Francisco lawyer James Silva, who laid the groundwork by reminding everyone that their activities were no less illegal than the time of Nixon, no matter what they thought the Ogden memo said. He ran through some basic precautions that were doubtlessly old news to everyone else in the room, but to which I paid specific attention: Keep your pot away from your cash because skunky-smelling money is a clue of what you're up to; don't agree to a search of your car during routine traffic stops (and for that matter, keep any weed you're transporting locked in the trunk or otherwise out of sight); and if you get arrested, don't say a word without a lawyer present. At one point, a kid who'd borrowed money from his dad to fly out from New Jersey, which just days before the expo had passed its medical marijuana law, began to incriminate himself during a long-winded question that Silva cut off from the podium.

"I should have maybe started with this, but everyone should realize that you don't know everyone in this room," he said. "It's open to anyone who registers, of course, so we usually have one or two members of our local law enforcement community in attendance."

Despite that word of warning, it became difficult to remember that the main topic of conversation was an illegal substance. The expo was my first full immersion into a crowd of True Believers, and I wasn't used to hanging around marijuana aficionados who weren't trying to convince me that pot should be legalized. That was considered to be a foregone conclusion with this crowd. By the very act of being there, I was presumed to be part of the community, someone who needed no convincing, and the wide-ranging discussions that weekend skipped entirely over the talk-radio topics of whether marijuana was addictive, or would lead to harder drugs, or would poison the children; those subjects were considered to be Cannabis 101, and we were in the advanced studies class. Throughout the weekend, we plumbed the depths of knowledge amassed over the course of decades by men and women who, by the very nature of their study and experiences, were criminals. For someone who's never gone very far below the surface of whether marijuana was good or bad for society, it was quite the education.

During the cultivators' presentations, for example, I felt like I'd snuck into a Ph.D.-level botany course. I didn't understand half the terminology and the discussion was way over my head, but I took copious notes, scrawling out phonetic spellings of endocannabinoids, tetrahydrocannabinol, cannabidiol, trichomes, and terpenes. There were presentations by growers who'd spent half a million dollars on complex hydroponic gardening systems, which deliver nutrients to plant roots through a liquid mixture rather than soil, and others who'd begun growing aeroponically, another soil-free technique that fertilizes roots using a fine, nutrient-rich mist. I learned for the first time that cannabis plants come in four species, but two are heavily cultivated and hybridized to produce a wide range of effects—*sativas* are known for their clear bell-like helium-headed highs, and *indicas* leaden the body and are responsible for the phenomenon known as "couch weld," which is familiar to anyone who really wants to get up and go make some popcorn but can't move off the sofa.

Thousands of strains of marijuana have been developed by outlaw growers who've crossed and recrossed plants to maximize their most desirable traits. This has resulted in specific highs that can be expected from specific strains, which is good for matching them to illnesses— what might be good for muscle spasms, for example, might not be as good for migraines. Crossbreeding also resulted in shorter plants that produce more weed in less time than in the past. These growers have done something amazing: They have developed marijuana that is customized to being grown indoors and with a yield and growth cycle that is perfect for commercial purposes. It's long been debated whether the science of cannabis would have come so far so fast if there hadn't been laws that drove growers indoors and forced them to innovate and experiment.

Throughout the weekend, I was struck by how seriously everything was taken, and more than a little impressed by the level of scholarship displayed by members of the audience. Detailed questions about molecular biology were answered in equally meticulous fashion. Audience members scribbled notes as if there was an exam on the horizon. Skeptical growers wary of such new technology as LED growing lights grilled product distributors about light spectrums and wavelengths. Arguments and discussions—including over such minutiae as whether or not to prune pot plants while they're growing— were civilized, but impassioned. Anyone hoping for a toking-circle and a sing-along were disappointed; there were one or two chuckles about someone having grown some "really good medicine," but the expo was all business.

As a newcomer to this community, that came as a bit of a surprise. Back home, where the industry was like a runaway train threatening to go off the rails, you couldn't escape the grumblings in the press that all this talk of "medical" marijuana was just a big scam. Colorado's attorney general, John Suthers, said as much a few years before, when he was a U.S. Attorney. "Medical marijuana is nothing more than a smokescreen, an excuse for lifelong pot smokers to get high," he told a TV reporter during the case of Dana May, a medical marijuana patient who suffered from reflex sympathetic dystrophy, an incurable nerve disease in his lower limbs that made it feel like his feet were in a deep fryer. In 2004, May was raided by the DEA, which confiscated all of his pot and his growing equipment. May was never charged, but he had all his medicine taken away, along with his means of growing more. Suthers didn't buy May's argument, or that of May's doctor, that pot was the only thing that eased his pain—May and others like him smoke for no reason other than "because they like to smoke marijuana," Suthers said. "They have been longtime marijuana users, and they like to smoke marijuana." May eventually sued for the return of his weed and his equipment, and he succeeded in getting at least the equipment back. It was the first time in U.S. history that the DEA gave back gear used to grow cannabis.

Many share Suthers's attitude, and its pervasiveness has grown in tandem with the medical marijuana industry itself. The complicating factor is that there is reason to believe it. There are plenty of people like May, in Colorado and across the country, who use the medical marijuana laws to find relief from serious illnesses. But there are a substantial number of people who enroll in their state programs whose reasons are more suspicious. In Colorado, about 90 percent of those on the medical marijuana registry are men whose average age is thirty-nine who are suffering an apparent epidemic of "severe pain"—I fit that demographic perfectly, and I'm living proof of how simple it is to get one's name on the registry. Most states have such a catch-all category, but not every one publishes the percentage of patients claiming specific illnesses—in fact, some states don't require patients to register with the state government at all. In California, obtaining a license and medical marijuana ID are optional—so it can be difficult to know how pervasive this is. But the same situation exists in Oregon, where of the 36,380 Oregonians with medical marijuana cards as of August 2010, 32,614 claim "severe pain" as their condition.

Of course there are legitimate "severe pain" claims, but as my own experience proved, it's a condition that's easy to fake. This is the heart of the problem with medical marijuana laws and why so many are torn over them—their very existence proves that voters support the idea of ensuring access to pot for those with a legitimate medical need, but no one envisioned a scenario in which healthy tokers would be able to shop with impunity at the corner weed emporium. This anxiety is born from two major factors—"forty years of bullshit," as Perlowin characterized the government's relentless fear-mongering about the supposed dangers of pot that has become as intractable a truth in the minds of most Americans as the sky being blue; and the fact that marijuana remains under lock and key as a Schedule I drug with no redeeming benefit, medically or otherwise.

Both of those reasons are why the medical marijuana issue is pushed so strongly by the legalization movement. Ogden's memo provided a gold-plated opportunity to thrust marijuana into the mainstream to demonstrate what pot activists have been saying for decades—that it's not only a relatively harmless substance that fails to justify the severity of penalties for its recreational use, but also legitimately useful in medical applications.

Richard Cowan, the former national director of NORML and one of the most forceful speakers of the weekend, admitted that the Ogden memo represented a loophole that the marijuana legalization community needed to step through before it closes.

"We need to take advantage of it," he said.

Changing the federal law and ending prohibition first depend on winning the hearts and minds of the average American, and there has been no better opportunity than through medical marijuana, Cowan said, pointing out that the hard part is behind them.

"If this were any other issue with this amount of support, politicians would be trying to claim they invented it," he said, referring to polls showing support for legalizing it for medical use at around 70 percent nationwide.

If there was a unifying theme among those at the L.A. expo that weekend, that was it. No matter whether they were in it for profit or compassion, the goal was to seize on both the opportunity afforded by the Ogden memo and popular support to demonstrate that marijuana isn't the evil bugaboo it's been said to be throughout most people's lifetimes.

Whether they could or not was an open question. As Perlowin says, "There is no roadmap for how to build a medical marijuana company," much less an entire industry, one capable of smoothly injecting itself under society's embedded prejudices against marijuana use as a *recreational* drug without backfiring so badly that it crushes the momentum afforded by the Ogden memo.

It was a precipitous moment in the history of the marijuana legalization movement. As much as the landscape in 2009 seemed like paradise to many, there was the high possibility of a backlash that could freeze everything in its place, or even reverse what progress has been made. Unrest was already manifesting in some places—Montana Sen. Jim Shockley was so fed up with the proliferation of marijuana dispensaries there that he announced plans to try revoking the citizen-initiated law. "It needs control, if not extinction," he said of the medical marijuana trade.

The ball was in the legalizers' court, but history has shown it hasn't always been adept at handling its challenges. The broad, multifaceted marijuana community tends to be as divisive and Balkanized as any striving for sweeping social changes. Throw in flamboyant personalities and titanic egos, and the results can be messy, often at critical moments.

For an illustration, one needs to look no further than the Medical Marijuana Education Expo itself.

ON THE SURFACE, the expo seemed to have gone off splendidly, but behind the scenes, mutiny was brewing. One of the reasons Perlowin looked so haggard, I found out later, was because he was in a pitched battle over finances and strategy with his second-in-command, a burly man named Cliff Perry. While the attendees enjoyed riveting "call to arms" presentations by Cowan and heard war stories from Robert "Bobby Tuna" Platshorn, who'd recently been released from serving a twenty-eight-year prison sentence for marijuana smuggling (which is currently a record), Perry and Perlowin were all but coming to blows.

There were differences in style, for one thing. Perry calls himself a pragmatist who took on all the myriad details of organizing the expo because Perlowin was too flighty to be depended on. That included paying out of pocket for so many things that he'd drained his checking account. Perlowin considered Perry to be a tight-fisted dictator trying to hijack the company. Worse, Perry later accused Perlowin of misleading interested investors by touting the expo as a raging financial success when in truth it was anything but—throughout the weekend, as Perlowin pitched his seminar franchise idea, he gestured around the room of about 150 attendees as proof of how much money there was to be made duplicating the event around the country. What the King of Pot never mentioned was that only about fifty people had actually paid the full $420 for the seminar series. The rest came for free, most likely because the expo was organized at the last minute. At least one person put down $100,000 for a license to put on a "King of Pot" seminar in Las Vegas, based partly on his belief that everyone in attendance in L.A. paid to be there.

The truth was, Perlowin's company was so broke that its credit card, used to pay for Cowan's and Platshorn's hotel rooms, was rejected when they tried to check out at the end of the weekend. Perry rushed to the rescue, but he'd paid for so much else by that point that he couldn't cover the bill—he had to talk MMI's lawyer into paying for the rooms.

For Cowan and Platshorn, it was just more proof that Perlowin couldn't be trusted. Both men left L.A. angry after learning that Perlowin tried to sweeten the deal for investors by telling anyone considering writing a fat check to a gang of former drug dealers that Cowan and Platshorn were both poised to join Medical Marijuana Inc. in some capacity, a detail Perlowin mentioned to me as well. In fact, Cowan heard from others that the King of Pot was supposedly working on a deal to buy Cowan's current venture, a marijuana research and development firm in Colorado Springs called Cannabis Science Inc.

"Frankly, I was a little bit disturbed at the conference when two different people came up and told me that they'd been told that MMI was going to acquire Cannabis Science," Cowan told me later. "There have been no—zero—conversations about that. They told me that Bruce was the source of that statement and that did not please me at all. . . . There were too many statements made [about a relationship between MMI and Cannabis Science] that were not factual."

The same was true with Platshorn, who said Perlowin flew him to L.A. from his home in Florida to discuss the possibility of Platshorn developing a training manual for MMI's investors. Once he learned more about the business, Platshorn wanted nothing to do with it. He suspected it was a con job meant to hype the company's stock so that its shareholders, most of whom are former drug runners, could unload their stock at a high price.

"I didn't want the legal liability and, very honestly, I didn't like the idea of basically scamming people, if not intentionally, then inevitably," Platshorn said. "[There's] no substance in the business. They want to sell learning centers, which is their default product now, but there wasn't so much as a training manual, a teaching manual, a business manual. There was nothing. Bruce wanted to take money from some of these people who wanted to buy territories. Maybe some of them decided [to invest] after they heard me speak. I hope not, because I told them I was not connected to MMI but was there to negotiate possible employment."

In the end, Perry wound up calling Perlowin a "rabid dog" and quit to start his own marijuana seminar business. Perlowin, for his part, was as optimistic and effusive as ever when I called him a few days later to try to figure out what happened.

The problem isn't him, he said. All that stuff with Perry was a big disaster, but also just the growing pains of a new business, nothing that would get in the way of changing the world. As for Cowan and Platshorn, that was nothing but a misunderstanding about a business model that was too complex to be easily grasped.

The real problem, he said, is that no one understands quantum economics.

IN TERMS OF an implosion, MMI's meltdown wasn't as dramatic as others. The worst result was that the King of Pot's crown was tarnished and another rift developed in the fractured landscape of those who should be allies.

Others have been harder to overcome. For instance, while Cowan was national director of NORML, he fired two employees, Rob Kampia and Chuck Thomas, who'd been agitating for organizational change. The two men went on to found the advocacy and lobbying organization Marijuana Policy Project (MPP) in 1995, which quickly grew in size and influence. While it would seem obvious that NORML and MPP should work together since they share common goals, Cowan and Kampia don't get along; when it became clear that the organizations couldn't work in harmony, Cowan resigned.

Over the years, Kampia embraced his role as a national spokesman for the marijuana movement, testifying before Congress and becoming a regular on cable news networks, debating drug policy with the likes of former congressman Bob Barr, former DEA administrator Asa Hutchinson, and former deputy drug czar Andrea Barthwell.

But when he wasn't under the glare of television lights, Kampia was apparently trying to get under the sheets with his own employees. In August 2009, Kampia and several MPP employees went to a local Washington, D.C., bar for a few happy-hour drinks after work; the next day, four full-time employees quit because Kampia hooked up with a female subordinate, the capstone of what many described as a pattern of intolerable boorishness. Three others left a few weeks later. Several employees spoke with reporters from *High Times* and described Kampia's actions as "predatory" and "morally reprehensible."

Salem Pearce, MPP's former director of membership, told the magazine: "This is all part of a pattern of behavior by Rob, who was known in the office for his sexually explicit comments and actions towards female employees and interns, particularly ones half his age and desirous of full-time jobs with MPP. Rob's willingness to jeopardize the organization for sexual gratification and his desperate attempts to keep his job sickened me and made me no longer able to work for him."

Kampia did indeed keep his job but took a three-week leave of absence to go to sex rehab. The scandal made national news and necessitated the cancelation of MPP's annual fundraiser, which was the only thing to do since it was to be held at the Playboy Mansion.

For marijuana advocates, the scandal was a gruesome embarrassment at a time when the national marijuana movement was most in need of sober leadership. But it wasn't the most regrettable example of the pot movement's ability to shoot itself in the foot. For that, we have to go back to Jimmy Carter's administration, just before the time when Perlowin moved his smuggling operation to California. It involved the rock-star swagger of NORML's founder, the country's drug czar, and an herbicide called Paraquat.

PRESIDENT CARTER, THE affable peanut farmer from Georgia, is remembered by history for many things—the energy crisis, the hostage debacle in Iran, wearing sweaters in the Oval Office so that he could turn down the heat and conserve energy—but for many people in the counterculture, Carter is the best thing to happen to the cannabis movement since Thomas Jefferson drafted the Declaration of Independence on hemp paper. This isn't due to any hard evidence that Carter smoked weed but because of his forthright stance against the harshness of laws pertaining to marijuana. Like the Shafer commission, Carter wanted to decriminalize possession and put the focus on drug treatment and rehabilitation. Despite being labeled as "soft on drugs" by his political opponents—and not to mention his admission, in a *Playboy* interview, that he'd "committed adultery in my heart many times"[1]—the nation was so repulsed by the still-fresh Watergate scandal that ended Nixon's presidency that it allowed this down-home Beltway outsider to squeak into the Oval Office by a vote of 50.1 percent to incumbent Gerald Ford's 48 percent. Carter was the first southern president since 1848, and he wasted little time working to make good on his campaign promises. Marijuana decriminalization was high on the list.

"Penalties against drug use should not be more damaging to an individual than the use of the drug itself," he told Congress in 1977. "Nowhere is this more clear than in the laws against the possession of marijuana in private for personal use."[2]

A man of his convictions, he surrounded himself with people who thought likewise, including his drug czar, Dr. Peter Bourne, who was controversial because he didn't view marijuana, or even cocaine, as very harmful. According to news reports from the time, it apparently wasn't unusual to pick up a whiff around the White House from time to time. For example, at a jazz festival on the South Lawn of the White House, pot haze hung so heavily under the canopies of trees and tents during the performances that it was hard to see the stage. Carter mingled with the musicians (many of them financial contributors to his campaign) while Secret Service agents feebly tried to wave away the cloud of smoke. Carter was friendly with Gregg Allman of the Allman Brothers Band and country singer Willie Nelson, both longtime pot smokers. Bourne once told a reporter (in a statement that he later retracted) that pot smoking among White House staffers was common.[3]

Against that backdrop, NORML, a relatively new advocacy group, enjoyed great sway and access on Capitol Hill. Formed with a $5,000 grant from Hugh Hefner's Playboy Foundation in 1970 by young D.C. lawyer Keith Stroup, NORML latched onto the Shafer report and lobbied relentlessly for marijuana decriminalization. NORML staffers were extremely popular among congressional aides and newspaper reporters, many of whom were happy to share a joint with the colorful lobbyists. NORML even began playing softball against a team from the White House.[4]

The mostly widely anticipated event of the year was NORML's annual Christmas party, which attracted all sorts of edgy celebrities like gonzo journalist Hunter S. Thompson, Playboy bunnies, *High Times* reporters, congressmen, and influential D.C. dealmakers. Getting zonked on drugs was part of the atmosphere. Bourne, the drug czar himself, attended one of these events but was nervous about being seen at a party where pot was smoked openly and harder drugs were in use as well.

For many years, Stroup cultivated Bourne as an ally in the war against the War on Drugs, hoping that Bourne's friendly stance toward marijuana would lead to wider social acceptance, decriminalization, and perhaps even all-out legalization. But the two didn't see eye to eye on everything, and what could have been a minor rift over a foreign drug-eradication program ended up contributing to Bourne's ignominious resignation in 1978 and very likely set back the decriminalization campaign by decades.

Starting in 1975, the United States spent millions of dollars supplying Mexican drug agencies with Bell helicopters equipped with herbicide applicators to quickly poison poppy fields and marijuana farms in the Sierra Madres. Previously, the unlucky soldiers on marijuana eradication duty were required to hike hours into the mountains and chop down the plants by hand, tedious and time-consuming work. Now, the choppers did most of the heavy lifting, spraying the pot fields with a strong chemical called Paraquat, an herbicide developed by Britain's Imperial Chemical Industries. While some of the helicopters sprayed the fields, others provided military support in case any farmers on the ground decided to shoot it out with the drug agents.

Paraquat was good at killing cannabis plants, but it needed time in the sun to work—at least three days exposed to intense sunlight. The Mexican growers found that if they harvested the marijuana immediately after the plants had been sprayed and covered them from direct sunlight, the chemical agent didn't seem to degrade the plants— therefore, they could include it with all the rest of the marijuana making its way into the U.S. market. At the time, most of the pot being smoked in the United States came from Mexico.

Paraquat is deadly to humans; even a small amount ingested into the body can lead to acute respiratory distress or death from fibrous tissue development in the lungs. Fatalities could occur within thirty days. Naturally, this caused quite a panic among the 13 million people estimated to smoke marijuana in the 1970s. Laboratories were overwhelmed with requests to test marijuana samples to look for Paraquat; a 1978 *Time* magazine article reported that a lab in Palo Alto,

California, received five thousand samples of marijuana and had to hire twenty-two new lab workers to handle the additional work. Twenty-eight percent of the samples contained some amounts of Paraquat. Even anti-marijuana politicians called for an end to the spraying program, fearing a widespread health crisis.[5]

That crisis never developed—in later years, the Environmental Protection Agency would learn that Paraquat burns up into much less toxic compounds when smoked. But Paraquat had a much longer-lasting effect on U.S. drug policy than an unfounded health scare.

Stroup, who worked for the Commission on Product Safety before forming NORML, was inspired by the consumer rights activities of Ralph Nader and saw one of his roles as advocating for the health and safety of marijuana smokers. That naturally included lobbying to change restrictive laws, but he also saw it as his duty to sue the government to end the Paraquat program. He put a lot of pressure on Bourne and took it as a personal affront that the drug czar considered the situation to be no big deal.

"It became one of these sort of non-issues that took on a life of its own," Bourne later told a PBS interviewer. He pointed out that the Paraquat was bought and used on marijuana by the Mexicans; the U.S. government was more interested in spraying the chemical on poppy plants from which opium is derived. The marijuana spraying was more of a Mexican freelance operation, albeit conducted with American-supplied helicopters.[6]

Unable to convince Bourne to adopt his viewpoint about Paraquat, Stroup resorted to personal sabotage, a move he later said was "the stupidest thing I ever did."[7] He called a newspaper reporter and told him that the country's drug czar had snorted cocaine at one of the NORML parties. Bourne, already under fire for having written a prescription for one of his staff members for a sedative using a fake name, denied the allegation but submitted his resignation. Stroup was fired by NORML for being a snitch.[8]

The accusation that the nation's drug czar was attending drug-fueled parties with Playboy bunnies did not sit well with the average American. At the time of his resignation, there was a grass-roots anti-marijuana movement under way that was being led by parents in Carter's home state of Georgia. Even before Carter was elected, Bourne recounted in the PBS interview, they were calling him soft on drugs because of his preference to treat drug users rather than lock them up.

"They'd made a lot of noise along the lines of, you know, 'Carter's too liberal on drugs. We don't want treatment. We want more aggressive law enforcement. These people aren't sick, they're criminals, and we want to lock them all up and put them in prison. Heroin isn't the issue, it's marijuana smoking by suburban white kids—our children—that we're worried about,'" Bourne recalled. "Quite frankly, Carter and I had regarded these people as pretty inconsequential gadflies that you see in politics but [who] are really of no particular consequence, and we essentially ignored them."[9]

But after Stroup's leak to the press, there was no ignoring them and others who seized on Bourne's resignation as evidence that the White House was being run by a bunch of potheads. Bourne saw it as a complete reversal of whatever momentum may have been building behind the decriminalization policies he and Carter were trying to encourage.

"I don't want to seem so egocentric as to suggest that the whole world revolves around me," Bourne said. "But I think the real turning point in this was the moment that I left the White House. It ended the era of the focus on dealing drugs as a public health issue. From the point after I left, it then became a political, law enforcement, and moral issue, and there were obviously other players like . . . the parents' movement and other factors. But if I had to point to any one moment when the whole perspective changed, I think that would be the perspective. . . .

"The objective was, can you appeal to suburban voters who have this rational or irrational fear about their children smoking marijuana? And that is what you want to appeal to."[10]

· 7 ·

Growing Pains and Ganja Gurus

"Never tell anybody about any garden."

— Jorge Cervantes, *Marijuana Horticulture:*
The Indoor/Outdoor Medical Grower's Bible, 2006

I began violating federal drug laws on Easter Sunday, after the glazed ham and a glass of wine and a mid-afternoon nap. I skipped dessert and the traditional evening stroll around the neighborhood and instead hopped in the car. I had an appointment with Abundant Healing's master cultivator, a woman who would hook me up with some live marijuana plants. My relationship with the owners of the dispensary next to the gym had grown since I hatched my plan to be a pot farmer, and they became my mentors.

Sonja Gibbons, the dispensary's master grower who knew everything about cannabis, met me at the dispensary and I then followed her pickup truck on a circuitous route meant to shake off any undercover cops that might be tailing us. We drove in circles and figure eights through the streets of an industrial neighborhood for about ten minutes before pulling into a dirt parking lot on the side of a warehouse, where we were greeted by a couple of friendly pit bulls guarding the place.

"You can never be too safe," Sonja explained of the long, winding drive that ended just a few blocks from where we started. She unlocked a nondescript metal door and punched a code on an electronic keypad to disable the alarm. Walking into the warehouse was like stepping inside the reptile house at the zoo, the warmth and humidity carrying a wave of green fragrance through the door before I'd even stepped around the corner and laid my eyes on a veritable jungle of cannabis. The door opened into a large room crammed with wide plywood tables. These were lit by several six-hundred-watt high-pressure sodium lights beaming artificial sunlight onto dozens and dozens of little baby plants in red plastic keg-party cups and taller, more mature ones in three-gallon pots. The fifteen-foot-tall walls were covered in plastic sheeting, and along one wall was a chest-high stack of organic soil in plastic bags. A thermometer said it was eighty-three degrees in the room, which explained why Sonja was dressed in cargo shorts and a David Letterman T-shirt even though it was nippy enough at dusk for me to wear a light coat.

This was the cloning and vegetative room, Sonja explained, and it was clearly where much of the day-to-day work occurred. Scattered about were cannabis reference books and troubleshooting guides; a supply of white jugs filled with fertilizer, mildew killer, and nutrients; and gardening tools, duct tape, and other bric-a-brac. The dogs followed us inside and flopped under the table onto overstuffed pet pillows next to where a boom box was tuned to a hip-hop station. Overhead, a flat-screen TV broadcast images from the outside security camera, and along the ceiling was a maze of shiny silver ductwork and noisy ventilation equipment hanging from bungee cords.

In this room, seedlings and young plants are lavished with intense light twenty-four hours per day. They live here for four weeks or more as they "vegetate," establishing healthy root systems and developing stems and nodes where buds will eventually form. Theoretically, cannabis plants can be kept in a perpetual state of immature vegetating if the light cycle isn't broken. Eternal sunshine allows them to grow quickly but also keeps them from maturing into flowering plants, which is beneficial for the cultivator, who can keep a constant supply of plants ready to begin their flowering cycles to replace those that are harvested, thereby producing a steady crop of marijuana every few weeks. Cannabis farmers call this sort of operation a "Sea of Green" because there are plants in every stage of development.

Vegetating plants are also important because from them new plants can be propagated, a process called cloning. While plenty of cannabis growers start their crops with seeds ordered online from Canada or Amsterdam, cloning offers a number of advantages. First, cannabis plants can be either male or female—in nature, the male pollinates the female, which produces seeds that germinate in the ground when the plant dies. In an industrial operation, male plants are not only worthless—they don't produce enough THC to bother harvesting them—but they wreak havoc on the females, at least from a marijuana cultivator's point of view. Pollinated females stop producing THC and spend all their energy creating strong, healthy seeds. This is excellent for breeding, hybridizing, and producing viable seeds, but not for producing killer pot. Potent marijuana is basically the result of sexually frustrated plants—females produce more and more THC and grow heavier and heavier buds, waiting for pollen to arrive to trigger their seed production. Unpollinated females that produce no seeds have buds that are nearly dripping with cannabinoids, which of course is the point; marijuana produced from such plants is called sinsemilla, which is Spanish for "without seeds."

Because seeds contain the genetic characteristics of both parents, there's a fifty-fifty chance that plants grown from seeds will be male. But cloning—cutting and rooting a branch from a known female—will produce a perfect genetic match to the plant, one that will also be female. Generally, clones grow more slowly than seedlings, and some connoisseurs will argue that they also don't produce buds as vigorously, but cloning is a way of guaranteeing an all-female population of plants in a grow operation. And if you manage to come into possession of a highly prized strain of marijuana with strong genetic traits, such as DJ Shorts Blueberry, you can grow the same great pot year-round. Many growers choose their best specimen of a particular strain and keep her in the vegetative state forever; her only job is to stay healthy so that she can be harvested for clones. This is called the mother plant.

Once the cultivator is ready to start flowering the vegetative plants, they are moved into a separate space where the light cycle is changed from twenty-four hours of sunlight to twelve hours of light and twelve of complete darkness. This is a mimicry of marijuana's natural outdoor life cycle; the shortening of days signals the plants that winter is coming and it's time to produce flowers and pollinate seeds so that the species will grow anew the following spring. Twelve hours of uninterrupted darkness changes the plants' internal behaviors, and the results of those behaviors are smoked around the world by millions of people.

We went into the flowering chamber through a fabricated hallway covered in more black plastic that acted like an airlock on a space station; the point here was to keep out any trace of light if the grower needs to enter the flowering room at "night." Even the briefest flash of light or an accidental flick of the light switch can stress marijuana, baffling them so badly that some have been known to spontaneously turn hermaphrodite, producing both male and female traits. Sonja keeps a little green LED flashlight on her keychain in case she needs to do some work during the lights-out hours. Green lights don't induce any type of photosynthetic activity in plants. On this occasion, however, we didn't need the green flashlight; we timed our visit to coincide with the plants' "daylight hours," which were actually during the evening, when the electricity rates were cheaper.

The flowering room was a humid forest of cannabis, some plants soaring over six feet tall, all of them waving in the breeze of several industrial fans placed around the cavernous space. Here the lighting was provided by about two dozen thousand-watt high-pressure sodium lights that could give you sunburn; they too hung from a system of bungee cords rigged to pulleys just a few inches from the tops of plants, some of which were dense with resinous buds the size of beehives.

"Some of these got too tall," Sonja explained as she pushed through the foliage along a small pathway between the ten-gallon planting pots, quickly getting lost in the branches. "We ran out of room to move the lights higher, so next time we'll keep them to a more manageable size."

She moved among the dozens of plants with the same type of care and grace as any other gardener in any other greenhouse the world over. Each of the plants was named, and their identities were written in Magic Marker on the pots, along with their strain. Sonja knew many of them without looking, though, and she stopped here and there to examine their iconic serrated leaves, murmuring little words of encouragement or diagnosis. "Looks like Sue here might have a zinc deficiency," she said, bent over to examine a few yellowish leaves; or, pointing to a freakishly huge purple bud the size of a small pineapple, "This is Daphne; she's probably got another two or three weeks to go."

Sonja is tomboyish and as laid-back as you'd expect a cannabis farmer to be, but when she starts talking about the particulars of her craft, she takes on a wonkishness you'd expect from an aerospace technician caught up in the geeky minutiae of thrust/weight ratios, forgetting that her audience is a layman. She'd been growing marijuana since she was nineteen, learning the basics and picking up advanced tips from a network of underground growers up and down Colorado's Front Range. These outlaw ganja gurus, and others like them throughout the United States, have nurtured the marijuana market for decades. Prohibition and law enforcement crackdowns are directly responsible for the advancement of indoor growing, requiring growers to develop more and more ingenious methods of cultivation and security. Luckily, their crop of choice proved well suited to evolving along with the needs of the grower—marijuana seems unusually adaptable to increasingly unnatural growing environments. Plants that grow outdoors under the sun can grow up to fifteen feet or taller and be as wide around as a child's wading pool; indoors under artificial light, they have been bred to stay about four feet tall and still yield a full crop of THC-laden buds. The plants under Sonja's care grow in soil, but many cultivators prefer to raise their plants hydroponically, in a liquid bath of nutrients that feeds directly into free-floating roots. More recently, some innovators have even eliminated the water, delivering life-sustaining and bud-producing nutrients to naked roots through an aeroponic mist. Nothing that the law has been able to throw at them has ever dented the industry's growth and innovation—not the threat of mandatory long-term prison sentences, and not the development of thermal imaging devices that cops use to sniff out grow operations based on a building's "heat signature." After decades of eradication efforts, marijuana is by far the biggest cash crop in the United States, estimated in a 2006 study to be worth $35.8 billion per year. That's more than the two largest legal crops—corn and wheat—combined.[1]

Now in her early thirties, Sonja has the science down cold. She talked of Northern Lights, Island Skunk, fertilizer burn, kola buds versus popcorn buds, staking, and flushing, but I was too enraptured to pay much attention to what she was saying. I'd only seen marijuana plants on posters and in photos, but here was the felonious flora in all of her glory on every side. They gave off a powerful but not unpleasant odor, a rich and loamy scent that reminded me of elementary school trips to working farms so we could see where food came from. The buds were sticky, leaving my fingers tacky with resin. I had the feeling that I was meeting an alien life form, one that I wasn't sure, at first, was benign. At first I didn't want to touch them because they seemed so delicate and majestic, but soon I was deep in the forest with the plants over my head, tickled on all sides by their slender leaves. My son's question kept running through my head: *Why is this illegal?*

WE WENT BACK to the vegging room to pick out some good ones for my fledgling operation. I chose two each of Mother's Finest and Mango, one Maui, and one DJ Shorts Blueberry; each plant was about a foot and a half tall. I seat-belted Elizabeth, Eve, Keva, Garnet, La'Hi, and Savannah into the backseat of my Ford Explorer like the toddlers they were, hoping that the dusk and the tinted windows would make it impossible for any passing cops to see inside. The car smelled like a Phish concert.

If your life ever gets boring, try this for some excitement—load up your car with live marijuana plants and count the number of times you might crash, speed, or just have the bad luck to stop at a red light with a cop behind you while driving six miles back to your house. Of course I had my well-thumbed doctor's recommendation on the seat next to me, but it didn't lessen the trepidation. In fact, it seemed more stupid than ever to expect this mimeographed, coffee-ringed paper filled with chicken scratch to get me off the hook if I were stopped. I drove through a notorious speed trap near the university with my cruise control on thirty miles per hour, and took every turn and curve along the route back to my house like a parent bringing his newborn home from the maternity ward. Indeed, my passengers had their very own nursery waiting for them.

It was fully dark by the time I arrived, but I still waited until the garage door had firmly sealed me inside before I got out of the car and transported the plants into the house.

"Eww, gross, Dad!" Turner had gone into full recoil at the first whiff of his new housemates, and he had the same look on his face as when he forces down a shot of cough syrup.

"What?" I asked. "C'mon, it's not that bad. I kind of like it."

"Good God, honey," Rebecca said, mimicking Turner's wrinkled nose and raising her eyebrows in a look I knew well. It said, *You better know what you're doing.*

The plants were in three-gallon plastic pots and fit perfectly in the shower pan under the fuchsia glow of the LED lights. They were mature enough to start their flowering cycle right away, but I wanted to give them another week or two just to be sure. After freshly watering them, then spritzing them with an organic mist to stave off any spores they might have picked up on their brief journey outdoors, there was nothing else for me to do. I just had to let them grow.

It was harder than you might think.

AT THE FORT Collins Barnes & Noble, you can buy a book about how to grow psychedelic mushrooms right off the shelf (the active ingredient in mushrooms is a Schedule I drug, meaning, like marijuana, they're considered dangerous and addictive with no medical benefit or safe dosage), but if you want any on cannabis cultivation, you have to ask a sales clerk, who keeps them behind the cash register as if they're porn. I bought a half dozen books that were written, thankfully, in "cannabis for dummies" style and devoured and bookmarked every one of them. Next to where I stacked them on my desk, I kept a notebook with a running list of new supplies I needed to keep my plants happy and healthy. Sonja accompanied me on a few trips to Way to Grow, the local hydroponic store, to stock up on liquid fertilizer, bigger pots for transplanting when I induced flowering, and other necessities. Those trips were always eye-opening, and I was staggered by the selection of grow lights and soil types and the endless varieties of plant food. I followed Sonja's suggestions and filled my basket with Neptune's Harvest and FoxFarm brand Big Bloom and Grow Big fertilizers. Every dude in line at the cash register was growing pot.

Way to Grow was out of pH paper to test the acidity of my tap water, so I went to a regular garden nursery to find some. The helpful clerk couldn't find any of the small paper strips on the shelves, but pointed out a few products used to test the pH level of soil.

"No, I'm looking for something to test the water," I said.

"The water," she repeated, confused as to why, assuming I was working on an outdoor garden and nurturing something harmless like peas. "What are you growing?"

I was afraid she would ask, but I had been to every nursery in Fort Collins looking for pH paper and all were sold out, so I leaned forward and semi-whispered: "Marijuana."

The clerk didn't have long to ponder it because from over my shoulder, I heard a voice say, "It's cannabis, dear. I can't stand when people call it marijuana." I turned to face a little old lady a foot shorter than me holding a basket full of flowers, seed packets, and other gardening doo-dads. She was wearing elastic-waist jeans, a denim work shirt, and a straw hat. "If you're on Fort Collins water," she was saying, "you're fine. My cannabis grows just fine with tap water, but I'm working in soil. If you're doing hydro, you might have to adjust it just a little. Have you tried an aquarium store, like PETCO?"

"No," I answered, "but that's a good idea."

She turned back to browse the aisles. "The grow stores around here are sold out of everything," she was saying. "I usually just go to Denver."

The clerk and I smiled at each other, and I headed to PETCO, where I found exactly what I needed in the fish department.

As soon as I got the plants into the grow room, I noticed that it had a glaring shortcoming. Because it was composed of only one temperature- and humidity-controlled space, I had nowhere to separately flower half the plants while keeping the other half in their vegging state. That was one of the proscriptions of the state law; as a state-certified medical marijuana patient, I could have six plants, but only three of them could be maturing at a time. That required different light cycles and therefore different growing spaces. My options were to construct a separate area to keep the vegetating plants—an enclosed temperature-controlled cabinet would work fine—or find someone for whom I could act as a caregiver, which would allow me to bring all six of the plants to fruition at once.

I was impatient to get going, so I opted for the latter—I called my buddy Nick, who'd been my partner in crime at The Med Shed.

"I need you to make me your caregiver," I told him after I'd explained the dilemma.

"Yeah, no problem," he said. "Can we do that? This isn't going to affect where I usually shop, is it?"

Frankly, I wasn't sure. It was one of the many occasions where I identified a shortcoming in the law that I might have otherwise missed if I hadn't been knee-deep in it and trying to adhere to its various dictates. According to the letter of the law, I was in violation already; I'd signed over my caregiver rights to The Med Shed in exchange for the free doctor's visit, so the only six plants legally in existence under my name were ones I'd never seen, growing wherever they cultivated their pot. Or were they? I'd also signed my caregiver rights over to at least three other dispensaries since that time, a typical matter of paperwork that comes whenever you visit a new place. According to the law, there's nothing wrong with this, except that I'm required to fill out a "change of caregiver" form and send it by certified mail to the health department so that (again, theoretically) they could keep track of who was caring for whom. Changing caregivers—or opting to grow for oneself—should cancel everyone who's claimed a patient's right to grow in the past. The trouble was, I wasn't aware of any mechanism at all for alerting the previous caregiver of the change. Talking to Nick was the first time I'd considered that. By going from dispensary to dispensary, changing caregivers all along the way, I was like Johnny Appleseed spreading cannabis plants in my wake. I'd magically turned the six plants that were legally allowed to exist in the state of Colorado under my name into thirty.

But I also knew that the chances of the health department learning about my activities were nil; I'd been a bona fide medical marijuana patient for nearly six months, and they still hadn't cashed the check I mailed with my registration information or issued my official license.

So while I knew that if Nick filled out the "change of caregiver" paperwork to make me his official marijuana supplier, it should technically nullify any other caregivers growing pot on his behalf, I also knew that in reality it would make no difference whatsoever. I just wanted the proof that I was growing three mature plants for me and three for him in case I was ever asked about it.

After that discussion, another complication dawned on me. The law also specified that in addition to the plants, I could legally possess as much as two ounces of pot, or four once I became Nick's caregiver—but what if, as I hoped, the plants produced more than four ounces? I'd been keeping tabs on marijuana busts throughout the country, and every story contained a police commander bragging about the volume and street value of the grow they'd discovered. Invariably, the cops base the so-called "street value" of the busts on an assumption that each plant discovered—whether male or female, seedling or ripe—will produce one to two *pounds* of smokable marijuana. Therefore, every suspect they take down was on his way to becoming a potential multimillionaire in a few short years. I didn't have to be familiar with this business long to know that whoever can grow two pounds of marijuana on plants that fit indoors would qualify for the Nobel Prize in botany, if there were such a thing. That's not to say that large yields can't be accomplished, but to be able to produce them consistently, with every plant a grower has rooted, is unlikely at best.

Police estimates of the value of marijuana are equally exaggerated. A bust in Philadelphia in early 2010 netted the police 131 plants, which they estimated had a "street value" of $1.2 million. That meant that if each plant produced a half pound of marijuana, the street value of Philly pot was more than $18,000 per pound. Considering that pot from California's Emerald Triangle, deemed to be some of the best in the world, was barely going for $2,000 per pound at the same time, the cops either didn't know the street value of marijuana at all, or the suspect's plants were all sprouting two-pound buds.

A similar report came from Michigan around the same time; police there discovered a warehouse grow operation with enough marijuana plants to end deforestation in the Amazon. The police commander was quoted in the local newspaper as saying that each plant confiscated was worth $8,000 because it would produce 2.2 pounds of marijuana.

These stories make great sound bites for reporters who know as much about marijuana prices as they do about the value of tea in India. But they're almost never rooted in reality. Growing cannabis is tricky business, and although every grower has fantasies that each seedling he plants will grow up to be a *High Times* Cannabis Cup winner, he knows better than to start borrowing money based on outlandish expectations. An outbreak of any one of dozens of diseases, mold infestations, or pests can quickly bring the value of one's crop down to zero. The biggest misconception is that any idiot can plant a seed, water it for a few weeks, and expect the floorboards to be groaning under the weight of dumbbell-size buds.

Naturally, I wanted to get as much pot as possible from my six plants, but I had no idea what to expect. As one grower aptly put it, trying to figure out how much your plants will produce is like trying to figure out how many apples you'll get from your apple tree. All I knew was that wholesale prices from growers like me to dispensaries was about $225 per ounce, or $3,600 per pound, and that's if the quality was very good and there was no fungus or mold in the buds, which can easily happen at the very end, when the harvested marijuana is drying and curing. I would be overjoyed with a total half pound of pot from six plants—that would recoup my investment and give me some pocket change.

The trouble was that a half pound of pot—eight ounces—is double what I'm legally allowed to possess. This loophole seems to have evaded everyone, even the local police. Back when the city council was deciding whether to ban dispensaries or not, they also considered new regulations for home growers like me. They were trying to avoid a situation like in the pot mecca of Arcata, California, where commercial operations were run from suburban rental homes, which played havoc with the housing market and public safety. In the end they decided to limit home grow operations to twelve plants, with only half flowering at once. (That assumed, of course, that there were two patients represented in order to comply with the individual limits of the state law.)

When one of the Fort Collins council members asked the police representative at the meeting approximately how much money a home operator harvesting six mature plants every two months could earn per year, he was told about $75,000. I quickly did the math and calculated this estimate to mean that, at current wholesale prices, the cops were guessing that each plant in this scenario would produce about nine ounces of pot. Under perfect growing conditions and with the right lights, this isn't unreasonable, and even some of the council members looked impressed, as if they too might entertain the idea of going into the pot trade. What no one pointed out is that the moment those plants are harvested, the grower would be breaking the law by exceeding the allowable limits of harvested marijuana.

Luckily, most of the people trying to decode how to comply with the law were medical marijuana patients and had just the thing on hand to deal with the headaches it produced. I had no such salve; I might have been growing pot, but I still didn't smoke it.

THERE WERE REASONS to fret over these details, as Chris Bartkowicz discovered when he overlooked almost all of them and ended up serving as a clear reminder to others in the state that the DEA is ready and able to come down like the hammer of the gods on anyone who isn't toeing the line. In his case, not only did he go on TV, virtually a dare for the feds to raid him, but he was growing more plants than he was allowed. Later, in court, the judge would tell him that he "miserably failed" to follow the state law, which I was trying to do with all of my might.

The Bartkowicz raid represented one of the high points of friction between medical marijuana establishments and law enforcement in Colorado. By most measures, the hapless grower who was briefly "living the dream" was an outlier, an isolated incident of someone who doesn't know what he's doing trying to make a big splash. Some tried to make him into a martyr, but the facts of his case—too many plants, two prior drug convictions, too close to a school, too cocky to keep himself out of prison—made it hard to whip up sympathy. The majority of dispensary owners are run by legitimate businesspeople with various reasons for getting on the ganja bandwagon. Some have serious illnesses, including one dispensary owner in Boulder who has brain cancer. They saw the Great Green Rush as a means of turning their secret gardens into legitimate businesses that could help others in need, and they took their responsibility to the marijuana movement seriously. To be sure, there were also plenty of dispensary owners in the early days who were clueless about running a business and gave the marijuana critics plenty of reason to complain. What everyone was trying to avoid was someone like Bartkowicz bursting onto the scene and causing an outrage.

And of course, that's just what happened. Sweetin was unapologetic about taking him down. "I enforce federal law," he told 9News, "and nothing has changed in federal law. Wanting the federal law to be different is not a great strategy."

Sweetin expanded on his viewpoint in an interview with *The Denver Post*.

"Technically, every dispensary in the state is in blatant violation of federal law," he said. "The time is coming when we go into a dispensary, we find out what their profit is, we seize the building and we arrest everybody. They're violating federal law; they're at risk of arrest and imprisonment."[2]

Not surprisingly, the medical marijuana community was up in arms at these comments; for many, the Ogden memo was read in its entirety for the first time only after the Bartkowicz raid. Indeed, it did not change existing law, or even constitute a hard policy that U.S. Attorneys were required to comply with. It was merely a suggestion, and furthermore it made clear that anyone trying to use states' compassionate laws as cover for illegal operations is fair game to suffer the full brunt of the law.

"To be sure, claims of compliance with state or local law may mask operations inconsistent with the terms, conditions, or purposes of those laws," the memo read, "and federal law enforcement should not be deterred by such assertions when otherwise pursuing the Department's core enforcement priorities."

It went so far as to outline certain characteristics of operations that could be open to prosecution, including having amounts of marijuana "inconsistent with purported compliance" with local laws, excessive amounts of cash, ties to criminal enterprises, evidence of money laundering, and other red flags. In other words, no attorney in his right mind would go to court waving a copy of the memo as a defense for his client's alleged crimes.

What bothered people more than the raid itself was Sweetin's ominous threat that "the time is coming" when "we arrest everybody." He later clarified that he simply meant that dispensaries were violating federal law no matter how compliant they were with state law, not that he was planning a D-day style invasion of the state's dispensaries. Still, many were outraged, interpreting his comment as a flat-out threat meant to instill fear in people who were using the medical marijuana law. Sweetin and his family got death threats over his comments, and his Facebook page was hacked; the hacker sent threats to his online friends.

"Certain people that don't like the government already decided that I was rogue and I needed to be killed," Sweetin said the following year. "One of the guys involved in the threats was a real killer [and investigated by the FBI], he wasn't a guy who was just outspoken. It's my job to be threatened, but it was a difficult time for my family. To think all these activists are just peace-loving Jimmy Buffett lovers, that's not entirely the story. I worked undercover in Miami [busting drug lords] but it wasn't until I crossed swords with the marijuana legalizers that this kind of thing happened."

The state's most prominent medical marijuana attorney, Rob Corry Jr., sent a letter to the U.S. Justice Department's Inspector General calling Sweetin a "rogue agent" and demanding that he be sacked; and Boulder Rep. Jared Polis sent a letter of complaint to Sweetin's boss, Attorney General Eric Holder, and Holder's boss, President Obama.

"Agent Sweetin's comment that 'we arrest everybody' is of great concern to me and to the people of Colorado, who overwhelmingly voted to allow medical marijuana," it read. "Coloradans suffering from debilitating medical conditions, many of them disabled, elderly, veterans, or otherwise vulnerable people, have expressed their concern to me that the DEA will come into medical marijuana dispensaries, which are legal under Colorado law, and 'arrest everybody' present. Although Agent Sweetin reportedly has backed away from his comments, he has yet to issue a written clarification or resign, thus the widespread panic in Colorado continues."

WHEN I FIRST read Polis's letter, I thought his invocation of "widespread panic" was a bit of a stretch. But that was before I had my own homegrown marijuana crop.

The first couple of weeks were a clandestine adventure. Very few people knew of my plans; one was my friend Mike, the photographer who met me for beers once or twice a week at a local tavern. He smoked pot practically every day and was recently fired from his job with the local newspaper. The two had nothing to do with each other, but because I was manufacturing his favorite drug, I was a welcome distraction from his job search. And because of his obvious expertise and his journalism background, he was the perfect person for me to debrief with. His enthusiasm for what I was doing was a needed boost of encouragement, because what I hadn't expected was the stress of growing pot.

For one thing, I had no idea if the plants were healthy or not. They seemed to be, but I was just following instructions from a book and watering and fertilizing according to the labels on the FoxFarm bottles. The literature stressed the importance of balancing nutrients, but didn't say how. As far as I knew, I was overloading the nitrogen and not providing enough phosphorous. Lately, I'd become obsessed with the concept of "flushing" the plants, a process by which you leach out all the built-up nutrients in the soil by essentially drowning them with five times the volume of water to the size of the pots. That seemed straightforward, but I wasn't sure when to do it; all the book said was to flush ten days before the harvest, but as a newbie grower, I had no idea when harvest might be.

But this paled in comparison to what kept me awake at night: The unmistakable odor of fresh pot soon took over the house. Once the plants began to flower on the twelve/twelve lighting cycle, they became dangerously fragrant, and for the first time, I questioned just how smart this whole idea was. Step into the house and you'd think we were breeding indoor skunks. Despite the ventilation in the grow room, the entire basement smelled like a wet hayloft. The aroma crept into all corners of the house, migrating through the heat ducts and seeping into the living room, the upstairs bedrooms, and the bathrooms. It was worse in the backyard, where the exhaust vent was located. Before the lilac bushes around the porch blossomed to disguise the smell, I prayed for rain all spring if only to keep my neighbors from mowing their lawns and weeding their gardens.

The smell of fresh blooming marijuana won't get you high, but it will definitely make you paranoid. Innocent visits from anyone became almost too much to bear. We'd long stopped answering the door if we weren't expecting visitors—every Jehovah's Witness or Girl Scout who came calling became a suspected DEA agent or undercover narc. I quickly associated the sound of the doorbell with the theme song for the TV show *Cops*. *Whatcha gonna do when they come for you?* My wife and I ran through every possible reason we might qualify for an otherwise routine visit from someone in authority and tried to eliminate them all. When I forgot to pay a photo-radar speeding ticket that came in the mail, I panicked for a week over a line in the notice warning me that failure to pay meant a law enforcement process server could come to my house to deliver the citation in person.

At night, I was afraid of everything: armed drug dealers breaking in to steal my stash, unannounced visits by out-of-state relatives, accidentally burning down the house. I lay staring at the ceiling, getting ghostly whiffs of maturing pot plants from the floor vent and interpreting every slamming car door in the night to mean the SWAT team was running up the driveway with one of those steel rams to knock down the front door.

Finally, operating on the principle of keeping your enemies close, I decided I would quit worrying about the DEA coming to me, and go to the DEA myself.

I made an appointment to talk with Jeff Sweetin.

· 8 ·

Unlocking the Doors of Perception

"[E]very cop is a criminal, and all the sinners, saints."

—The Rolling Stones

The Drug Enforcement Administration's Denver office building is a steel-and-glass mirrored cube situated on a little grassy hilltop in Englewood, an area just southeast of downtown. You can't just show up there and hope to get anything accomplished; the complex is ringed with a high iron fence, and visitors without appointments won't even get through the metal detector before being turned away. Jeff Sweetin's office is on the fourth floor, and as Special Agent in Charge—meaning he's the boss of eleven DEA field offices in Colorado, Wyoming, Utah, and Montana—he gets the sweetest spot in the building. The floor-to-ceiling windows face north and west toward the grand vista of the Rocky Mountains. Making the view all the better is another little grassy hill just across the street that's just big enough to obscure the interstate and most of the suburban sprawl leading to the foot of the mountains, giving the impression that there's nothing between the DEA and snow-peaked Mt. Evans but wide-open prairie.

Sweetin knows better. Denver is a city filled with drugs and drug dealers, and it's his job to catch them.

"Denver is a very active place," he said, as both of us sat side by side in front of a desk that's the size of my son's bed. "Denver is a very lucrative place for drug-trafficking organizations that are outside the United States."

I wasn't sure what to expect of this career drug agent who has been with the DEA since 1986, working first in Miami and Washington, D.C., before taking charge of the Denver bureau in 2002. For the marijuana advocates, he was the worst sort of nightmare, a cop with a federal badge who in their estimation had gone off the reservation and waged jihad against marijuana smokers in general and medical users in particular.

But Sweetin insisted that's not the case. He has bigger fish to fry, he said, and frankly, the medical marijuana industries in Colorado and Montana, the two medical marijuana states under his jurisdiction, have become huge distractions and headaches.

"I'm not the weed collector for the state," he said. "We get calls all the time about, 'Hey, I think there's a huge marijuana grow next door to me.' If we're not careful, the de facto regulation by the federal government of the medical marijuana industry could become all we do. Based on our resources, we could spend twenty-four hours a day trying to regulate the medical marijuana industry, and that's not what we're here for and really it's not what we do best."

While his assistant was dressed in a typical G-man suit, Sweetin, clad in a salmon-colored polo shirt and khaki pants, looked like he had a tee time after our meeting. He's lean, on the verge of being gaunt, the sort of physique that ultra-marathon runners have, and he was wearing Velcro ankle weights. We talked for more than an hour, and he was friendly and open, but also obviously frustrated at how he's been portrayed in the wake of the Bartkowicz raid. It became clear that on his enemies list, a close second to the drug runners he pursues is the media.

"I firmly believe Bartkowicz is going to jail because of the media in this town," he said. "They were the ones that told him nobody is going to enforce federal law. You go ask a hundred people in the big dispensaries prior to [the Bartkowicz arrest], 'Aren't you worried about the DEA coming in?' They would have told you, 'Obama's not letting them.' ... I had [reporters] on the phone every day and I would say, 'Guys, listen, you need your readers to understand there is no mulligan. You need to understand what the guidance [contained in the memo] says; it's on our Web site.'

"When I make statements like, 'Listen, we're not going after dispensaries, but they're all in violation of federal law,' people panic," he continued. "That's when people threaten to kill us and blow up our building. We have never [busted] a dispensary. That would be like us going out and arresting a guy for selling joints at the high school. That's not our job; that's not what our mandate is. But it's still a violation of federal law."

The mandate, as Sweetin described it, is to take down the big drug-trafficking organizations, especially those with foreign ties. In the past, those organizations were most often found in the border states and those with open coastline, like Florida. But the one hallmark of criminal organizations that has been consistent since the time of Al Capone has been adaptability, and many of those groups have moved their operations inland.

"Because we've upped our enforcement activities along the Southwest border, it's smarter for organizations to move inside the United States a little bit and get away from the borders," Sweetin said.

"[If] you can pay somebody to bring dope across the Southwest border, you then can pay somebody—rather than deliver it to your stash house in El Paso—to drive it ten hours up I-25 and go to Denver. If you had a choice to live in Laredo, El Paso, or Fort Collins, where would you live?"

Historically, marijuana smuggling has gone hand in hand with the trafficking of other hard drugs, and it's no surprise to anyone that violent organized crime syndicates control the market and are reaping billions. Even Harry Anslinger, in an interview with *Esquire* magazine in 1968, conceded that the prohibition he initiated against pot had been a boon to gangsters far and wide. "One cannot help but think in retrospect that prohibition, by depriving Americans of their vices, only created avenues through which organized crime gained its firm foothold," he told the magazine.[1]

Combined, the illicit global drug market is worth some $320 billion annually, about 1 percent of all global commerce. Drug money accounts for a full 10 percent of the Mexican economy, and violent drug gangs in Mexican border cities have waged a violent years-long siege of such cities as Juarez in an effort to keep that money flowing. In 2009, 2,600 people were killed in Juarez in cartel-related shootings, bombings, and assassinations, making it one of the deadliest cities on earth. The gangs derive much of their cash from cocaine and marijuana, but marijuana is the most lucrative. While cocaine has a higher street value, it must first be bought from the Colombians, giving it a smaller profit margin than pot, which is controlled by the cartels all the way from planting to distribution. According to the U.S. State Department, marijuana production in Mexico increased 35 percent in 2009; pot grows on an estimated thirty thousand acres there.[2]

But the drug cartels don't always smuggle pot from Mexico to Denver and other cities; they often grow it here, under the canopy of the state's ample forestland. Marijuana plants linked to Mexican gangs have been found growing in Golden Gate Canyon State Park, located in the foothills west of Denver, and Pike National Forest, sixty miles southwest of the city. The U.S. Forest Service created a minor uproar in 2009 when it warned hikers and hunters to be on the lookout for cultivation camps, which the agency said could be identified by being on the lookout for discarded tortilla wrappers, Tecate cerveza bottles, and Spam tins, as well as campers playing Hispanic music. Many took this as a disparagement against law-abiding Hispanic campers, but the invasion of U.S. national forests by Mexican drug cartels was hard to deny in light of similar discoveries in the woodlands of California, Washington, Oregon, and Idaho, among other states.

The canopy they're hiding under now, Sweetin said, is that of the medical marijuana law.

"I am convinced they see Colorado as a phenomenal opportunity, and why wouldn't they?" he said. "It is only a matter of time before we find organizations that are closely linked to violent Mexican cartels that are supplying these dispensaries. I often ask myself, with the new demand created by this law, can enough marijuana be grown in Colorado by legal—'legal' under state level—caretakers and growers to supply the demand? I don't really know the answer. My suspicion based on my experience is we'll never know, because the cartels will rush to supply that. And they will undercut the [local] growers; they'll find a way to get some of that money.

"I know right now that there are probably hundreds of large marijuana grows in this city," he said. "If I wanted to find them and I put my people on it, we could easily find them. That's what we do. Is that worthy of my effort? I doubt it. . . . What we do is we look at who the criminal organizations are. That may well lead to evidence that they're supplying dispensaries. When that happens, everyone involved is going to jail. But we're not going to investigate every grow and work backwards. The resources that would take are unjustifiable."

Like many top law enforcement officers, Sweetin sees medical marijuana as a farce and a charade, a "red herring" whose end goal is overall legalization for recreational use. Cagey, well-funded advocates preyed on voters' natural "sympathy about sick people" to dupe the state, he said.

"Are the guys who wrote this law the same that wrote the one in California?" he asked rhetorically. "Yeah, and every time they do it, they learn. This one in Colorado is perfect because it amends the constitution. . . . Once you amend the Colorado constitution, you can't change that legislatively."

Sweetin was building steam—talking about Mexican gangsters, he was clinical and matter-of-fact, but once the topic moved to the medical marijuana law, he grew more and more agitated.

"The law is unenforceable," he continued. "Go talk to some of the police chiefs about what it would take to go into a grow that has a thousand plants . . . and actually prosecute those people for a violation of the existing state law. Because [the police] have to keep those plants alive. How do you do that? That's all funny in the media, but do you want to dial 9-1-1 and have the Douglas County Sheriff tell you, 'I can't send anybody; all my guys are out watering the plants?' And, 'They got some that are dying; they've got leaf blight?'"

Sweetin's complaints were familiar. He'd succinctly encapsulated the anxiety and frustration of most people who look at medical marijuana laws with alarm, articulating every criticism I'd heard, from bogus goals about compassion for patients that masked the real agenda of eventually legalizing recreational use all the way through law enforcement's relative inability to prevent them. But he also touched on an argument long used by the marijuana legalizers: If pot were no longer criminal, and it was regulated and taxed for legal sale, in much the way that liquor is, wouldn't that wipe out the black market and deal a blow to organized crime?

Sweetin isn't convinced. There are black markets for all sorts of legal products, he said, from untaxed cigarettes to Canadian toilets that flush more water than American commodes. Because cannabis is a plant that has proven capable of growing anywhere, from my basement to yours, it will always be available outside of regulated channels if only so that users can avoid the hassle of paying taxes.

"There is the perfect black market for OxyContin" despite being highly regulated, he said. "You see heroin users trying to buy Oxy, and Oxy users trying to buy heroin. They're addicted; they're an addicted population."

And that seems to be the core of his complaint—Americans are already far too hooked on intoxicants, whether it's caffeine or heroin, and legalizing pot, including for medicinal purposes, would make yet another intoxicant more accessible and would "send the wrong message" that getting high is no big deal. To Sweetin, it's a very big deal. The message he would send?

"I think sobriety is a cool idea," he said.

So does Colorado's top state law enforcement officer, Attorney General John Suthers, the man who, as a U.S. Attorney, told reporters that medical marijuana was "a smokescreen." In early 2010, Suthers was actively working with lawmakers to draft a new set of rules that would clamp down on the runaway pot industry in Colorado. I'd met him not long before the meeting with Sweetin, and he told me proudly that he'd never in his life been intoxicated on anything. He didn't smoke, obviously never used drugs, and has only had, at most, a few sips of beer or wine on special occasions.

He's also worried about medical marijuana sending the wrong message.

"Teenage use of marijuana is a function of two things: accessibility and acceptability," he said. "What I mean by acceptability is how it's perceived as a normative behavior. What we are doing, in my opinion, by putting dispensaries on every street corner and letting a twenty-two-year-old student who plays on the intramural football team go in and get it—the message that it sends to his little brother [is] that this is wholly normative behavior.

"If *you* start today smoking marijuana," he said, pointing at me, "odds are you will not quickly progress to other things. If you start today as a twelve- thirteen-, fourteen-, fifteen- sixteen-year-old teenager, odds are that you will be a hard-core drug addict."

This is absurd, but whether he actually believes it or not is almost immaterial. When a typical parent hears something like this from the state attorney general, he or she will take it as fact. They wouldn't be inclined to look up back issues of the *American Journal of Psychiatry* to read about the 2006 University of Pittsburgh study that found that kids who smoke pot before using other substances, both legal and illegal, were no more inclined to become a "hard-core drug addict" than those who hadn't.³ Or the 2002 Rand Corporation study cited earlier, or an April 2010 Australian study of World Health Organization data showing that "the 'gateway' pattern at least partially reflects unmeasured common causes rather than causal effects of specific drugs on subsequent use of others."⁴ In other words, there are reasons other than pot itself why kids who smoke marijuana may or may not use other drugs.

This makes sense when one considers the vast number of people who've survived smoking a joint as a teen without becoming a hopeless addict to other substances.

But people like Suthers and Sweetin are imbued with automatic credibility because of their positions, especially when compared with people they consider to be just a bunch of criminal potheads instituting medical marijuana laws that Suthers calls "state-sanctioned hypocrisy."

Sweetin sees it the same way.

"What we're really doing right now is that we are reversing decades and decades of investment in drug education," he said. "We tell kids when they grow up, drugs are bad, just say no. . . . What you're starting to see is huge confusion, lessening of stigmas. It's an attitude of, 'Wait a second, if you told me that heroin, cocaine, and marijuana were bad, and now you're telling me that marijuana is medicine, were you lying to me? What about these other drugs?'"

For marijuana advocates, that's precisely what they hope will happen—the confusion, from their point of view, stems entirely from the government's refusal to distinguish marijuana from other drugs. But Sweetin had veered away from discussing DEA policy and priorities and was now into the realm of his personal opinions.

"I think it's a dangerous drug," he said. "I think it causes people to [become addicted]; for kids, it changes their brain functions, their brain development; for adults, it causes emotional issues. So I think it's unnecessary.

"The dangers of smoking far outweigh the benefit you could get from smoking a marginal weed," he said. "Listen, when I speak, I have to be factual. And I should be, because I represent the government of the United States. When [marijuana advocates] speak, you wouldn't believe it. They've got studies I've never even heard of. What about the AMA, or [the American Academy of] Pediatrics?

"We as a government believe, keep researching," he said. "We lose nothing through research. . . . [Marijuana advocates] paint the picture that there's some sinister government force out there, that we have just decided, even though we know it's good medicine, to keep that from people."

IT IS TRUE that the American Academy of Pediatrics has long opposed the legalization or decriminalization of marijuana, primarily on the assumption that marijuana would be easier for kids to get hold of if it were taxed, regulated, and age-restricted in the same way as beer and wine, as opposed to the current climate in which it's completely prohibited. But the National Center on Addiction and Substance Abuse at Columbia University reports that half of all kids between the ages of twelve and seventeen said that they can score some weed within a day, and a quarter say they could get it within the hour.[5]

As for the American Medical Association, it had fundamentally altered its longstanding position on medical marijuana on November 10, 2009, five months before Sweetin and I had this conversation. For the first time since Dr. William Woodward spoke on behalf of cannabis in 1937, the AMA called on the Justice Department to consider freeing marijuana from its federal restrictions in order to encourage the sort of rigorous tests and studies Sweetin says do not exist. The AMA stressed that its position should not be seen as an endorsement of existing medical marijuana programs, or the legalization of marijuana, but to facilitate further study. It might seem lukewarm, but its previous recommendation in 2001 was that the federal government keep marijuana in Schedule I; the new recommendation now seeks a review of its classification.

"Results of short-term controlled trials indicate that smoked cannabis reduces neuropathic pain, improves appetite and caloric intake, especially in patients with reduced muscle mass, and may relieve spasticity and pain in patients with multiple sclerosis," according to the report of the AMA's Council on Science and Public Health.

As for the perception that there is some "sinister government force" keeping what it knows is good medicine away from people who need it, that view is rather justified—the sinister force would be the DEA itself.

In 1972, NORML and other groups petitioned the DEA to reschedule marijuana out of its restrictive Schedule I category so that doctors could prescribe it to their patients without fear of arrest for either party.[6] The petition bounced from court to court for more than a decade until it finally wound up in front of the DEA's own administrative law judge, Francis Young, in 1986. Hearings on the petition spanned nearly two years.

An administrative law judge acts in the same manner as a criminal or civil court judge, only the role is to preside over disputes between government agencies and parties that have allegedly been aggrieved by that agency. Young's role was to weigh facts, take testimony under oath, and issue a ruling on the matter at hand. In this case, the question was whether or not the cannabis plant, as a whole, could be moved from Schedule I to Schedule II under the Controlled Substances Act, whether there was a currently accepted medical use for marijuana, and whether there was an acceptable level of safety in using marijuana in medical situations.

Throughout weeks of testimony, Young heard from dozens of physicians and their patients—including those who suffered from cancer, glaucoma, multiple sclerosis, and other illnesses—who described how smoking marijuana helped them cope with treatment or mitigated their symptoms. He heard evidence indicating that doctors from coast to coast regularly, and illegally, recommended that their patients smoke pot to deal with chemotherapy and other causes of violent nausea. He was presented with marijuana's historical uses in a wide variety of illnesses and learned that there hasn't been a single fatality connected to its use. The court documents are voluminous, and they provide one of the best bodies of expert medical opinion on marijuana's safety and efficacy in existence.

Suppressing nausea has long been touted as one of the most miraculous uses of marijuana as medicine, and the testimony Young heard made it clear that the nausea experienced by chemotherapy patients is not like the nausea one gets from an upset stomach or even food poisoning. Chemo-induced nausea is a thing unto itself, a violent full-body retching induced by the introduction of poisonous chemicals that oncologists hope will kill cancerous tumors before they kill the patient. Nausea can last for days and can be fatal—constant vomiting makes it impossible to keep down food and medication, making starvation a real risk. And often, nausea will be so severe that some patients would rather discontinue treatment and die than to endure it.

One description of how wrenching nausea can be came from a Coloradan who testified before Young, an eighteen-year-old cancer patient named John James Dunsmore. Active in sports like basketball, Dunsmore began noticing a painful bump on his left leg that sometimes made his leg so stiff that he had to limp. An X-ray revealed what he described as a "ratty mass" of tissue around his leg bones, which doctors diagnosed as osteogenic sarcoma, or bone cancer. The prognosis wasn't good. The tumor was dense, well formed, and infecting the bones, muscle, and tissues of his leg. Dunsmore was told that amputation was probably the only way he would stop the cancer, but that they might try aggressive chemotherapy first.

"My father and I went back to the Ronald McDonald House in Denver, where we stayed during my outpatient trips to Children's

Hospital, and had a long talk," according to a record of his testimony reprinted in the book *Cancer Treatment and Marijuana Therapy.* "I like sports a lot. After some hard thinking, I decided to give chemotherapy a shot. Maybe I could save my leg. My dad gave me his support. It was worth a try."

Father and son were given a long list of side effects they could expect from the chemo, and vomiting and nausea were among them. After discussing medication options to help with the nausea, they agreed to try Ativan, an anti-anxiety drug that is often given to patients who become so stressed over the anticipation of vomiting from chemotherapy that they vomit anyway out of sheer fear. Dunsmore said one of the reasons his father agreed to using Ativan is because one of its side effects is memory loss. "There would be a lot for me to forget," Dunsmore said.

His father surprised him by asking the oncologist what he knew about marijuana. The doctor and a nurse told him that some cancer patients found relief from marijuana to the degree that the nurses sometimes kept pot brownies on the ward. But the doctor also mentioned that the FDA had recently approved a synthetic THC drug called Marinol, basically a marijuana pill that was developed in an attempt to mimic the effects of smoked marijuana. It wasn't yet on the market, however.

There was another option for obtaining prescription marijuana—a little known government-run program administered by the U.S. Food and Drug Administration. The Compassionate Investigational New Drug program began in 1976 after a glaucoma patient sued for (and won) the right to smoke pot for his illness; at its peak, it enrolled thirty patients with various illnesses who received pre-rolled joints from the federal government's private stash at the University of Mississippi, which runs the only legal pot farm in the United States, for research. President George H.W. Bush ended the program in 1992 when AIDS patients, seeking marijuana's help to boost their appetite and quell their nausea, flooded the government with applications. Only three of the original patients who were grandfathered into the program are still alive and still picking up a big drum of NIDA-supplied pot from federal pharmacies each month.

Even though it was still in existence at the time of Dunsmore's cancer treatment, his doctor had no idea how to enroll him in the program because it was so secretive and complex; in the end, Dunsmore's dad ended up finding some pot from another source.

"They told me chemotherapy would be bad," Dunsmore testified. "They didn't tell me how bad 'bad' was. I started throwing up about two hours after they started giving me chemotherapy. I stayed sick for seven days. For the first couple of days I just threw up. When there wasn't anything to throw up, I threw up bile. When there wasn't any more bile, I got the dry heaves."

Dunsmore didn't eat anything for seven days after his first bout with chemo and quickly shrank from 185 pounds to 130. One of the drugs used in his treatment was cisplatin, one of the most nausea-inducing drugs used in chemotherapy, which can also cause kidney and nerve damage. Smoking pot didn't eliminate Dunsmore's vomiting, but it made being treated with cisplatin more tolerable.

"I know marijuana helps with the vomiting," he said. "Sure, I throw up. Almost everyone getting cisplatin throws up. But there are lots of ways to throw up. Throwing up with marijuana is a lot easier than the kind of throwing up that happens when I don't smoke marijuana.

"Then there's eating," he continued. "Without marijuana, I can't. Simple as that. . . . When I smoke marijuana, the tightness in my tummy goes away. Then I get hungry. Not just a little hungry, but really hungry. It's great to be hungry, to be able to eat."

Finally, Dunsmore gave Judge Young his opinion about marijuana's safety: "Is marijuana safe? Asking a chemotherapy patient taking cisplatin if marijuana is 'safe' is a lot like asking the guy who gets run over by a Mack truck if the wind's too strong. Compared to the anti-cancer drugs and other anti-vomiting drugs, marijuana is real safe."

In the end, chemo didn't save his leg—the amputation, though, saved his life—but he told Young that he wouldn't have been able to fight as hard as he did for it if it hadn't been for marijuana.[7]

Young also heard from numerous doctors who testified to the prevalence of cancer patients illegally medicating with marijuana as far back as the early 1970s, sometimes at the encouragement of their physicians, but just as frequently with their silent, tacit approval. This trend was seen in Washington, D.C.; Kansas City, Missouri; Tucson, Arizona; and other areas of the country, but with much prevalence in San Francisco.

"As of the spring of 1987 in the San Francisco area, patients receiving chemotherapy commonly smoked marijuana in hospitals during their treatments," Young wrote in his ruling on the case. "This in-hospital use, which takes place in rooms behind closed doors, does not bother staff, is expected by physicians and welcomed by nurses who, instead of having to run back and forth with containers of vomit, can treat patients whose emesis is better controlled than it would be without marijuana. Medical institutions in the Bay Area where use of marijuana obtained on the streets is quite common, although discrete, include the University of California at San Francisco Hospital, the Mount Zion Hospital, and the Franklin Hospital. In effect, marijuana is readily accepted throughout the oncologic community in the Bay Area for its benefits in connection with chemotherapy. The same situation exists in other large metropolitan areas of the United States."

Testimony was also given about marijuana's medical use for people with paraplegia, quadriplegia, and muscle spasticity. Young heard of the case of Valerie Cover, an athletic young mother married to a U.S. Navy officer who developed multiple sclerosis in her early twenties. MS is a lifelong debilitating disease with no known cure; it strikes the message-carrying nerve fibers in the brain and the spinal cord. Symptoms vary from person to person but can include lack of coordination, impaired mobility, paralysis, muscle spasms, and tremors. Cover tried all the normal therapies, including treatment with two MS drugs known to be of only marginal help, but was eventually declared totally disabled by the Social Security Administration. Her life as she'd known it had effectively ended, and she was confined to bed or a wheelchair; to get around her house, she often had to resort to pushing herself while sitting on a skateboard.

Within five minutes of smoking a joint provided by her neighbor—who'd heard that marijuana was good for preventing vomiting, which Cover also struggled with—Cover stood up unaided. Three months later, she was walking without assistance, regaining lost weight, and caring for her children again.

Another case was that of young Irwin Rosenfeld, who began suffering at age ten from a rare disease called pseudohypoparathyroidism, which caused him to develop bone spurs all over his body, which could become malignant at any time. Over one's lifetime, hundreds of these can develop, causing extreme pain as they rub against bones, skin, muscles, and even organs. Rosenfeld couldn't sit, stand, or lie in any one position for very long, and lifting and walking caused him extreme pain. Tearing muscles and bleeding were regular occurrences. By the time he was nineteen, he was taking massive doses of a small pharmacy's worth of muscle relaxants, powerful sleeping aids, and the strong drug Dilaudid, a painkiller similar to morphine and heroin, which he took three to four times a day. He spent much of his time in a drug-induced fog.

In college, Rosenfeld smoked a joint in a classmate's room and sat with him to play a game of chess. Absorbed in the game, he suddenly realized he'd been sitting in the same position for more than an hour, something that was normally impossible. He began smoking marijuana regularly and found that his pain relief was far superior to the man-made drugs he'd been taking. Rosenfeld was one of the patients who applied to, and was approved for, the FDA investigational new drug program that supplied marijuana to select patients, even though the doctor who assisted with the application insisted he remain unidentified. He didn't want to end up in prison.

At the end of the marathon stretch of hearings in 1982, Judge Young was quite convinced. He ruled that the evidence supporting marijuana's practical uses for cancer patients and those with painfully debilitating diseases, muscle spasticity, and multiple sclerosis was overwhelming. (Glaucoma didn't fare as well, at least in terms of the plaintiffs presenting enough hard evidence that a substantial number of doctors used pot to relieve the intraocular pressure that glaucoma induces, which can lead to blindness.)

Furthermore, Young was convinced by the testimony that synthetic THC capsules like Marinol are a poor substitute for smoked marijuana, which is the opposite of arguments heard from the DEA today—smoked marijuana, or "marginal weed," as Sweetin referred to it, is routinely derided as crude and unnecessary because of the existence of Marinol.

"Marijuana cigarettes in many cases are superior to synthetic THC capsules in reducing chemotherapy-induced nausea and vomiting," Young wrote. "Marijuana cigarettes have an important, clear advantage over synthetic THC capsules in that the natural marijuana is inhaled and generally takes effect more quickly than the synthetic capsule, which is ingested and must be processed through the digestive system before it takes effect. Attempting to orally administer the synthetic THC capsule to a vomiting patient presents obvious problems—it is vomited right back up before it can have any effect."

And as for marijuana's safety? Young could barely say enough about it.

"The most obvious concern when dealing with drug safety is the possibility of lethal effects," Young wrote. "Can the drug cause death? Nearly all medicines have toxic, potentially lethal effects. But marijuana is not such a substance. There is no record in the extensive medical literature describing a proven, documented cannabis-induced fatality. This is a remarkable statement. First, the record on marijuana encompasses 5,000 years of human experience. Second, marijuana is now used daily by enormous numbers of people throughout the world. Estimates suggest that from twenty million to fifty million Americans routinely, albeit illegally, smoke marijuana without the benefit of direct medical supervision. Yet, despite this long history of use and the extraordinarily high numbers of social smokers, there are simply no credible medical reports to suggest that consuming marijuana has caused a single death.

"In strict medical terms," he continued, "marijuana is far safer than many foods we commonly consume. For example, eating ten raw potatoes can result in a toxic response. By comparison, it is physically impossible to eat enough marijuana to induce death.

"Marijuana, in its natural form, is one of the safest therapeutically active substances known to man."

It's worth repeating that Young was a DEA judge ruling against the DEA itself. Young, however, didn't have final authority, only the power to recommend a switch from Schedule I to Schedule II. Implementing that recommendation was up to one person, DEA Administrator John Lawn, who had the power then and there to end the debate about marijuana's use as a medicine by turning it over to the medical community for investigation.

By this point in the story, Lawn's decision not to should come as no surprise.

PERHAPS THE MOST amazing thing about Young's recommendation isn't necessarily that a law enforcement bureaucrat promptly tossed it in the trash, but that almost all of the testimony was given with barely any knowledge of how marijuana actually works its magic on the human brain.

THC was discovered in the mid-1960s, but it wasn't until 1988 that a researcher at St. Louis University School of Medicine discovered the specific receptors in the brain to which THC—and only THC—attaches. If the field of molecular biology were known for stop-the-presses-style breaking news, this discovery would have qualified. A scientist named Allyn Howell found that these receptor cells act like empty spaces in a jigsaw puzzle waiting for the just the right piece to complete the picture—in this case, THC. When it slips neatly into place, it triggers a series of events in the brain that are only just coming to be understood.

The question then became why would the brain be specifically wired to accept such an exceptionally unique chemical compound, one that, to that point, was known to exist only in pot? In the words of scientists Raphael Mechoulam and Lumir Hanus: "It was quite unacceptable to most neuroscientists that the brain will waste its resources to synthesize a receptor in order to bind a constituent of a plant." Only students of relentlessly bland and humorless scientific reports would pick up on the fact that a sentence like that in a study about molecules is the equivalent of Archimedes losing his senses and first shouting "Eureka!" when studying gold alloy. The hidden glee points to what Mechoulam and Hanus hypothesized: It isn't the singular chemicals of a plant the human brain had prepared itself to welcome into its cellular network, but a naturally occurring (or endogenous) compound that had yet to be discovered.

Mechoulam and his colleagues were the ones who found it: the brain's first identified endocannabinoid, which they appropriately named anandamide, meaning, in Sanskrit, "bliss."

Anyone who has ever smoked pot will attest that the effects span the senses. Colors appear sharper, sounds are more intense and acute, one's body becomes lighter or heavier, thoughts are freed to roam with little or no connection to linear principles, and time stretches out like a long piece of warm taffy. The scientists connected these sensations to specific brain functions affected by cannabinoids—they reduced pain, impaired motor skills, induced short-term memory loss, and stimulated sensory perceptions.

And they do a lot more that, as most stoners know; the effects of smoking a good joint aren't just physical but mental, cuing all kinds of crazy connections, new truths, psychic insights, and raw emotions.

There are few better written descriptions of this phenomenon than that by Mr. X, the pseudonym adopted as legal cover and reputation-protector by America's preeminent astrophysicist and astronomer Carl Sagan, when he penned an essay about getting stoned in 1969 for the book *Marihuana Reconsidered.*

"Sometimes a kind of existential perception of the absurd comes over me and I see with awful certainty the hypocrisies and posturing of myself and my fellow men," Mr. X wrote. "And at other times, there is a different sense of the absurd, a playful and whimsical awareness. Both of these senses of the absurd can be communicated, and some of the most rewarding highs I've had have been in sharing talk and perceptions and humor. Cannabis brings us an awareness that we spend a lifetime being trained to overlook and forget and put out of our minds. . . .

"There is a myth about such highs: the user has an illusion of great insight, but it does not survive scrutiny in the morning. . . . If I find in the morning a message from myself the night before informing me that there is a world around us which we barely sense, or that we can become one with the universe, or even that certain politicians are desperately frightened men, I may tend to disbelieve; but when I'm high I know about this disbelief. And so I have a tape in which I exhort myself to take such remarks seriously. I say 'Listen closely, you sonofabitch of the morning! This stuff is real!'"

One of my own most vivid memories about being high was in how everyday objects took on a subtle new lifelike quality, almost as if they were sentient, self-aware beings. I would notice for the first time the craftsmanship of the design inlaid in the kitchen tile, or newly appreciate the powerful, simple grace of a water glass. The things around me wouldn't animate or morph, like in a Disney movie where the stupefied homeowner discovers that his silverware can talk and has been leading a life of wild adventures with the teacups each night. That's LSD. Marijuana provided me with just enough of a subtle perception shift to see everything with a dash of new vibrancy and enhancement. The chair across the room would become the most quintessential Chair in the universe, a masterpiece of design and function existing throughout my days with a quiet noble pride I'd never appreciated or noticed. The closest I've come to replicating the sensation without taking a hit off my old Greensboro roommate's green bong has been by staring at one of those 3-D posters long enough for it to suddenly spring to life. People who don't have the patience to experience the effect don't get it—to them it's just a weird flat picture that gives them a headache. People who *do* get it know that there's so much more just under the surface.

I was experiencing this sort of perception shift with the entire issue of marijuana, the difference being that it wasn't wearing off. Drew, Joey, and Dave, the proprietors of Abundant Healing, were no longer just a trio of unlikely partners trying to untangle the complexities of starting a new business that was hated by half the community, but integral parts of the whole cellular biology of the marijuana movement. It was an organic thing with tendrils in the most unlikely corners of society; the old lady giving me advice on the pH of tap water was as much a part of the greater whole as those in Denver and Sacramento and Washington, D.C., who lobbied politicians and spoke before television cameras. The more I looked, the more the evidence of this organism detached from the two-dimensional world of my everyday life and floated slightly above it to let me know it was there, just like the seemingly random patterns on the 3-D posters suddenly coalescing into wholly unexpected and fascinating works of art.

"The cannabis scene has always been here," a volunteer with Denver's NORML chapter told me once. "You're just seeing it now."

How true. In the beginning, my biggest fear in growing cannabis wasn't getting arrested, but being scorned by people who might learn about my secret garden. The opposite proved to be true. Mike and I, during our weekly beer-drinking get-togethers, would often let our pot conversation get carried away and realize, way too late, that our voices were booming around the tavern, the full details of my horti-cultural activities overheard by everyone. Not only did no one ever reach for a torch or pitchfork, but we most often ended up befriend-ing a fellow cultivator or an old ganja vet. When a neighbor finally approached me, as I feared would happen eventually since my house emanated a green stench all way out to the sidewalk, it wasn't to threaten a call to the police but to lean in and whisper conspiratori-ally, "Hey, when can I take a look at what you're growing?" And when I came clean to the parents of my son's best friend so that we could still host summertime sleepovers—in his second-story bedroom, nowhere near the basement—it was no more controversial than if I'd said we'd be serving vegetarian food at our house from now on.

"I've got no problem with that," said the dad. "Hell, I'd much rather catch them smoking a joint some day than drinking beer."

I felt like Winston Smith, the hero of George Orwell's *Nineteen Eighty-Four*, who, just by opening his eyes, realizes that not everyone surrounding him is a brainwashed automaton who believes Big Brother's lie that "We've always been at war with Eastasia." They've just been cowed into acting as if it were true.

But the ultimate awakening of how near to me the marijuana debate has always been came when I called my parents at their home in Virginia. They're both in the medical field, and I wanted to ask my father, a radiologist with years of experience working with cancer patients, if he'd ever run across anyone who used marijuana to cope with the symptoms of chemotherapy.

"As a matter of fact, I have," he said. "Why don't you call your aunt?"

·9·

First, Do No Harm

"We ask cooperation on the part of the federal government by not imposing an unnecessary burden which in the end falls on the sick."

—Dr. William Woodward of the American Medical Association, opposing the Marihuana Tax Act in testimony before Congress, 1937

In 2003, my older cousin Cynthia was diagnosed with mesothelioma at age thirty-five. At that time it was a little-known cancer that attacks the protective lining of the body's organs. It's most commonly caused by exposure to asbestos, but no one really knew how it invaded my cousin's body. Research into mesothelioma has come a long way in the past few years, but when Cynthia was diagnosed, the treatment options were limited.

"We went to Sloan-Kettering and they knew zilch," my Aunt Cathy told me when I took my father's advice and called her a few days later at her home in Long Island, New York. "She was given heavy, heavy-duty chemo, cisplatin and gemcitabine. . . . Temporarily, as is common with all cancers, the chemo shrinks the tumors for a while, but then most of the time [the cancer] comes back. And then it's not very helpful. So Cynthia had a year's worth of heavy-duty chemo, maybe sixteen treatments, then was given a break of maybe seven, eight months, and then her lung area filled up with fluid again.

"And unfortunately, she decided—and we went along with—going back on the chemo, which just was devastating," my aunt sighed. "The last six months of chemo [were] horrible. It made her really, really, really sick."

Like many chemotherapy patients, my cousin lost some of her hair, but she had such thick, long dark locks that she kept most of it. But she was chronically fatigued and nauseous, and she eventually developed neuropathy, numbing of the hands and feet. She also developed hearing and vision loss.

When she was diagnosed, I hadn't seen Cynthia in many years. My best memories of her were from childhood, especially the times when a whole troop of my cousins (I had fourteen) would visit our house in the Philadelphia suburb of Secane, Pennsylvania. Family gatherings had our fathers and uncles smoking cheap cigars out in the yard and drinking cans of Pabst around a hand-built picnic table, while the mothers and aunts filled plastic picnic bowls with potato salad and pulled the foil tops off acidic orange drinks for us kids. We, in the meantime, were all over the neighborhood, riding bikes, looking for locust shells on the tree trunks, or playing with action figures in the mud.

Of all my cousins, Cynthia was normally the quietest and most reserved. She wasn't shy, but an observer. As a young teenager, she had an adult's ability to pick up nuance and humor where other kids her age never would. I remember her best as someone with an introspective soul, and with the heart and eye of the artist she later became. She was very beautiful.

As happens with families, ours drifted apart. My parents moved my younger brother and me to North Carolina, and I moved to Colorado when I was twenty-three. But I'd lost touch with my cousins long before then. I haven't seen most of them since the days of those backyard barbecues; others I might run into for only an hour or two over the course of five or six years, and usually then only by happenstance. This drifting was nothing personal. No bad blood. It's just something that happened.

Even while Cynthia struggled with her illness, I knew few details. I heard them all for the first time when I called my aunt.

Her first round of chemotherapy was just a precursor to the suffering that was to come. The more damaging regimen that came after the seven-month reprieve destroyed her red and white blood cells. Cynthia required blood transfusions; $2,000-per-shot injections of the anti-anemia drug Procrit, which is usually associated with chronic renal failure; and white-blood-cell booster Neupogen, which causes bone pain.

"The chemo just destroyed her," my Aunt Cathy said. "She was hospitalized easily once a month for a week."

When she wasn't hospitalized, Cynthia lived with my aunt in suburban New York. My cousin was a freelance writer and a poet who devoured books on the Renaissance, literary masterpieces, and Russian history. She gardened when she could, kept company with her cats, grew some Chia Pet herbs on the windowsill, and maintained a handwritten journal of her experience with cancer.

"Someone called from Sloan-Ket," Cynthia wrote in an entry dated November 23, 2003. "My chemo starts promptly, well, not promptly, but around 2 p.m. on the day after Thanksgiving. . . . I have my acupuncture at 12:30 (call to check on that tomorrow) and then off to the Poison Lab. I feel like [Danish writer] Isak Dinesen as the Baroness returned home to take the arsenic cure for syphilis; it, the chemo, the cure, will either kill me or heal me."

In another entry, she wrote: "Perhaps from now on most of my days will be spent in bed; as a refuge from chemotherapy, from the things and people that make me anxious. Feeling particularly anxious today—ovulating & its swelling & pain. . . . I ask you, how can this poisoned body keep producing an egg each month when it is becoming difficult for me to stand longer than five minutes?"

The journals were also infused with Cynthia's smart humor that transported me immediately back to our childhood, remembering the older cousin who chased me, my brother, and her brother through the backyard threatening to hug and kiss us. Apparently, her doctors were of European background and she referred to them as the "Eastern Bloc," as in "[I] apologized for not acting on his suggestion that I contact the Eastern Bloc sooner" when she developed a fever and needed to be admitted to the hospital. And once she wrote of her lunch menu: "Mother is making an egg for me. . . . I just ate a piece of cheese and two and one half crackers with some Dilaudid, morphine-Contin and a Dr. Pepper. I guess I should really have the egg."

Of course there were darker times as well.

"My mind has dismissed any chance of love, marriage, and family," she wrote, "and the desire for them is dissipating in my heart as well. I don't even believe I wish to be well again. This, certainly, is a bad sign: resignation. I think I'm ready for nothing. I have no plans except to have my portrait done before I die, and to see New Orleans once more."

At some point during this wrenching ordeal, "friends and relatives"—which is as specific as my aunt wanted to get—recommended that Cynthia try some marijuana for relief from pain and nausea. Like most of America, New York does not allow marijuana use for any reason, and those who bought and delivered the pot broke the law to do so. But no one cared. They were only concerned about helping Cynthia endure her chemo.

"It was so charming," my aunt recalled. "People volunteered to teach her how to roll it, and we had, you know, not parties, but someone would come over and we'd sit at the dining room table [rolling joints] and it was a lot of fun. Sometimes they were too fat and too big and too long and too short and all that. Cynthia used it primarily for nausea. She hated nausea, as many people do. If you smoke marijuana for nausea, then you can obviously eat a meal.

"People would bring it over and we would pay a couple hundred dollars," she said. "I'm sorry to say, I don't know anything about amounts, an ounce or two or something. At one point, I went up to the local store and bought little pipes and little papers."

My aunt said she never hesitated when marijuana was suggested; it never crossed her mind to say no, and the fact that it was illegal was completely immaterial if it meant alleviating her daughter's suffering.

"She took a puff or two and her nausea went away immediately," Cathy said.

Cynthia wrote about one of those experiences in her journal.

"After chemo, I came home yesterday and was very sick," my cousin wrote on April 17, 2004. "All the fluids, cold, made my bowels run for two hours. My nausea was terrific so I took a Kytril [an anti-nausea pill], which didn't work, and then three tokes on my MJ"—and here she wrote in all capitals—"AND IT DISAPPEARED INSTANTLY. I then fell asleep. Mom and I have decided to work to legalize marijuana for cancer patients who can use it. If I find that's not going well, I would give it away free to cancer patients who need it. Enough of these idiotic 'wonder drugs' that take care of nausea. Foolishness. Still tired, so going to doze."

Because of its illegality, marijuana wasn't always an option. When my cousin was so sick that she had to be admitted to the hospital, she couldn't use it. And my aunt worried about some drug deals because she was concerned for those who would be making the transaction; she didn't want them to blemish their careers with an arrest on pot charges.

One time, my aunt got the drugs herself.

"So I placed this call and I had to meet this person in New York City," she said, "so I jumped on the Long Island Rail Road and we were communicating on cell phones because the person was in a car outside Penn Station. Now, I'm not good with directions—I don't know the northeast, southeast corners of anything—but somehow I walked out the right exit and there was the car, so I got in."

As she was telling this story, I was picturing it in my mind. My aunt is now seventy years old and stands about five feet four inches tall. She's my mom's older sister, but they could be twins. They look alike and sound identical, so as she was telling me of her New York City pot deal, I couldn't help but picture my own mom, on a cell phone with her marijuana connection, wandering through the cavernous, bustling station looking for the right exit, then ducking into a car at the curb to make the transaction.

"I got the marijuana and paid my money," my aunt continued, "and as I was leaving, this person said, 'Now, it's in the plastic bag, make sure it stays in there. There are cops in there with drug-sniffing dogs.' But I didn't care. Nothing matters, believe me.

"I would do it again," Cathy said. "I would recommend it to anybody; I would give it to anybody. Anything that makes somebody feel better, when they feel that shitty, [if] it so clearly, clearly makes somebody feel better. She wasn't high; it goes straight to your brain and it takes away, in her case, the nausea. And the nausea medications, if they worked, would take hours."

In fact, while we were on the phone, my aunt remembered that she still had a bottle of the anti-nausea drug Marinol, more than five years old, in the refrigerator: It was a prescription for sixty pills, and there were still fifty doses of the synthetic THC drug left.

"I now remember that she tried them and she said they took too long," Cathy said. "Today, I will finally throw these out. There they go, in the trash can."

My cousin put a halt to her chemotherapy in January 2006.

She died at home at age thirty-eight on April 27, 2006.

I watered my plants with more reverence after that conversation. They were flowering now, with little furry buds emerging in dense clusters along the stems and between the leaves. Those leaves are probably as familiar as rose petals throughout the world, and their spiky silhouette is an enduring sign of the counterculture, of rebellion against authority. I realized that what they symbolized was truer than ever. Or, more precisely, it's as true today as it ever was; it's just that now I'd come to understand what the revolution is all about. While my cousin's friends and relatives were scurrying around the New York underbelly like common criminals, and my elderly aunt had to run a gauntlet of drug-sniffing dogs to broker a drug deal so that my cousin could have some relief, I could walk into any dispensary in the state of Colorado and choose my medicine. In New York and thirty-five other states, people who need marijuana can't get seed-choked Mexican schwag without risking their lives trading with street dealers, while in fourteen others, practically anyone who wants it for any reason at all can have their pick of the best-quality hydro-grown sinsemilla in an atmosphere that preserves their dignity.

Far from being scandalized at what Colorado Attorney General John Suthers called the "state-sanctioned hypocrisy" of the current medical marijuana law, I couldn't be happier for it. If this is what it takes to eventually force the government to do the right thing and at least reschedule marijuana so that doctors can prescribe it, then so be it. Prior to the big explosion of dispensaries lining many local streets in 2009 on account of the Ogden memo, half the people in Colorado weren't even aware we had a medical marijuana law, or even that there was such a thing as medical marijuana. If it takes public uproar over the fact that some potheads are now buying their weed from a dispensary than from a street thug to raise awareness about what my cousin and countless others have gone through thanks to total prohibition, I'm all for it. Those potheads are serving their purpose, although I doubt they know it.

What has become abundantly clear in my time in the world of cannabis is that attempts to decriminalize it the "right" way, through rescheduling petitions and presidential commissions and appeals to the courts, have been a worthless waste of time.

The mortal fear these plants inspired at the very upper reaches of the U.S. government—and indeed within every municipality from coast to coast—could be wryly laughed off as the ultimate cosmic joke if the stakes weren't so high for people who may benefit from them. Studying cannabis and reaching back through history to mark the points at which each objection to its very existence had collapsed and was replaced by yet another argument that would eventually prove to be equally weak had given me an entirely new perspective on this debate. The very plants growing in my house had been accused of causing almost every calamity except global warming. They were first said to make you an insane killer, but that hardly proved to be true. Insatiable sexual hedonism never panned out. Bill Gates, Ted Turner, Arnold Schwarzenegger, and even Barack Obama—onetime pot smokers all—disprove the terminal apathy accusation. Addiction potential is less than that of the cocoa bean. Escalation to harder drugs—which, by the way, implies that marijuana is less harmful than every other controlled substance—is unfounded. The chance of dying of overdose is zero.[1] What's left for those still grasping at the vapor of reefer madness? Only the illogical concept that admitting that marijuana prohibition had been a terrible, foolish mistake, which should be reversed so that it can help ease the suffering of the critically ill, is somehow sending the wrong message to our children.

It's exactly the message we should be sending to our children.

When I began my self-education into the mythology of cannabis, I was at first amused by the absurdity of the arguments used to prohibit it and by all the colorful characters who populate its history. That gradually faded to dismay, and then to frustration. The marijuana advocates who are trying to reverse an insane policy of frivolous waste, personal destruction, and medical immorality by seizing every opportunity at their disposal are not running a con game. The con is in perpetrating the lie that *they* are somehow threatening lives and well-being by demanding a commonsense approach to cannabis laws.

The government, clearly, is hell-bent on keeping marijuana just as illegal as it is today no matter how convincing the evidence that doing so is harming its citizens.

President Obama, once such a hope for the marijuana movement that it co-opted and tweaked his campaign slogan as their own—"Yes

We Cannabis"—has proven to be just as anti-pot as any president before him.

And that is probably why, in spring 2010, California voters were fed up enough to place a full legalization measure on the November ballot, known as Prop 19. It's not the first time a state's citizens have tried to legalize marijuana—Californians voted down a legalization bid in 1972, and similar efforts in Nevada and Colorado in 2006 also failed—but this one looked as if it had a true chance of passing. By early August 2010, a SurveyUSA election poll showed it leading 50 percent to 40 percent with 10 percent undecided.[2] If it passed, California would have been the first jurisdiction in the country to legitimize commercial cannabis production for any use at all.

Obama's drug czar, former Seattle police chief Gil Kerlikowske, spoke to the California Police Chiefs Association in a closed meeting on March 4, 2010, to address this and other aspects of the federal drug policy, and said, "Marijuana legalization—for any purpose—is a non-starter in the Obama Administration."[3]

In his remarks, Kerlikowske addressed numerous topics regarding marijuana to explain the government's position; primary among them, to prevent it from getting into the hands of children. Thankfully, he didn't bring up the canard again about marijuana being a gateway drug, but he had several other concerns, including that smoking pot interferes with learning, can lead to dependence, and can impair motor skills.

He's quite right about all of those things. Marijuana is a powerful narcotic that, despite its prevalence and low toxicity, should not be taken lightly, especially by adolescents and developing young adults. I'll even second Kerlikowske's points—based on my experience in college, if I'd have smoked pot in high school with the same determination, I never would have graduated. As unfocused as my mind was during my adventures in 1991, studying and learning would have been next to impossible. But I have yet to hear any marijuana advocate suggest that pot should be available to teens and children unless there was a bona fide medical need. In fact, their argument is that the "utter failure" of the War on Drugs (to use President Obama's own description) has done nothing to stem pot's availability to adolescents who want to get hold of some. As pointed out earlier, a 2009 study found that half of those between the ages of twelve and seventeen said they could get some pot within a day, and a quarter said they could score within the hour.[4] Yet the same study showed that it was harder for teens to get hold of beer and prescription drugs, which are government-regulated and have restricted availability. Somehow, these statistics serve as proof for marijuana opponents that prohibition should be continued.

Legalizing marijuana and treating it in similar fashion to alcohol will not prevent it from getting into the hands of those it shouldn't. I believe what DEA chief Jeff Sweetin said when he predicted that there will always be a black market for pot; it's too prevalent and too easy to grow to regulate entirely. But the current system puts every cent of the money it generates into the hands of criminals, some of whom are waging an actual drug war on the U.S. border with Mexico. It seems far saner to take the money currently being spent busting adult pot smokers and domestic growers—including those who do so only for medical reasons—and pour it into an honest education campaign targeted squarely at adolescents in order to discourage their temptation to toke up. We currently take our kids to Miller Park to watch the Milwaukee Brewers while enjoying an MGD Light, and where does the responsibility fall to teach kids right from wrong when it comes to alcohol consumption? On parents. How can parents be expected to properly educate their children about the *real* facts about marijuana when the government won't acknowledge them itself? Parents who blindly parrot the government line—"We've always been at war with Eastasia"—are doomed to raise children who will eventually hear otherwise and seek out the information for themselves.

✤

KERLIKOWSKE, OBAMA'S DRUG czar, addressed numerous other topics, such as how legalizing and taxing marijuana wouldn't generate enough revenue to cover the social costs of what is assumed to be greater availability (and, ergo, greater instances of abuse). Those social costs include increased health care, lost work productivity, crime, and other expenditures. Illicit drug use in the country already accounts for $180 billion in social costs, he said, and noted that alcohol and tobacco don't generate nearly enough revenue to offset their unique social costs.[5]

The truth is that no one knows how much tax revenue could be expected under a legalization scenario—no one has ever taxed it before. It's a commodity that would probably be very sensitive to tax rates because the black market for marijuana is clearly very well established: Taxing it too much would push users to the secondary market—or, in other words, where they get it today. The California State Board of Equalization estimated that if pot were legalized in California, the state could see $1.4 billion in annual state sales tax.[6] But that estimate is just a guess based on current market value of $300–$450 per ounce. There's no telling what prices will do in a typical economic environment; they could collapse, a possibility that was pointed out in a recent study by the Rand Corporation, which, doing some admitted guessing of its own, estimated the cost of an ounce of weed could fall to $38.[7] Or it could go higher than it is currently; no one knows. Another 2010 study by Harvard University economist Jeffrey Miron put the estimate for California tax revenue under a legalization scenario around $259 million per year.[8]

What Kerlikowske didn't address when he spoke to California's police chiefs was the estimated *savings* from legalizing marijuana if states were no longer required to investigate, arrest, prosecute, and incarcerate pot offenders. Miron put that number at a staggering $13.7 billion nationwide, with the states saving the bulk, $10.4 billion.[9]

"Legalization eliminates arrests for trafficking and possession," Miron said. "Second, legalization saves judicial and incarceration expenses. Third, legalization allows taxation of drug production and sale."

He estimated that eight states, including California, could save more than $1 billion each if they stopped enforcing marijuana prohibition laws.[10]

Kerlikowske did, however, emphasize the president's renewed focus on drug prevention and treatment, a new shift toward handling the matter of drug abuse in the United States from the perspective of public health and safety, rather than one that relies so heavily on law enforcement. It's an approach that he said encouraged him to retire the phrase *War on Drugs* once and for all.

Yet just a few weeks later, President Obama released his drug control budget, which indeed increased spending on the sorts of programs Kerlikowske promised, but it also devoted two-thirds of its $15.5 billion budget to law enforcement, a record increase in both spending and the percentage of the overall budget going toward cops and courts, larger even than under his predecessor, George W. Bush.

Business as usual.

MEANWHILE, BACK IN Colorado, business was quite unusual. While Kerlikowske was telling California cops that legalization was a nonstarter, the pot business was going gangbusters in the Rockies. Dispensaries had a months-long head start on the politicians, who had to wait until their legislative session began in January before they could consider what, if anything, to do about dispensaries. And in that time the industry had done nothing but grow. A California company called Daily Buds rented out the half-million-plus-square-foot Colorado Convention Center in downtown Denver and staged what was at the time the nation's largest Cannabis Convention, drawing around

100,000 people, more than twice the number who attended the Great American Beer Festival, which had previously been the city's largest annual draw.

A California dispensary chain called The Farmacy, famed for its Whole Foods–like approach to decor and customer service, was one of the first out-of-state venues to open a location in Denver, joining an unruly gaggle of competitors that truly spanned every taste. For a sense of adventure, one could visit a ramshackle trailer painted in a garish Day-Glo green in a dirt parking lot on South Broadway—long referred to as "Broadsterdam" by that point, due to its density of dispensaries—or for a more Zen experience, there was The Apothecary of Colorado, which was decorated like a combination Scientology retreat and Russian bath house.

The local alternative newspaper, *Westword*, posted an online ad for a marijuana dispensary reviewer, a help-wanted item that received media attention as far afield as China and as mainstream as *The Tonight Show with Conan O'Brien*. "Our first applicant replied within five minutes—fast work for a stoner," wrote editor Patricia Calhoun in an online column. "Our first media response came a few minutes later—really fast work for a journalist."

By midyear, the nation's first cannabis college to be accredited by a state's agency of higher education opened in Denver. Greenway University offered degrees in bud tending, cultivating, and business management. "It's the first time in history in the medical marijuana industry where someone can have some type of validation from a state entity," CEO Gus Escamilla told me when I called to ask about the school. "We have the ability to offer government money to help fund educational programs and it really puts us into a higher platform. We can give grades, and have transcripts held by us and by the state."

Although it is the first such facility to be recognized as legitimate by a state educational agency, Greenway is not the only cannabis college in the United States. Oakland, California, is home to Oaksterdam University, a place where budding ganjapreneurs can learn everything about the marijuana business from seed to sale. Oakster-dam has a total of four campuses: in Oakland, Los Angeles, North Bay, and Flint, Michigan.

Like many other new arrivals, Greenway started in California but moved to the new Promised Land in Colorado and is planning a campus in New Jersey.

"Colorado is truly setting the standard for the entire United States, and the entire United States is looking to Colorado for guidance and perspective," Escamilla said. "Hands down, it has now become the epicenter."

Colorado was even luring ganjapreneurs from what had previously been considered cannabis heaven: Amsterdam. American business-man Adam Dunn, who moved to the Netherlands twenty years ago to open seed distributor T.H. Seeds and a hemp clothing company, was enticed to branch back into the New World because Colorado was proving to be more permissive than even pot-friendly Amster-dam.[11] The Netherlands forbids growing cannabis; Colorado not only allows it, but has enshrined it in the state constitution.

The same type of barn-burning activity was happening in other medical marijuana states, but it was ebb and flow in terms of whether advocates or opponents held the upper hand, depending on the section of the country. Montana, for instance, became a battle zone. Dispensaries in Billings were firebombed on the night before a city council voted to extend a moratorium on such businesses, and an anonymous parents' group papered elementary schools with fliers for the children to take home, encouraging their parents to support an effort to repeal that state's law, which had passed with 62 percent of the vote in 2004.

In Los Angeles, the city council approved restrictive zoning rules for marijuana businesses that forced more than four hundred of them to shut their doors; it inspired some Cheech and Chong–type prank-sterism, such as when a dispensary on wheels (think of it as an ice cream truck that sells pot instead of popsicles) infiltrated the victory parade for the L.A. Lakers, who'd won the NBA championship, handing out marijuana lollipops and beating a hasty retreat before the cops caught wind.

In New Mexico, the state's Department of Health Medical Advisory Board revved up the medical marijuana law to consider adding new qualifying illnesses to its already lengthy list of sixteen; and thanks to all the heavy media attention medical marijuana was generating from coast to coast, new light was shined on one of its more controversial inclusions, post-traumatic stress disorder, which was added in January 2009. New Mexico is the only state to have done so, but the new round of scrutiny set off a chain reaction of events. First, the Veterans Administration, which treats the majority of PTSD cases in returning war veterans, forbade its federally funded doctors from recommending a federally prohibited drug to its military veterans, citing department rules under which the VA could deny patients pain medications if they're found using illicit drugs. This became a brief cause célèbre for reform proponents, and after only a few weeks of stonewalling, the VA caved in. VA patients in medical marijuana states are now allowed to receive doctor's recommendations to use medical marijuana for PTSD.

Michigan saw an outburst of "cannabis clubs" opening across the state, operations that are legally hazy at best; Michigan's Medical Marihuana Act specifically prohibits the sale of pot but allows approved caregivers to charge for the cost of recouping their growing expenses. Hence, all sales at the cannabis clubs are claimed to be legal by their operators and declared to be in violation by state and local officials. The matter will likely be settled in court in the future, but in the meantime, several Michigan cities have banned the clubs outright through vaguely worded ordinances outlawing activities that are federally prohibited, which selling marijuana obviously is. That led to the threat of a lawsuit by the American Civil Liberties Union, which is using the October 2009 Ogden memo as leverage to argue that the cities are violating patients' rights, since the memo indicated such persons wouldn't be prosecuted under federal law.

In Maine, voters approved possession of medical marijuana in 1998 but provided no way for patients to access it. In the fall of 2009, nearly 60 percent of voters approved a plan to create six state-run dispensaries; one was to be run by a former sheriff who has long been an outspoken advocate for marijuana legalization.

Down the road in Vermont, however, things are different. Like Maine, its 2004 law did not mention dispensaries or a distribution system for its 187 medical marijuana patients—a bill that would have created such businesses was killed in the state senate over a disagreement about how many were needed with fewer than two hundred people on the registry. Lawmakers opposed to a dispensary system pointed to Colorado as evidence of how easily it could be abused.

Activity on this issue was just as impressive in the non–medical marijuana states. Several introduced legislation to consider joining the club. By the summer of 2010, eight states had pending legislation or ballot measures to legalize medical marijuana: Arizona, Illinois, Massachusetts, New York, North Carolina, Ohio, Pennsylvania, and South Dakota. Many more introduced bills that died at some point during the 2010 legislative session, but which activists promised to revive in the future. Those included Alabama, Delaware, Iowa, Kansas, Mississippi, Missouri, Tennessee, Wisconsin, and Virginia.

Meanwhile, all eyes were on Colorado, whose state legislature had been working since January 2010 to settle on rules governing medical marijuana dispensaries. State politicians were truly in a no-win situation. No matter how badly many of them may have wanted to, they couldn't undo the medical marijuana law; as part of the state constitution, only another vote of the citizens could change it. The best they could hope for on a state level was to create a framework of reasonable regulations that wouldn't impinge on the rights contained in the constitution. By the spring of 2010, even some dispensary owners were clamoring for rules—the growth in the industry had exceeded all expectations and threatened to backfire. Many communities in

Colorado voted to ban, either permanently or temporarily, medical marijuana dispensaries, or regulate them into oblivion with zoning regulations that banished them to industrial parks or warehouse districts. The city of Centennial shut down a dispensary called CannaMart using an argument that became common in Colorado and in other medical marijuana states: CannaMart was said to be in violation of Centennial's land use code, which prohibits activities that are against federal law, including selling marijuana.

Centennial's argument seemed perfectly logical—even the judge who ruled on the lawsuit CannaMart filed agreed that the dispensary violated federal law *and* the land use code by selling pot. But he ruled that it's not Centennial's job to enforce federal law; that was up to federal agencies.

"The city of Centennial cannot use the potential violation of a federal law to order a business legally operating under our state constitution to cease and desist its business," District Court Judge Christopher Cross said.[12]

It was another victory for medical marijuana, but these individual triumphs began adding up to fuel the impression that potheads were running amok throughout the state with no one capable of stopping them. Dispensary owners knew the state legislature had the power to make their lives hell if it wished, by passing onerous regulations that could easily put them out of business. Law enforcement, with Colorado Attorney General John Suthers leading the charge, proposed a bill that reinstituted the five-patient-per-caregiver cap, which would have effectively ended the entire dispensary phenomenon; it simply wasn't cost effective to open a retail outlet that served only five people. Several pro-marijuana groups began their own lobbying effort—they realized that *some* regulations were inevitable and they wanted to have as much input as possible.

Freshman Sen. Chris Romer, son of former Gov. Roy Romer who had aspirations to higher office, was among those state leaders who took up the charge. Shortly before the legislature convened, he penned an optimistic column for *The Huffington Post* in which he saw nothing but sunny skies in the forecast.

"We would be the first state in the nation to create a patient-focused model," he wrote, "and would thus become a national leader forging the way towards successful regulation and dispensing of medical marijuana. There are many interested parties coming together to craft this policy, but as long as we focus on helping patients . . . while appropriately regulating the market, I have no doubt that we can creatively and successfully formulate a common sense policy that works for Colorado."[13]

It wasn't long before Romer got a better education of the entrenched battlefield he was wandering onto. Finding common ground between cops and pot peddlers, no matter what the end use, would be a first in the nation's history. Marijuana advocates wouldn't easily give up the ground they'd gained, even if many agreed that regulations would help professionalize the industry in the minds of critics. Because of marijuana's outlaw status, many communities weren't even sure they could collect sales tax on it. The more proactive dispensary owners applied for sales tax licenses and contributed to their communities' revenue, but since it wasn't required anywhere in existing law, they did so voluntarily. Those who were truly seeking to legitimize medical marijuana as an industry looked forward to some reasonable rules that would weed out the shadier characters giving them a bad name, but there was a limit to what they would agree to. In that, they had the law on their side, even if it was broadly worded and open to abuse. And they also had a powerful advocate who would ensure that the law was followed to the letter.

As in every medical marijuana state, the permissive laws spawned a number of professionals who specialize in the industry's peripheral needs, such as carpenters and electricians who added grow room construction to kitchen remodeling on their list of offerings. Perhaps no specialized profession was as important as the lawyers, however. In Colorado, dozens of attorneys made medical marijuana the primary focus of their practices, and none was as out front and visible as Rob Corry Jr., whose skill in defending his clients and keeping state agencies in line with the details of the medical marijuana amendment was matched only by his ability to attract media attention to himself and his cause. When I mentioned to Jeff Sweetin that I was meeting with Corry, he predicted Corry would find some way to turn it into a media event.

"Rob's a good lawyer, but the fact that you're interviewing him will be on the news," he said. "He doesn't do anything without the news finding out about it."

That's true, but Corry hardly sees it as a bad thing. Publicity equals awareness, and Corry has spent much of his life trying to educate juries, police departments, district attorneys' offices, reporters, and the public about a topic he's felt passionately about since he was a teen. He began specializing in medical marijuana cases when he moved to Colorado from California in 2001. He was Dana May's attorney, the medical patient whose reflex sympathetic dystrophy made him feel like his feet were boiling if he didn't have marijuana to give him relief. Corry won the case and compelled the DEA to at least return May's growing equipment if not his pot. It was that case that led Suthers, who at the time was the federal prosecutor Corry faced, to declare medical marijuana to be a "smokescreen."

"That was sort of my first big media case," Corry said. "In the criminal defense practice, nine clients out of ten want zero media attention. They want to keep it as quiet as possible and who can blame them? But the rare client who's willing to get media attention, I'm also willing to help them with that as well. We were on TV [during the May case]; we got a ton of action."

Corry is a constitutional lawyer who, in his words, "already had a longstanding relationship with marijuana dating back to age 14," before he developed his reputation as one of Colorado's premier medical marijuana defense attorneys. Despite his admitted recreational use—and the psychedelic posters on the walls of his office—Corry wouldn't set off anyone's 420 radar with just a glance. He and his then-wife Jessica, who is also an attorney, are lifelong conservative Republicans. After receiving degrees at Stanford University and the University of Colorado at Boulder, Corry was the majority counsel to the U.S. House of Representatives Judiciary Committee and Constitution Subcommittee. Jessica Corry was a press secretary for GOP stalwarts like Tennessee Sen. Fred Thompson and Maine Sen. Olympia Snowe, as well as the U.S. Senate Governmental Affairs Committee, and she is a frequent guest commentator for the libertarian Independence Institute. NORML and other marijuana activist groups have lauded both for their legal activism.

Although Republicans and conservatives in general are typically among those who favor marijuana legalization the least in national polls—both all-out legalization as well as for medical purposes—the Corrys see themselves as truer to the core values of the GOP than the GOP itself.

"From a principle standpoint, if Republicans are not in favor of ending the drug war then they're totally hypocrites and they're departing from their small government mentality, in my opinion, and I'm still a registered Republican," Corry said. "War should not be a perpetual thing; it is impossible to eradicate marijuana. It will never happen. Singapore has the death penalty for it and you can still get it there. It will not be eliminated by any amount of governmental activity, and I think the past seventy years must have proven that. But we still continue the insanity. In my opinion, the GOP has got to be the party to end this and we're not. Actually, we're worse than the Democrats. Both parties are horrible on the issue but the Republicans are probably worse than the Democrats currently. We're taking a totally anti-freedom position."

It's an argument Corry has been making since childhood. Growing up in Iowa, he was no less clean-cut than he is today, with his impeccably coifed blond hair and crisp courtroom attire, when he first smoked pot at age fourteen during a sleepover at a buddy's house. In fact, his friends often compared him to Alex Keaton, Michael J. Fox's stridently conservative character on *Family Ties*. Corry and his friend spent the night getting stoned and listening to Rush, Led Zeppelin, Pink Floyd, and Jimi Hendrix on the record player. He remembers that it was easier to get pot in Iowa in the 1980s than it was to get beer, and he had no fear about smoking up for the first time.

"Despite the DARE-type preaching that I had been subjected to, I was a scientific thinker and thus knew that the police and schools were lying to us all about marijuana," he said. "I had little fear of marijuana since I had seen first-hand many people use it dozens of times with no apparent ill effects."

Corry said he used marijuana with moderate frequency during high school, but not during school hours—that time was taken up with numerous activities, including the student newspaper, presiding as president of the chess club, competing on the swim team, and getting into student government. As speaker of his student house of representatives, he led a mock charge to legalize marijuana, which might not seem very challenging among high school students, but it set the stage for the arguments he would make later in his career.

Since 2001, Corry has had a hand in dismantling every barrier put in the way of the state medical marijuana law. He represented CannaMart in its lawsuit against Centennial, and he successfully sued the state to overturn the health department's arbitrary five-patient cap on caregivers, the legal precedent that was more responsible than any other in clearing the way for retail distribution and the proliferation of dispensaries. He and other lawyers have successfully defended clients who had more marijuana plants than the state law allows (by relying on another provision of the law that allows patients to grow or possess more than the legal limit if they can prove it's medically necessary) and have even gotten marijuana growers who weren't registered as patients off the hook. Not only did he make history by having the DEA return growing equipment to a marijuana defendant, he did himself one better by having local law enforcement return actual marijuana, on more than one occasion.

"I ended up kind of building a string of victories in getting medicine back for patients who had their medicine seized," he said. "Back then [in the mid-2000s], that was news, going to the Denver Police Department and picking up an ounce of pot and walking out of the police department with marijuana in an evidence bag. Nowadays, you can barely get the news media interested. Just last week I picked up two pounds from the Arapahoe sheriff, which is extraordinary, because Arapahoe County is a law and order suburban Republican county, and they coughed up two pounds. I got only the *Denver Post* and 9News, and nobody else bothered to show up for that. It's becoming routine."

Like many others who champion the cause of medical marijuana, Corry sees it as a means to eventually legalizing marijuana outright. Throughout my investigation of this issue, nothing caught me so continually off guard as these admissions that the marijuana critics are correct, at least on this point: Medical marijuana is an important issue in and of itself, but it is being used as a vehicle for broader acceptance with the hope that it will eventually be legalized in the same way as alcohol and tobacco.

"The way I see it is that the patients will never be safe until it's legal for everyone," he said. "Until it's legal for everyone—for recreational, spiritual, for any purpose—the patients are always going to get caught up in this mentality of 'you're not really a legitimate patient, you're faking it, you're lying about your medical condition just so that you can get marijuana.' They're also going to get caught up in this unique-to-marijuana principle that you can only have what is medically necessary. There is no other medicine or commodity that has that. You can have forty kegs of beer sitting in your garage and no one is going to say that you have an excessive amount of alcohol, or you could have a hundred OxyContin, the amount that can kill six horses, sitting in your medicine cabinet and nobody is going to say you've got an excessive amount. Until it's legal for everyone, the patients are never going to be safe because they'll be caught up in this netherworld.

"The analogy that I used is that Rosa Parks and other civil rights pioneers began with the most politically palatable venues, such as buses and lunch counters, things that dealt with most people's day-to-day lives," he continued. "Integration of whites-only private country clubs and golf clubs were not where they began. That was decades after Rosa Parks, when civil rights pioneers integrated private golf clubs.

"The same thing with this. We're looking to legalize marijuana. We start with the medical as the most politically palatable route. It just so happens that there is an immediate collateral benefit to suffering patients who need what is literally a miracle."

When we met in April 2010, Corry was planning an appeal to the Colorado Supreme Court on a marijuana case, but his other big priority was to keep tabs on what was happening at the state capitol building—Chris Romer and other lawmakers were refining their bills, and it was Corry's job to let them know that he was watching their activities carefully.

Almost regardless of what the politicians did, he fully expected to take them to court.

· 10 ·

Coming Soon to a Neighborhood Near You: Auditors With Guns

"I have always loved marijuana. It has been a source of joy and comfort to me for many years. And I still think of it as a basic staple of life, along with beer and ice and grapefruits—and millions of Americans agree with me."

—Hunter S. Thompson

As state lawmakers were beginning to cultivate their knowledge about this new alien industry that seemed to have taken over the state, I was busy with my own cultivation in the basement. The Mango and the Mother's Finest plants had zoomed toward the ceiling, standing nearly four feet tall after seven or eight weeks on the twelve/twelve light cycle. I was worried about the Blueberry and Maui, which had grown to only half the height of their sisters, but Sonja, who visited from time to time to see how things were going, told me that modest growth can be one of the characteristics of those particular strains. They weren't producing nearly the same amount of fat, sticky buds as the other plants, but what they were growing looked good to her experienced eyes. The trichomes, once milky white and crystalline, had begun to turn amber on most of the plants, signs that THC production was beginning to peak. The Blueberry was the most charming of them all—I could squeeze the little buds and the scent of fresh blueberries would be on my fingertips for the rest of the day.

In fact, the scent of marijuana clung to me at all hours of the day and night. I met my buddy Mike at the bar a few weeks before the plants were fully mature, and he turned toward me sniffing the air.

"I can smell you coming, man," he said, and a fellow sitting a few stools away raised his eyebrows at his beer and nodded in agreement.

"Really?" I asked. I was completely immune to the smell, but that I reeked like my old apartment back in Greensboro didn't worry me too much; I'd long gotten over any fears that someone might call me out as a drug dealer, considering that Mike and I openly discussed my cultivation operation every Monday and Thursday from the barstools for the sake of anyone who cared to listen. My confidence in the legality of what I was doing had solidified, and I knew I had only a few more weeks until it was time to harvest my plants and I could quit worrying about having them seized by the police.

But the pervasiveness of the pot fragrance suddenly had me concerned that both my wife and son were probably carrying it with them to work and school. So far, we hadn't aroused any inquiries from authorities, but the new worry was the possibility of getting a call from the school guidance counselor or safety officer who'd tagged my innocent son as a burgeoning pothead because he smelled like he just burned a joint behind the athletic field.

In fact, nothing could be further from the truth, from all the evidence I could gather. If I'd had any concerns that growing pot in the house would make Turner any more curious about getting high than he otherwise might, they were scuttled in the days and weeks following our "marijuana as medicine" conversation. It seems a sort of reverse psychology had taken effect once he became a teenager, one in which anything Dad was interested in was automatically written off as stupid and boring. On occasion, I would drag him down to the grow room and fawn over the plants, describing for him the photosynthetic effects that were producing the buds, explaining the still-mysterious-to-me nutritional elixirs lined up on the bathroom counter, and wondering aloud at the chemical magic the buds contained and all the unknown potential still to be unlocked by science. Turner couldn't have been less interested if I were showing off my newfound love for collecting rare coins.

"Great, Dad," he'd say, humoring me with mock interest until he could escape to something—anything—more exciting. Could I have found the cure for teenage drug experimentation?

IF MY *EAU de cannabis* was good for anything, it was to fit in with the right crowd that had gathered at the golden-domed capitol building in Denver in late April 2010, when public testimony was to be heard on Chris Romer's medical marijuana bill, one of two scheduled to be voted on in the coming weeks. The hearing was held in the Old Supreme Court Chambers, a stately two-story room painted in rosy hues with cream-colored Renaissance columns stretching toward the stained glass windows ringing the upper perimeter.

"Check it out," the dude seated behind me said, pointing to the centermost pane of glass. It depicted one of Colorado's founding fathers accepting a long pipe from a Native American chief. "They're smoking the peace pipe, bro."

From the smell of things, they clearly weren't the only ones, but by then, the clinging odor of weed had stopped seeming out of place in gatherings like this. It was one of the few occasions that everyone on both sides of the medical marijuana debate was together in the same room. Pot advocates outnumbered the cops, but their presence was no less noticeable; whereas the activists hugged one another and chatted in the aisles as if waiting for a concert to start, a long blue row of sheriffs, prosecutors, and police chiefs sat stone-faced in the back row, breathing deeply and trying to conceal their contempt behind leaden expressions. Defense lawyer Rob Corry wandered through the crowd, finishing a foil-wrapped burrito from the cafeteria on the ground floor, and Laura Kriho, who had formed an advocacy and education group called Cannabis Therapy Institute, was there too, mingling with the local NORML members and others who had done their best to influence the composition of the main bill Romer would introduce.

Once again, it was a testament to how important this crowd considered the occasion that they arrived precisely on time. I'd spent months hanging out with all sorts of marijuana users, and the only time the punctuality gene was triggered was when their presence was required at a governmental hearing. But this time, they could well have afforded to be late—before the marijuana bill was heard, the committee considered another matter, something having to do with requiring home builders to install low-flow toilets and other water-saving measures in newly built homes. So for about an hour, a hundred stoned hippies, a handful of wheelchair-bound medical patients, and sundry dreadlocked activists sat quietly beside a squad of graven-faced cops listening to testimony about toilets, including details about the flushing habits of one senator's family members.

It was worth enduring, however. The bill to be heard was seventy-eight pages and dense with all sorts of new rules and regulations. Dispensaries, which had until then operated with barely any rules, would be made fully transparent. Owners and employees would be required to have clean criminal records and to open their financial ledgers (both business and private) to a level of scrutiny unseen in other industries. This was an effort to weed out criminals and those with ties to organized crime or, at the very least, with shady sources of operating income. In order to remain in business, they would have to have the blessing of their local municipalities in the form of a local operating license, as well as a license issued by the state. The fees involved had yet to be determined, but it was assumed they would be hefty.

A key provision of the bill was the requirement that dispensaries grow at least 70 percent of the product they sold; the other 30 percent could come only from dispensary-to-dispensary sales. This was an attempt to ensure that the marijuana being sold could be accounted for. Currently, there was no telling if dispensaries were selling Mexican weed smuggled by the cartels and enriching violent gangs south of the border; if the pot sold was smuggled from California, where the volume of product on the market had already started impacting wholesale prices there, leading growers to look for buyers elsewhere in the United States; or if it was grown legitimately by locally owned operations like my friends at Abundant Healing. The intent was sound, but it promised to make life hard for dispensaries that didn't currently have their own grow operations. Starting one would be expensive, as would the additional cultivation license the bill required. Finally, there was a third level of license required for those who wished to manufacture edible products like pot-infused cookies and brownies.

The bill bestowed the Colorado Department of Revenue with the task of implementing rules for dispensaries and carrying out inspections to be sure the dispensaries were following those rules. At a meeting of medical marijuana businesses in mid-April, Chris Romer, the bill's most outspoken champion in the capitol, quipped about these inspections by warning dispensaries that "auditors with guns" would be showing up on their doorstep frequently, demanding to weigh the product, inspect the sales records, and ensure that everything was aboveboard.

A critical component was the so-called "opt-out" provision, which allowed local municipalities the freedom to vote to ban dispensaries altogether.[1]

A separate companion bill tightened the screws on doctors—no longer would patients be able to go through a four-minute farce of an appointment like I'd done. Future recommendations had to be based on a full physical examination, and the diagnosis would no longer be able to take place somewhere as disreputable-sounding as The Med Shed or any other location where medical marijuana is sold. Doctors would be forbidden from receiving payments or perks from dispensaries or holding an economic interest in them, and they couldn't offer discounts to patients in exchange for buying their pot from preferred providers.[2]

Overall, the vision projected by these new laws was one of a closed system wherein private businesses with the financial clout and the requisite level of patience to comply with myriad details could flourish, while providing patients with enough choices of dispensaries that there was a competitive incentive to keep prices low, and at the same time bowing to local sensibilities if communities decided marijuana dispensaries were not for them. In addition, it preserved individual patients' rights to grow their own marijuana, or for caregivers to do it for them, although it reintroduced the five-patient cap on these caregivers—anyone who wanted to grow for more than five patients had to incorporate as a dispensary and commit to the regulatory gauntlet that it entailed.

The bill was unprecedented in American history, a road map for legitimizing and controlling the for-profit sale of marijuana, a revolutionary concept.

Naturally, almost everyone hated it.

FROM THE VERY beginning of the dispensary boom, cops in Colorado did not know which way was up. Therefore, they didn't have any idea what to propose in terms of a legal solution. Their cop genes gave them only one involuntary reflex: to bust the living hell out of everyone. But that was no longer an option, and they found themselves short-circuited with confusion and anger. Revoking the medical marijuana law wasn't possible from a legislative point of view—that could happen only through a citizen revolt resulting in a new vote to repeal the law, or if the U.S. Supreme Court deemed it unconstitutional. The only choices for cops were to advocate clamping down as firmly as the constitutional law would allow or throw up their hands and cave in. Even as staunch an opponent of medical marijuana as Colorado Attorney General John Suthers considered the latter an improvement over law enforcement's current state of impotence.

"I would prefer legalization to the state-sanctioned hypocrisy that we've embraced right now," he told me. "I just think it's unhealthy from a societal point of view to have 22-year-olds going in and lying about their medical condition to get this stuff. That bothers me a great deal, and having doctors cheating and all that stuff. The moral ambivalence involved in that is very troubling to me. I would prefer straight-up legalization."[3]

Short of that, Suthers preferred a system that instituted an across-the-board five-patient-per-caregiver cap, which is illustrative of the overall law enforcement myopia this debate produced.[4] That would indeed wipe out the dispensary industry and seem to solve the problem on an "out of sight, out of mind" level, but with 105,000 patients and counting on the registry by the summer of 2010,[5] it would put in its place at least twenty-one thousand mini-dispensaries serving only five patients each. These would be operating in suburban basements and generating their revenue tax-free—meaning Colorado would have followed the precise course as Arcata, California, the community that was falling apart because of home-run marijuana grows that were operated completely out of sight from a state regulatory agency.

Law enforcement did get some concessions in the bill, including the opt-out provision, which Suthers personally testified on behalf of during the hearing in the capitol. And cops' lobbying helped shape the legislation concerning new oversight of physicians.

For the marijuana advocates, however, there was far more reason for concern. Romer himself admitted that half or more of the dispensaries in business at the time of the hearing would be wiped out by the provisions in the bill. Either they wouldn't stand the scrutiny into their owners' criminal backgrounds, the fees would be too far out of the reach of the more modest operations, or they wouldn't be able to comply with the provision that they grow their own marijuana.

Kriho and her group, the Cannabis Therapy Institute, decried the bill as a "monstrosity" and lobbied for its defeat. Her preferences for regulation were enshrined in a draft bill she'd penned in November 2009, which essentially allowed dispensaries to open shop anywhere that any other retail or commercial business was allowed with no restrictions, a pure free-market model whose only regulation included a requirement for for-profit dispensaries to collect sales tax.

"It was very, very minimal," she said. "Mostly just definitions on what a medical marijuana business is and leaving the zoning up to the locals. What we would favor, if anything, is just simple registration of caregivers, because right now there's no mechanism for caregivers to register in this state to be protected."

Kriho said she offered her draft legislation to Romer early in the process and that he "didn't even look at it," leading her to suspect the fix was in.

"Every law enforcement officer in the country is watching this case and has been watching and they've all been involved in the planning of it and they all wanted to see how much Colorado is going to be allowed to get away with," she said. "And [law enforcement] got away with everything as far as I can see."

Kriho wasn't alone in griping about the bill—most people who sat through the marathon hearing, which lasted until after midnight, were dismayed about the number of fees, the requirement to grow most of their own marijuana, the restrictions on felons, and many of the other details. As the hours wound on, the initial excitement among marijuana advocates turned to a dark frustration as it became clear that the bill was going to clear the committee and be forwarded on for a vote.

"Nobody else [in any other industry] has to put up with this kind of abuse," Kriho continued. "The environmental guys ahead of us? I ran into one of those guys down at the bar and I'm like, 'You guys have got it easy, you're talking about how many times you flush your toilet and then we come in and we've got every district attorney on the Front Range, twenty cops, and the attorney general [lined up in opposition].' Nobody else has to put up with that kind of abuse."

TRUE, BUT THE low-flow toilet industry is completely legal and has never had to overcome allegations that their products cause insanity. In the end, both bills passed the legislature and were signed into law by Gov. Bill Ritter on June 7, 2010. They didn't go into effect immediately, but instead laid out several deadlines for compliance of certain provisions. Dispensaries had until the end of Sunday, August 1, 2010, to apply for their state licenses after completing a thirty-plus-page questionnaire regarding finances and personal details of employees. The final tally was impressive, considering Romer's estimate that at least half the dispensaries in Colorado would fold in the face of the regulations: 717 dispensaries applied for licenses, as did 271 manufactures of "infused products" and 1,071 grow operations. These applicants also had to submit their licensing fees at the same time, earning the state of Colorado $7.34 million by Monday morning.

But, indeed, not everyone could participate under the new rules. Pierre Werner had owned one of the more luridly named dispensaries in the state, Dr. Reefer, in the heart of Boulder, and he may well have been the sort of dispensary owner the lawmakers had in mind when they crafted the law to exclude felons. I met Werner on April 20—the infamous *four-twenty*—which is something of an international day of armistice between cops and potheads that sees hundreds of thousands of marijuana smokers gathering on campuses, in front of state capitol buildings, and in other public areas to toke up at exactly 4:20 p.m. In reality, the toking goes on all day long, and one's risk of arrest is directly proportional to the number of like-minded people in the immediate vicinity. With strength in numbers, cops at the larger gatherings give up the hopeless task of writing tickets or making arrests and simply stand around waiting until 4:21, when they can start clearing people out. I went to Boulder in 2010, the site of one of the largest gatherings in Colorado; I'd never been to one before and figured that, with marijuana growing in my very basement, it would be wrong not to. True to nature, I didn't smoke anything, but I hardly needed to. On a broad and stately quad on the University of Colorado–Boulder campus, at least ten thousand stoners of every stripe had begun gathering as early as noon to enjoy the day's activities. Hula-Hoops swirled around tie-dyed hips, crazed skeletal hippies twirled around in a trance to wild bongo music, and in every direction, someone had a pipe, bong, or joint between their lips. The air was leaden with pot smoke, and ringing the whole area was a gang of cops looking on with bored detachment.

Dr. Reefer had the good fortune of being located directly across the street from this gathering, and there was a steady stream of traffic going through the doors; perhaps the only comparably busy store in the area was nearby Cheeba Hut, a pot-themed deli that was curing the munchies as quickly as people could get through the door. Werner had invested a lot of money in neon signs, and we stood chatting in their glow while trying to make room for his customers.

Werner appeared in Boulder at the height of the Green Rush after having already made headlines in Nevada and California. Colorado was his third chance to find a place to make a living off a state's medical marijuana law. He'd reportedly run a dispensary in Santa Barbara, California, until he was raided and shut down by the DEA; then he and his mom operated a medical marijuana referral service in Las Vegas called DrReefer.com, through which they connected prospective patients to doctors. Somewhere between those two ventures, he also tried to walk naked from California to Vegas and was subsequently diagnosed with bipolar disorder. He was given lithium, which he said turned him into a "zombie," but found more solace in pot, which his mother later told an AP reporter he'd smoked when he was younger.[6] Although it's one of the medical marijuana states, Nevada doesn't allow marijuana sales, even to patients; Werner disregarded that detail and grew the maximum of seven plants each for some two hundred patients. He was busted with what he called a "significant" number of cannabis plants and convicted of intent to distribute marijuana, a felony. The moment he was off probation, he moved to Colorado. Standing there shoveling money into his till on April 20, he must have finally felt like his Dr. Reefer empire was gaining traction.

At the appointed moment, a great throaty cheer arose from the thousands on the quad, and with it a cloud of pot smoke as dense as a blimp, temporarily making it impossible to see from one end of the gathering to the other. Surely it could be seen from passing aircraft; the cloud blocked the sun for a few moments before drifting away, as did the extremely stoned congregation that sent it heavenward.

A few months later, I happened to be in the neighborhood and decided to pop in to Dr. Reefer to see what Werner thought of the passage of House Bill 1284. He was in a much more despondent mood, slouched behind the cash register, idly toying with a glass pipe; as a felon, he'd have to sell the store.

"I don't know," he said, his feet up on a countertop filled with White Widow, Purple Urkle, and Island Sweet Skunk. "I'm out of it, I guess. I don't know what I'll do." He ended up selling to a new owner; Dr. Reefer is still in business, but the "doctor" himself has drifted off into the ether.

Since there was no accurate accounting of how many dispensaries were in the state before the passage of the new laws, much less a list of who owned them, it's impossible to say how many people like Werner were forced out of business, either by their criminal backgrounds or by their inability to comply, in some way or other, with the new requirements. It's hard to know how to feel about someone like Werner being excluded from the club of qualified dispensary owners. On one hand, on paper he doesn't seem to be the sort of person you'd expect to join the Chamber of Commerce and to sponsor 5K runs for charity. But on the other hand, who's more qualified to run a marijuana business than someone with a marijuana record?

After HB 1284 became law, the most qualified marijuana cultivators
were by definition felons who simply hadn't yet been caught.

"What we saw was the whole illegal drug industry become legal
for a brief period of time. Everybody became law abiding and paid
their taxes and everybody was happy about it and now they're going
to go back underground," Kriho said when we met for a lunch of
tacos and beers not long after I last saw Werner. "They were legal for
a year and now they're going to be criminals again."

She also wondered if the new law would eventually take the wind
out of the legalization movement.

"That was the other interesting thing," she said. "Instead of there
being a dozen of us cannabis activists around the state, all of a sudden
we had five thousand activists. But the people didn't know the history
of the whole thing. They didn't realize that they were part of a political movement, that they were part of a civil rights struggle. So all
these dispensary owners are scratching their heads and going, 'How
did I get reamed so badly?' But you have to realize that you are part
of a political struggle, part of a civil rights movement. You came into
it for a very brief period of time, but it's stretched way back behind
you.

"It's going to continue moving forward because the people who've
been doing it for years, we see this as just another bump in the road
on the way to legalization," she continued, "but for all these people,
who invested all their money in this business, it's a little bit more serious for them. We'll see how many of these people stay activists, stay
involved. One of our gripes over the years has been the growing
community not supporting the legalization community financially.
They never did, and they didn't this year when they're making lots of
money, and I assume that when they go back underground they're not
going to support us again either."

It's easy to get all grim and militant when hanging out for too long
with Kriho; she was just one side of the coin I'd seen tossed for so
long in this issue, so I went to speak with Brian Vicente, who is both

an attorney and the director of the medical marijuana advocacy group Sensible Colorado (which was formed through a grant from the Marijuana Policy Project). Depending on who you asked, either Vicente was one of the more reasonable marijuana advocates who saw the value of compromise in eventually obtaining the larger goal of legalization, or he was a sellout. He didn't even seem quite sure when I met him in an un-air-conditioned office a few blocks from the capitol.

"It's tough when you're battling every day and you lose these battles and at the end of it we come out with this bill and I felt kind of dirty about it," he admitted. Vicente was at the capitol nonstop for five months, building coalitions, taking meetings, and trying hard to lobby for as good a deal as possible for medical marijuana patients. In the end, he and his group ended up opposing the bill, but nevertheless, he sees it as more of a victory than others.

"We should remember that the initial discussions [among lawmakers] were 'how can we destroy dispensaries?'" he said. "We went in with that playing field and we got them to regulate dispensaries. I wouldn't say I love 1284, but it's an absolute landmark piece of legislation."

I asked him about the divide I'd witnessed among those striving for the same cause, not only on the state level but nationally. The examples were consistent everywhere I looked. Kriho, for instance, is hesitant to work with a group called the Medical Marijuana Business Alliance because they won't change their name to the Medical *Cannabis* Business Alliance, with Kriho citing marijuana's supposedly racist roots. In Montana, the two pro-marijuana members of a legislative panel studying that state's regulatory scheme are openly at war with each other. Jason Christ, who runs a network of traveling marijuana clinics, is rarely seen or photographed when he's not toking from a two-foot-long pipe he carries with him everywhere; not surprisingly, he's an advocate of loose regulation. Tom Daubert, who was behind Montana's 2004 medical marijuana law, openly accuses Christ of "exploiting [the law's] problems and loopholes, registering thousands in one day," even as Christ is standing next to him.[7] It's the NORML vs. MPP fight replicated everywhere I look.

"We can look at this as any other industry, sort of like do Coors and Bud spend their time attacking each other?" Vicente says. "I think marijuana will follow a path just like every other business. At least for now, this is becoming so much more normalized and standardized and the infighting is going to go away. The question is will the infighting prevent us from making progress? Because it really has in other states. If you look at Oregon and Washington, you have great activists there, really top notch. They hate each other. They can't accomplish anything."

Vicente is proud of what was accomplished in Colorado, even though it falls far short of many people's hopes and although there are matters that he considers to be flatly unconstitutional that will eventually be challenged in court, primarily the ability for communities to vote to ban dispensaries altogether. At the time of our meeting in the summer of 2010, a handful of small towns had approved such votes for November; should they pass, there is little question that either Vicente or Corry, or both, will be involved in yet another precedent-setting lawsuit. In the end, Vicente said, it's important to look at what has happened: Colorado has made history.

"It's an absolute landmark piece of legislation," Vicente said. "Colorado will have the most sophisticated regulated medical marijuana system of any in the country. It also allows for an endless number of dispensaries as long as you can comply with the state and local authorities. I think in some ways it's a template for other states."

Plus, look at what the state gets out of the bargain, he added—in addition to $7.34 million in what amounts to found money from licenses (not to mention $9.45 million in individual application fees by 105,000 patients paying $90 each, per year), there is a yet-to-be-calculated amount of sales tax that will begin rolling in, a hundred new jobs in the Department of Revenue to oversee the industry, and a nearly tenfold increase in jobs at the health department to handle the registry.

"Our state now has a real incentive to grow and develop and to keep regulated marijuana sales happening," Vicente said. "If we can get through the next year or two—and we don't have gun battles in dispensaries and dispensaries are actually caring about patients and paying taxes and following every rule and providing other wellness services and are viewed as contributing members of the community— if we can get through a year or so of implementing this new law, I think we'll be in a position to say the sky didn't fall and we can increase the tax base and the employment base one hundred-fold. I think Colorado is poised to do that.

"At the end of the day, we have what we have and we'll work to make it better. But we should realize that it is one of the best, probably *the* best, medical marijuana law on a state level in the country."

A FEW WEEKS before the new legislation was passed, I was in Aspen at a place called the Hunter Bar, drinking a beer with Bobby Tuna, the infamous pot smuggler who holds the record—at least for now; it's sure to be broken—for having served more time than anyone on a nonviolent drug offense, twenty-eight years in the federal penitentiary. Bobby is well into his sixties, but so is Keith Richards, and on this night, he shared the same rock-star status as the legendary guitarist. One after another, homeboys in hip-hop caps and baggy pants edged up to shake his hand, and at least half took the opportunity to slide him some homegrown bud. Or try to, anyway—"Hey, Mr. Tuna, I would really be honored if you'd take this Purple Kush me and my cousin are growing out in Grand Junction, you know, just to say thanks and all"—but Bobby, aware that he wouldn't survive to see freedom again if he were pinched with so much as a burned roach, would always politely defer: "That's really not a good idea, kid, but thanks." Somehow it was assumed that I was his flunky, and if I held out my hand, without saying a word, the kid would drop the offering in my palm. I ended up with nearly a half ounce of weed. Everyone in the bar was stoned out of his gourd.

The occasion for Bobby Tuna's visit, and mine, was the first of a planned annual competition among Colorado's dispensaries, the Aspen Cannabis Crown. On display at a nearby hotel were 141 strains of Rocky Mountain–grown marijuana, each competing for the title of best bud in Colorado. I'd been immersed in cannabis culture for months and had no real interest in seeing yet more marijuana, but I couldn't pass up the chance to see it practically on public display, right there in a hotel ballroom in full view of any cop who cared to wander in. It was still pretty mind-blowing to me that Colorado had advanced acceptance of marijuana more in seven months than anyone had managed to do in seventy years.

The events were split between two hotels, the Gant and the St. Regis. The pot was confined to the former, the partying to the latter. During the day, "judges"—who were really anyone with medical marijuana cards who'd cared to lay out a few hundred dollars to sample all the strains—cadged a few grams of pot from all the hopefuls, fired up a bowl, and scored their impressions on a ratty little tally sheet. Technically, there was to be no "medicating" in public, but that was apparently more of a suggestion than a hard rule. I ran across one judge, a kid from Denver who knew pot like Gordon Ramsay knows food, blowing smoke rings in a breezeway between the pool and the tennis courts. He didn't care about getting high, he said; he and his girlfriend were conducting market research in advance of opening a dispensary of their own.

The "no medicating in public" rule was also ignored at Hunter Bar, which has a large open patio accessed from the street by first descending a large outdoor staircase, as if you're entering a subway station. Sitting under the moonlight with joints being passed at every table, I was just waiting for the cops to appear over the edge to throw a large net on everyone below. But the only arrest I saw that weekend was of some poor kid who tried to scoot through the lobby of the St. Regis, which had forbidden marijuana on the premises, while trying to conceal a large glass jar full of buds under his shirt. Assuming he'd stolen it, hotel security jumped him right near the front doors and kept him pinned to the carpet until the cops could come. He was booked for possession and the Cannabis Crown contender was destroyed; Aspen had made its point—don't blatantly disregard the rules set up in advance and everyone will get along fine.

Otherwise, Aspen that weekend was something like Nirvana, and it was one of the few occasions where there was no visible tension among those in attendance, a real who's who in the pot world. Defense lawyer Rob Corry and his wife were there. Rick Cusick, the associate publisher of *High Times*, paid a visit, and Anita Thompson, Hunter S. Thompson's widow, dropped in throughout the weekend. Bruce Perlowin, the King of Pot, ran a booth not far from Bobby Tuna's, but as far as I knew they weren't sniping at each other. Even the competition—which many assumed would be rigged in favor of sponsoring dispensaries—seemed to go off amicably. The best bud in the state was deemed to be the Kandy Kush, entered by Rocky Mountain Remedies from Steamboat Springs.

This was the sort of kumbaya I had been expecting all along. It was almost as if those in the movement had allowed themselves to simply sit back and bask in what had been accomplished for a long easygoing weekend before heading back to Denver to bang heads over laws and regulations and other bummers. From the geriatric drug runner who'd kept the country fueled with pot during the dark days to the brash young hustlers growing the mad mountain chronic, everyone seemed tuned in to how cool it was to just hang out with a beer and a pipe at a public outdoor bar or by the pool at a hotel in one of the ritziest towns anywhere and get seriously Rocky Mountain high without any hassle at all.

I let my thoughts get carried away in the haze and thought that, if all went well with my harvest and I could improve my cultivation skills beyond the level of blind luck, I might try to convince the fellows at Abundant Healing to enter one of my strains in next year's competition. There's no prize whatsoever beyond bragging rights and some gaudy statue, but it would be a nice accolade to include on the wall of my office in the basement, along with all of my other professional accomplishments: Cannabis Crown, First Place. I'd even settle for honorable mention.

I never seriously considered entering the thing, but it was fun to fantasize. And it wasn't until a few weeks after I'd talked to both Kriho and Vicente that it occurred to me, quite out of the blue, that it would never happen for legal reasons. By passing its new laws, the state of Colorado had completely torpedoed my burgeoning business plan—small-timers like me were no longer allowed to sell to dispensaries because of the requirement that dispensaries grow their own. I could grow all I wanted for my own benefit, but my personal benefit from marijuana is a big goose egg. I'd been cut out and it hadn't even occurred to me.

Worse, I was now racing the clock to get my plants to harvest—the dispensaries had until September 1 to start complying with the grow-your-own rule, meaning that if I could cut it and cure it in time, I still had a few weeks to squeeze in under the wire. With luck, I could at least recoup my investment.

In a worst-case scenario, I'd be stuck with a bunch of pot that, like the handful of weed I brought home from Aspen, would be doomed to sit in my cabinet as a novelty, pulled out when my son has kids of his own and wants to tell the story of that time Grandpa grew weed in the basement.

Misty Mountain Hop

Of every tree of the garden thou mayest freely eat;
but of the tree of the knowledge of good and evil, thou shalt not eat of it.

—Genesis 2:16–17

The chimes of the doorbell echoed through the house like the chords of a horror movie, stretching through the living room and reaching downstairs to where I sat on the sofa surrounded by freshly cut marijuana. It covered the coffee table in front of me and littered the carpet, tiny, sticky clippings of stems and leaves in one pile and a little mound of bright green buds like fuzzy caterpillars in another. Mike and I raised our eyebrows at each other, neither of us acknowledging out loud what we'd just heard. We just pretended it hadn't happened and returned to the task at hand, trying by force of silent will to make whoever it was vanish in a puff from my doorstep as if they'd never existed. It was like pretending you hadn't seen the "check engine" light flash on the dashboard while driving across Death Valley. Now was not the time for visitors.

Harvest day was on a Friday in June, and it involved just as much planning as any other phase of my cannabis project. The literature had served me well to that point, and most of my reading material stressed the importance of staying vigilant all the way to the end. "The process of harvesting, drying, and curing is perhaps the must underestimated aspect of cannabis cultivation," warned an article in the *High Times Grow Guide 2010*. "How, when, and where you cut, dry, and store your buds can make a big difference in the final product."[1]

I'd bought a pair of well-lubricated, spring-loaded pruning shears at Way to Grow, earning myself a thumbs-up look of accomplishment from the cashier; all of the employees have perfected the art of talking about cannabis without really talking about cannabis. The shears were key—I expected to be hunched over branches and buds for most of the day, and the shears were going to get gummed up with psycho-active resin very quickly into the process, so having a good comfort-able pair was important. I then loaded up on a bunch of airtight mason jars that I would loosely fill with buds after they'd dried so that they could cure. That part of the process was as much an art form as any other; curing evens out the moisture so that the buds dry evenly inside and out. Carefully curing your weed by sealing and opening the airtight jars a few times a day for as long as two weeks avoids the final pitfall of the growing process: the terrifying possibility of pollut-ing your final product with fungus. Curing is also hard for most growers because they're eager to fire up a bowl and enjoy the fruits of their labor, but I didn't have that temptation. Last, I picked up a box of surgical gloves to keep my fingers from getting too sticky and a bottle of alcohol for general cleaning and tool maintenance. Imple-ment-wise, it was all systems go.

But the most important thing was something I couldn't pick up at Way to Grow or Home Depot: privacy. It was summertime, and in typical years the house would be a teenage way station as Turner and his friends shuttled through for Gatorade and Doritos either to or from the basketball court or the baseball diamond at the park down the street. It was going to be a hot, crystal-clear day, but I'd told him the evening before that today was a day to just batten down the hatches and stay indoors playing Xbox or watching TV—there would be way too much incriminating behavior going on downstairs to risk detection on the eve of victory. Telling my teenager to be a couch potato for the day was the easiest part of the entire growing process. By the time Mike came over with a six-pack around 10:30 that morning, Turner was still deeply asleep and, if history were any guide, would stay that way for another two hours.

The need for privacy was more than just because we would be busy and didn't want to be disturbed. For the first time since I had started this whole basement operation, I paid closer attention to the warnings about the unmistakable odor of bud. The *High Times* article contained a very frank caution that seemed aimed directly at me: "Beware: At harvest time, your girls will never smell sweeter or more pungent, an otherwise pleasing aroma that unfortunately can be overpowering enough to alert the neighbors to what you've been doing in your basement over the past few months."

Pot stench had been the hands-down biggest stressor of the entire experience. I'd foolishly thought the bathroom exhaust fan I'd installed in the grow room would direct the odor outside, where it would quickly dissipate into the atmosphere. Wrong. My biggest advice to wannabe cultivators is to invest in an activated carbon filter or ozone generator, expensive pieces of equipment that are worth their weight in peace of mind.

But even a carbon filter wouldn't have prevented the overpowering bouquet that was released as I clipped and trimmed all around the heart of the plants, emitting into the air fragrant essential oils called terpenes, hydrocarbons that are found in numerous plants and used in perfumes. Within an hour of the harvest being under way, you'd have thought Bob Marley and the Wailers had been living in the basement for the past year. I don't think I could have stunk up the entire house with a stronger odor if I'd been slaughtering swine in the kitchen and rendering the carcasses.

We popped open a couple of beers, put some Pink Floyd on the stereo for atmosphere, and settled into a good routine—Mike cut off the branches and I trimmed the buds, a learned skill, but one that I quickly mastered. The point was to cut down all the leaves poking out of the buds down to the stem, if possible, and shape them into their appealing and conical shapes; the trick was to strike the right balance between not cutting off too much of the little leaves (they were thick and sticky with resin) but not leaving so many that it looked like you were trying to thumb the scale when they were weighed. It was tedious, but fun.

The doorbell rang again. Whoever it was wasn't going away.

"Maybe it's the UPS guy or something," I said, stripping off the gloves and taking a quick swallow of beer, thinking it might be my last for a while if the cops had finally arrived. Normally, I would have ignored the bell, but when Mike came over, I'd absentmindedly left the big front door open, leaving only the screen door barring the entry. That, of course, is the universal sign that not only is someone home, but that the occupants aren't opposed to visitors.

I climbed the basement stairs and peeked my head around the corner from the living room, half expecting to see Jeff Sweetin standing at the threshold, crossing the last T on the federal search warrant in his hand, his probable cause being the faint whiff of pot I'd left on the upholstery of the chair in his office. Instead, I saw one of my son's sassier buddies, a kid I'll call Dwayne, bouncing impatiently from one foot to the next, a baseball mitt in one hand and a bat in the other. Behind him at the curb, his grandfather was leaned over the passenger seat waving in my direction, already starting to pull away now that he knew someone was home to take charge of the kid. At least he hadn't walked him to the door.

Even as I was crossing the living room, Dwayne was stepping inside. "Hi, Greg!"

"Heeeeyyy," I replied, trying to think fast. Of all Turner's friends, Dwayne was the one we'd specifically tried to discourage from summertime visits. We didn't dislike him; on the contrary, during the summer, he was practically family. I'd come down for breakfast one morning last year after he'd spent the night and found him sprawled across the sofa watching *SportsCenter*. "Morning, Greg," he'd said. "We're out of oatmeal."

He reminded me of Gary Coleman in both stature and moxie, and he is unusually smart and inquisitive for a thirteen-year-old, a dangerous combination at that moment. I'd been very judicious about which of Turner's friends' parents we'd included in our small circle of confidants, but Dwayne's weren't among them. The primary reason was that Dwayne was a natural chatterbox whose conversational skills are best described as loquacious. It's not so much that I didn't trust him to keep a secret from his vast social network, but more that I knew he was incapable of it. Handing him a conversational nugget like that and telling him to keep it quiet was like handing him a candy bar and telling him not to eat it.

Plus, he was on to me. Early in the growing cycle, he'd made a quick stop at the house to pick up Turner so that they could ride bikes around the neighborhood and he'd told him, "Your house smells like pot."

Loyal to the end, Turner had just said, "Huh, that's weird," and sped off on his bike before the conversation went further.

And now here he was, standing in the foyer, two feet away from where I stood, reeking of weed and wearing a *Big Lebowski* T-shirt that was covered in flicks of resin and little triangles of marijuana leaves that had stuck to me like bits of tape. Apparently, there had been a miscommunication between him and my son; Dwayne thought they were scheduled to hit some fly balls. It was too late to do anything about it. The grandfather had already driven off, and I couldn't just turn him away.

"Go wake him up," I said, pointing upstairs toward Turner's room and backing away quickly. "I'll be in the basement working on an important article, so you guys do what you want, but don't come downstairs no matter what, OK?"

I trimmed faster.

HARVESTING MY PLANTS elicited mixed feelings. Obviously, they were meant to be cut down and gotten into shape so that they could be smoked and enjoyed, but I'd grown attached to them. The more I learned about their truly magical and mysterious qualities, the more I came to respect and revere them, something I hadn't anticipated. Before I brought them into my home and shared my basement with them, I expected to regard them as ugly and distasteful. I'd seen plenty of pictures of cannabis and hadn't exactly been rendered breathless. They look like the sort of plant that, if encountered on a nature walk, you'd give wide berth, as if it could prick you or give you a rash. Before I got to know them up close, I thought cacti were more attractive.

Now, though, I understand why *High Times* runs a glossy center-fold each month, like *Playboy*. By the time it came to harvest them, I looked at these cannabis plants much less as an exploitable commodity, as I did at the beginning, and much more as a spiritual enigma. The plant kingdom is teeming with species that affect human physiology and most have been cataloged, recorded, and studied, if only to see if they are dangerous or can be useful. Atropa belladonna, or deadly nightshade, has the power to kill. Aloe has the power to soothe. Potatoes have the power to sustain. Marijuana has powers that are barely understood, but its most obvious—the power to alter our consciousness and gain insight into different realities, however fleetingly—has led only to an expensive, destructive, and hysteria-filled campaign to wipe it off the face of the planet without any apparent desire to understand it at all. If it were possible to patent a plant (and it's not) there is no question that some pharmaceutical company would long ago have taken up the legalization cause itself in order to embark on the estimated $800 million it takes to shepherd a new drug through the labyrinthine FDA approval process.[2] Were cannabis newly discovered today, it would be hailed as a potential miracle whose secrets should be unlocked as swiftly as possible; instead, it's dismissed as, at best, a "marginal weed" and marked for extermination.

So we're left with this: a suburban dad growing it in his basement and living every moment in fear of even children knocking on the door. At least I have the benefit of living where I do. The medical marijuana industry in Colorado (and everywhere else where it's permitted) may be in its infancy—one marked by a certain degree of chaos, false starts, and frustrating setbacks—but it's already done more for my understanding of what cannabis is, and could become, than anything I'd known prior to the summer of 2009. Aside from providing relief to those who would benefit from cannabis's palliative effects, it seems to me that the greatest advantage of laws like these is to nurture an environment in which curiosity can flourish and knowledge can be shared. As much as I found occasion to gripe about one pot faction or another's complaints and grievances, the truth is that I learned something new from each person I discussed this topic with, a level of open discourse that is—at best—significantly more difficult to find in states where marijuana remains as outlawed as ever. Sitting in a Denver café with *Westword*'s dispensary reviewer, I was going on and on about my experience cultivating marijuana, speaking in a regular conversational tone, when he looked at me as if he'd just thought of an interesting bit of trivia.

"You know," he said, "it would have been impossible for us to sit here and have this conversation even a year ago."

Indeed, and fifteen years ago, without the protection afforded by medical marijuana laws, the risk simply would have been too great for me to do what I've done—indulge my curiosity about this forbidden substance through hands-on experience. And that's if I'd even had that curiosity in the first place. As it was, it was the outrage and the uproar over marijuana hitting the mainstream that brought the issue to my attention. Had it not been for the "sham laws" decried by practically every politician in the country, it's quite likely I would have gone through life as ignorant about cannabis as the government intended me to be.

When I first drove home with a carload of pot plants, I was mortified at the prospect of getting caught. The fear was due more to the perceived shame of being identified as some subversive pothead than any legal repercussions. But three months later, when I loaded up a shoulder bag filled with six quart jars of manicured pot and drove over to Abundant Healing, I felt enlightened, like the member of some special group who'd been let in on an amazing secret.

It was a slow day at the dispensary when I arrived, and Dave was the only one of the owners around. We sat on a leather sofa in one of the back offices and I pulled out my weed.

"Wow," he said, examining a long Mother's Finest bud under a pocket magnifier. "You grew this? This looks pretty good. Let's go put it under the microscope."

He fired up the laptop in the pharmacy and stuck the end of the lighted scope onto the bud. The screen was filled with the microscopic trichome forests nestled in the folds and valleys of the sample, most of them amber or clear, with a few milky ones scattered about. Dave pointed out how the color of the trichomes indicates the maturity of the plant; the clearer the trichome, the more potent the THC. The skill is in harvesting the plants at just the right moment because not all the trichomes mature at the same time—the rule of thumb is take the plants when the trichomes are about 75 percent clear or amber. I'd nailed it on all but one sample; the Maui could have used another week or so before being harvested.

"But hell," he said, "I'd smoke it. For your first grow, I give you an A minus."

That was consolation for the fact that my yield had been terrible— out of six plants, I'd only managed to produce two and a quarter ounces when I'd hoped for at least eight, and I'd given Mike the extra quarter so that I could stay within the limits of what I was allowed to possess under the law. There are any number of reasons my plants failed to meet expectations; I could have screwed up the nutrients, which was a good possibility considering I had never figured out what I was supposed to be doing other than following the instructions on the label. Or I could have stunted the plants once when I didn't fully close the grow room door one night, allowing light from the adjoining office to leak in for twelve hours when it should have been totally dark. But Sonja said the most likely reason was the LED lights. An old hand who'd grown pot for more than a decade, she was pretty sure they were too weak to bring out the plants' true potential, no matter that the light spectrum was supposedly perfectly calibrated.

"Think about it," she told me, "you're trying to duplicate the power of the sun. Next time, you should get one of those 600-watt HID lamps."

The only trouble was that I wasn't sure there would be a next time. I still had a few weeks to sell my product to a dispensary before the deadline by which they would have to grow their own, but if I wanted to continue to grow as a commercial endeavor, I'd have to register as a dispensary or partner up with an existing one. That would involve fees, a background check, a financial-record search, and all sorts of hoops and barriers to navigate. Considering I had no plans to expand my grow room to accommodate more plants, I doubted it would be worth the trouble.

I also soon found that it was not worth the trouble of many dispensaries to deal with a stranger peddling a suspiciously insignificant amount of pot. Abundant Healing wasn't in the market because Sonja had also recently harvested and they were fully stocked with the strains I had to offer. That put me in the odd position of trying to sell weed door-to-door, cold-calling dispensaries. There were numerous disadvantages to this approach. First, no one knew me, and many didn't seem inclined to make a new acquaintance, preferring to deal with their existing network of suppliers. Second, with the grow-your-own deadline looming, most dispensaries had either already closed the loop on their supply, or they were trying to liquidate their inventory in anticipation of not being able to comply with the new regulations and going out of business. Finally, those who entertained the deal were interested in pounds of marijuana, not two piddling ounces. I came across as exactly what I was—a newbie grower who'd used the medical marijuana law to turn a buck and was now desperate to unload my stock before the boom fell.

Striking out on every front with the dispensaries, I changed tactics and turned to the place where everyone goes to sell things these days. I put an ad on Craigslist.

THE AD WENT up on July 27, 2010, under the For Sale: Health & Beauty category. Titled "Extra meds for sale, organic and cured," it was short and simple, with a list of the strains I had and a price breakdown based on what Dave had told me I could expect at wholesale rates, about $250 per ounce. I had no idea how advisable this approach was, but I wasn't the only pot salesman on the site. At the bottom of the ad, I included the line, "MUST have photo ID and valid MMJ card or paperwork; I've got mine, be prepared to show yours," in an effort to at least filter the potential responses to only those from legitimate patients.

My e-mail inbox didn't exactly explode with interest, but I got five or six replies rather quickly. Most were barely literate—"wut up dawg, howz bout dem meds?"—but one seemed promising. It was from a guy who said he had an official red card, not the ragtag paperwork that most patients were still carrying. I'd actually gotten my red card in the mail a few weeks before, nine months after The Med Shed submitted my paperwork. The guy also said he wanted to inspect the goods, which raised his credibility at least somewhat in my eyes (would an undercover cop think of that detail?), so through a series of e-mail and text messages, we arranged delivery the following evening, what they would call "the meet" on *Law & Order*.

I had no idea if what I was doing was even remotely legal, but I was pretty sure it wasn't specifically prohibited. I read the medical marijuana law and the newly passed legislation line for line trying to find some clue, but found nothing to indicate that patient-to-patient sales were prohibited.

Still, it seemed pretty shady when I loaded the car with pot and my wife yelled after me that dinner would be ready in thirty minutes, "so don't take too long with your drug deal." The address was in the student ghetto not far from campus, a neighborhood of once-nice homes that had gradually gone to seed after consecutive semesters of hosting block-wide keg parties for a few decades. I circled the block in all directions, looking for signs of a SWAT team staged to take me down when I showed up, but all looked normal.

The house I entered was a carbon copy of the apartment Joe and I shared in Greensboro, at least in terms of decor and occupancy. Posters of The Beatles, Led Zeppelin, Phish, and Pink Floyd were tacked to the wall over a third- or fourth-hand sofa, whose cushions were tangled up with tie-dyed blankets and some well-worn pillows. The wide coffee table was littered with beer bottles and bongs, and I had to step over a tall pile of sneakers and sandals that all but blocked the front door. A giant plasma TV dominated one corner of the room, the floor in front of it littered with DVDs of live Phish concerts. The patient, whom I'll call Tyler, was a mirror image of myself at his age, which I guessed to be around nineteen or twenty. All he lacked were the dreadlocks.

"Hey, man," he said in greeting, gesturing me to the love seat. "Thanks for coming over."

He showed me his driver's license and his red card, which were both in order. Same guy in the picture, same name on both documents, same address. While he "wow, man'd" in admiration over the pot (apparently, Dave hadn't been just pumping my ego; I really did grow some nice weed), I tried to identify some clue as to his illness, if any, but there were no pill bottles, leg braces, or wheelchairs in evidence. I suspected he suffered from the same thing I did, "severe pain," but who am I to say? As far as I know, he has inoperable cancer or Crohn's disease or lupus or something that wasn't obvious with just a glance. Regardless, it wasn't my job to diagnose him; the red card was evidence that *someone* had, and if it's good enough for any dispensary in Colorado, it was certainly good enough for me.

"Dude, how long have you been growing?" he asked, genuinely impressed. "These are some sick meds."

"Oh, I've been growing a little while," I said, feeling suddenly like Walter White, the mild-mannered chemistry teacher–turned–meth cook in the TV series *Breaking Bad*, a drug dealer who had no personal experience with the product he manufactured and sold. Maybe cannabis cultivation really *was* as simple as following the instructions.

The deal took less than ten minutes. Tyler was impressed enough that he opted to stock all the way up to his legal limit and buy all two ounces. He handed me a curled roll of $20 bills, which I had no problem counting right in front of him before I stood up from the love seat. It seemed like what was expected.

All told, three months of stress and anxiety netted me $500. Compared to what I paid in equipment, grow gear, fertilizer, soil, and construction materials—to say nothing of the building time, watering duties, stress, and anxiety—I was still $300 in the hole.

If I ever find a way to do this again, I thought as I pulled away from Tyler's house feeling like I'd come full circle in my personal marijuana journey, I'm investing in a sodium vapor light.

OF COURSE, I didn't sell Tyler *all* of the marijuana I grew. I kept a few grams of some strain or other that had rolled away from its pile and that I found on the carpet in the basement. I put them in a spare glass jar and kept them in the kitchen cabinet next to the tea.

Throughout my brief career as a pot cultivator, I was tempted time and again to fire up a joint and experience firsthand the things I'd been reading and studying about. I certainly had my choice of strains from which to choose—I had a handful of Jack Herer (the late "hemperor" had a strain named in his honor) and Purple Kush from Aspen, and a miniature dispensary's worth of other samples and small purchases I'd made whenever I went to check out a dispensary. Other than trying once to make some cannabis tea, they'd gone untouched (the tea was a failure, mainly because I didn't know at the time that THC is not very soluble in water; it *is* soluble in oil, so the experts suggest boiling marijuana in milk and butter first and then adding tea and other ingredients to create a chai-like concoction).

Any hesitancy I felt to indulge in the product of my new hobby had nothing to do with cultural indoctrination about marijuana's moral repugnance. I'd gotten over that long ago. What I hadn't gotten over were the disappointing experiences I'd had at the hands of Joe's infamous green bong. Back then, I had no idea how to approach marijuana or what to expect of it. I huffed down bong hits like I was chugging beers, and largely anticipated the same results. Now, though, I had a much more profound respect for the weed I'd surrounded myself with for most of a year. I knew better.

So one day, when I had the house to myself, I crumbled up those wayward grams and rolled a nice straight joint. I took a glass of red wine out onto the back porch (along with a big glass of water; morbid cottonmouth is not something one forgets easily) to see if the fierce wind shaking the cottonwood trees and dragging dark storm clouds down from the mountains would produce any rain. Just in case, I pulled one of the weather-beaten Adirondack chairs under the porch from the lawn and settled in to watch the storm.

I lit the joint and took a long, slow drag, letting the smoke cascade carefully into my lungs. It tasted much smoother than I remember from the old days, and I silently congratulated myself on producing more smokable weed than whomever Joe used as a source back then. I held it in my lungs, picturing little cartoon cannabinoids as they were sent on their way through the alveoli into the bloodstream and

232 • POT, INC.

toward the brain, then exhaled a thin plume of smoke to dance in the rafters over my head before being ripped up on the wind. I took another little half-hit and stubbed the joint out on the railing.

It was peaceful in the backyard despite the thrashing branches and the first big spits of raindrops hitting the deck. My feet were up on the railing and crossed at the ankles, and it wasn't long at all before they seemed weighted and weightless at the same time. The sensation crept through my body, emanating from my chest, and soon my arms and neck felt the same way, like dense iron objects cast loose in zero gravity. I guessed from the effect that I'd smoked one of the *indicas*, probably Mango, since I hadn't detected any hints of blueberry while rolling the joint. Within five minutes, I felt that if I closed my eyes I could levitate off the chair.

But there was too much to see and experience for that. The yard had become a full symphony orchestra before my eyes, with each individual leaf, branch, insect, and raindrop adding its own visual and aural flourish to what was building to be a true nature's crescendo welling through the trees around me. There are wind chimes on every corner of the porch and the storm was peeling notes from all of them, sending them tinkling like confetti through the air, where they mingled with the applause of the rainfall. A hummingbird left a low vibrato wake through the building downpour as it deftly carved a fast path across the yard toward shelter; the grapevine and the berry bush bounced like wild animals beating their breasts at the sky.

The colors were fantastic. All the leaves were green until you looked more closely. Then they were yellow and silver and black and blue, but *together* they were green, the best green ever, punctuated with small explosions of red berries and purple flowers. The wind died off, and for a moment, the rain fell straight down in a curtain of water. The trees swayed back to their centers like musicians adjusting their posture for the next movement. Then the next wall of wind hit and set everything into motion again. I was rapt with wonder.

There was no paranoia this time, no worry that someone would appear at my elbow and expect me to answer their questions or to explain myself or to justify why I sat there, getting misted with rain and feeling the giant hand of the storm closing around my little bubble of protection under the porch. There was just awe at the perfect synchronicity of the choreographed chaos unfolding on the stage in front of me.

Everything had its place and fulfilled its function. That included me. I was part of the harmony, sitting there with my wine and my wet feet, my only role to witness this newly discovered beauty, and to enjoy it.

My back, by the way, had never felt better.

Epilogue

A Sea of Green From Coast to Coast

"What a long strange trip it's been."

—The Grateful Dead

Friday the thirteenth is considered by many a day of bad luck, and for those who are opposed to and alarmed at the spread of permissive legislation making its way across the United States, May 13, 2011, lived up to its reputation. But for pot activists, it was more reason to celebrate: That's the day Delaware became the sixteenth U.S. state to adopt a medical marijuana law, with Gov. Jack Markell signing a bill allowing for three dispensaries to supply pot to qualifying patients and permitting those patients to possess up to six ounces every six months. As was the case with each of the states, Delaware had its unique features—patients weren't allowed to grow pot themselves but had to get it from one of the state-approved dispensaries.

Just two days before, Maryland took a half measure, with Gov. Martin O'Malley signing a bill protecting medical marijuana users from arrest, but not legalizing it.

And on that same day, May 11, 2011, New Hampshire tabled a bill that was similar to Delaware's legislation. New Hampshire had come close to passing a medical marijuana law in 2009. Both the state House and Senate passed a bill that would open three dispensaries and allow patients to possess two ounces of marijuana to treat the symptoms of their illnesses, but Gov. John Lynch vetoed it. An attempt to overturn the veto fell short by only two votes. The latest measure was shelved under threat of what Lynch promised would be another veto if the bill reached his desk.

One thing was clear: The debate over medical marijuana showed no signs of slowing down.

The flurry of mixed news in early May was welcome enough after crushing disappointment at the ballot box the previous November. California's Prop 19, which would have legalized adult possession of marijuana for any use and allowed local governments to tax and regulate it, was defeated 53.5 percent to 46.5 percent. For months leading up to the vote, it looked like it would make history and pass—had it, Californians would be free to smoke pot for any reason they wished, whether for chemotherapy or surfing. But it didn't. In the wake of the election, in typical form, there was no shortage of people offering their opinions of what they would have done differently.

Mason Tvert is the director of a Colorado-based pro-marijuana group called SAFER, an acronym for Safer Alternative for Enjoyable Recreation, which reiterates the organization's mission statement that pot is safer than booze. Even before Prop 19 was defeated, he thought its campaign relied too heavily on arguments about how taxing marijuana could help California's hemorrhaging economy, which faced a $19.1 billion deficit for the fiscal year beginning July 1, 2010. Tvert thought the focus should have been on the fact that marijuana is safer and less harmful than alcohol.

"The focus of their campaign, they decided, was tax revenue. 'We can solve the budget crisis,' this and that," he said. "Well, first of all, what happens when there isn't a budget crisis in four years and maybe marijuana is still not legal? Your argument is now gone and no one learned anything."

Tvert is young and looks as if he could star in a Judd Apatow movie, but many an opponent has misread his portly and sometimes disheveled appearance to mean that he's only half-bright. They make that mistake only once. Tvert is one of the smartest people I've met in this industry, our paths first having crossed in Fort Collins in 2004.

SAFER was brand-new at the time, an idea of Tvert's and Steve Fox, the director of government relations for the Marijuana Policy Project. MPP funded the new organization and told Tvert to find an area in the country where the message that pot was safer than alcohol would resonate the most and begin campaigning. As it happened, tragically, that area was Fort Collins. During the fall semester of 2004, a Colorado State University sophomore named Samantha Spady, an honor student, drank herself to death during a night of partying. Her blood alcohol concentration was 0.43, five times the legal limit.

Just a few weeks later, Lynn "Gordie" Bailey, an eighteen-year-old freshman at the University of Colorado–Boulder, also died from acute alcohol poisoning after a fraternity pledging ritual. Newspaper reports say he drank the equivalent of seventeen shots of whiskey in thirty minutes.[1]

SAFER ran campaigns at both universities to reduce the campuses' penalties for marijuana possession to no more than the penalties for possessing alcohol. The referendums both passed easily, the student populations happy to endorse SAFER's argument that no one has ever died from smoking too much pot. After those victories, Tvert spearheaded the successful 2005 campaign to legalize marijuana in Denver. He knows a thing or two about running successful campaigns.

"Rather than just saying 'marijuana should be legal, let's get it out of the black market,' all we need is to make sure more people understand and appreciate the fact that it's safer than alcohol," he said, pointing to his organization's statistics that in 2004, two-thirds of people who were asked thought marijuana was as harmful or worse than alcohol. "If you're these people in California right now saying we can generate tax revenue, the opponents can say, 'but it's going to hurt people.' That's a different conversation. What you have in California is one side saying 'we can make money' and the other saying 'at the cost of hurting people.'

"It's not just a matter of convincing people that they should support making it legal, but also breaking down that opposition to the point where, if [opponents are] crusading to save the children, then they've got to pick and choose," he continued. "Given all the talk in [Colorado] about medical marijuana, it's really amazing that right now prescription drugs are the number one cause of unintentional death in Colorado. Beyond traffic accidents. You'd think that the number one cause of unintentional death would be the thing that everyone is freaking out about, not that some doctor has written a hundred [recommendations] for medical marijuana. Guess what? He is also writing hundreds of prescriptions for legal drugs that are fucking killing people. It's insane."

Unfortunately, it wasn't just the marijuana opponents that Prop 19's backers had to convince: News reports leading up to election day were also filled with disheartening signals that California's marijuana movement was disintegrating from within. Debate raged among growers in the Emerald Triangle counties of Northern California about whether legalizing pot would ruin their gravy train. Laura Kriho, the Colorado hemp activist, predicted there might be trouble among the cultivators months before the vote.

"One of our gripes over the years has been the growing community not supporting the legalization community," she'd told me in Boulder in May 2010.

In the best of times, Mendocino County pot would sell for $5,000 a pound. In 2010, with the Great Green Rush sprouting more competition than ever in neighboring states, growers were having trouble selling it at $2,000 an pound, or the dirt-cheap price of $125 an ounce. The pot farmers were alarmed at the Rand Corporation report predicting (based on guesswork) that, if legalized, marijuana could plummet in price to as low as $38 an ounce, less than the cost of a tank of gas. In the end, most voters in the Emerald Triangle counties went against the measure.

Election day wasn't a complete loss, although it took a few weeks to know it. Arizona passed its medical marijuana law, Prop 203, by the thinnest margin of any state so far, becoming the fifteenth state in the club. When the news broke in late November after a hand-count of the ballots, few were more surprised than Arizonans themselves—particularly those who had campaigned to pass the law. The vote count was a nail-biter. Prop 203 was declared dead on election night, the victim of a strong anti-pot campaign spearheaded by the governor's office. But days later, after all the early and provisional ballots had been counted, the measure squeaked by with a margin of 4,341 votes of 1,678,351 votes cast.

Arizona's admission into the club of permissive states is even more remarkable considering how thoroughly the campaign for Prop 203 collapsed in the critical weeks leading up to election day.

One might look at the numbers and guess that there were still limbs on the battlefield weeks later, the result of a pitched battle between equally equipped forces. In reality, the anti-203 forces commandeered the airwaves, outspent their opponents, and controlled the message. Broke and disorganized, "Yes on 203" voices were heard only when reporters deigned to call for a response to the latest list of state leaders opposing the measure—or, worse, during profile pieces of the sketchiest dudes they could find itching to open a dispensary should 203 become law.

Dr. Sue Sisley, who works for the University of Arizona College of Medicine and was deeply involved in every step of the Yes on 203 campaign, sounds like she's describing a miracle when recounting the hurdles medical marijuana proponents faced as the race came down to the wire. The most critical was a lack of money. Local proponents had counted on a last-minute cash infusion from their helpers at Marijuana Policy Project, the largest national marijuana lobbying organization in the country, to fund an eleventh-hour advertising blitz. That money never came.

However, earlier campaigning proved critical.

"Basically we had a really robust signature drive [which was funded by MPP] and got more signatures than any other ballot proposition," Sisley said. "[MPP] was with us the whole time but then, after the signature drive, Peter Lewis, their big funder, dropped out. We were just floating from April until November. We were literally just trying to fly under the radar."

Though the victories on behalf of legalizing pot for medical use continue to ripple across the country, the factions within the movement are no less fractured and frequently disorganized as ever. Lewis, the billionaire philanthropist who helped pass California's law in 1996 and the big money behind MPP's various campaigns, as well as its former chairman, split from the organization in July 2010. It was more fallout from the sex scandal involving MPP's executive director, Rob Kampia. After three months of unpaid suspension, he was reinstated during what *High Times* called "a contentious conference call meeting of the nine-person board."

"The close vote on his potential return was followed by the resignation of at least two board members, one immediately and one within twenty-four hours," the magazine reported.

Lewis's withdrawal was a gut-blow to the organization. He'd given it $3 million in 2007 alone; when he took his money elsewhere, MPP was forced to lay off ten of its twenty-nine staffers, and Kampia told *High Times* that the group was back to 2004 levels of staffing and financing. That left efforts like the one under way in Arizona in the lurch.

With no cash, the Arizona campaign could do nothing but coast on favorable polling leading up to the election. A public relations team—a Phoenix firm hired by MPP—counseled Yes on 203 to lay low and let good poll numbers speak for themselves. The trouble with that strategy was it gave the impression that Prop 203 was cruising to victory, making it hard to raise money to defend against the inevitable counterstrike.

"All the polling was misleading," Sisley said. "We were enjoying like 65 percent support from the Arizona voters, but the problem was that completely disabled our fundraising capability. Nobody was giving us a dime. The campaign director was making sure we didn't look vulnerable. He never wanted to make a big public [appeal for funds] because he didn't want our opponents to smell blood in the water."

Whether they smelled blood or not, the opponents, led by a group called Drug Free Arizona and bolstered by support from Gov. Jan Brewer (as well as practically every district attorney and sheriff in the state), came out strong. Brewer held three different press conferences decrying the initiative, and Yes on 203 couldn't afford to respond.

"A lot of people under [Brewer] started falling in line and chanting the same rally cry," Sisley said. "We had thirty sheriffs come out against it and the health department was firmly against it. [Drug Free Arizona] managed to raise a lot of money and came out with a bunch of commercials that really hurt us because they went unopposed, basically. All their rhetoric, nobody challenged it. All we could do was rely on free publicity from the media, whenever they were willing to interview us.

"There were a lot of things playing against us," Sisley continued. "The governor's race was very uninspiring. Everybody was embarrassed by Jan Brewer, but because the Democrat was so disappointing, none of the Democrats really came to the polls, and none of the young voters came to the polls. Most of the young voters you talk to didn't even know 203 was on the ballot because we didn't do any education. That was painful."

Sisley wasn't alone. She learned from activists in South Dakota—where a medical marijuana initiative, Measure 13, was walloped in a 63.3–36.7 percent defeat—that financial fallout from Lewis's split with MPP wasn't confined to Arizona.

"They told me that they had the same problems from MPP," she said. "MPP basically said, 'We'll be with you every step of the way, make sure you don't have to raise any money.' They guaranteed a huge media buy at the end with several hundred thousand dollars to try to fight off any opposition. So we didn't get to do any media buys at the end and we basically just floated through. I was very frustrated."

Steve Fox, the director of government relations for MPP, agreed that Lewis's departure left a funding gap that couldn't be filled and that the lesson moving forward is to not rely so heavily on single funding sources.

"Yeah, it's no secret that we put half a million dollars into Arizona to draft [Prop 203], have lawyers look at it," Fox said during a visit to Denver after the election, where he spoke at an event called the Mile-High Marijuana Summit. It was a sort of postmortem debriefing on various legal efforts around the country and was notable in that the word *medical* was left out of the event's name. About a hundred people attended. "We created what's a pretty great twenty-four-page initiative that would have created 120 dispensaries immediately. We paid for that, we paid for the signature drive, but yeah, then one funder pulled out and we were left really sort of hanging."

At the time of the summit, the votes were still being counted, although Prop 203's opponents had already declared victory. But even though the tables were later turned, it was somewhat bittersweet for Sisley, who would have preferred the wider margin of success that a last-minute media blitz might have ensured. Although she is quick to point out that Prop 203 probably wouldn't have passed without MPP's initial financing of the signature drive, the razor-thin victory margin doesn't exactly scream "mandate."

"We start out with no money," she said. "The campaign was depleted and now the implementation process starts out with zero funds and all the genuflecting to the health department. But we actually have a seat at the table now."

Arizona was the only big success story during an election that many hoped would be an even bigger turning point for marijuana in the United States than the Green Rush of 2009 had been. In Colorado, it was an equally disappointing election. Twenty-six municipalities had taken advantage of House Bill 1284's opportunity to opt out of medical marijuana altogether and had ballot measures to ban dispensaries from within their borders. Some of the biggest voted to do so, including the city of Aurora, the third largest city in the state, and all of Douglas County. Only seven rejected the proposed bans, but among them was El Paso County, the most populous and home to county seat Colorado Springs.

Brian Vicente, of Sensible Colorado, put the best spin on the outcome as he could.

"Yesterday, Colorado voters in several cities and at least five counties acted with great compassion in endorsing the regulated sale of medical marijuana to ill community members," he said in a press release. "With these votes, these communities have helped ensure that their neighbors have safe, community-based access to the medicine they need.

"Unfortunately, certain municipalities voted to ban dispensaries— effectively cutting off safe access to medicine for patients in those communities," continued Vicente. "Medical marijuana patients in these communities will not be able to access medicine from regulated storefronts, and instead, will be forced to seek medicine from the black market or from local, unregulated grows. These communities also will not benefit from the jobs and considerable tax revenue that these regulated centers generate."

The legal wrangling continued well after the election, with a group of patients asking the Colorado Supreme Court to overturn large portions of HB 1284 as unconstitutional (the court refused to hear the case in January 2011), and with local skirmishes breaking out here and there over bans implemented in communities large and small. As of this writing, in November 2011, there has yet to be a decisive court challenge to the constitutionality of a community's ability to ban dispensaries.

LONG AFTER MY marijuana was gone and I'd gotten over the clenching fear of the doorbell, I answered the door to find a tall guy in cowboy boots and a bolo tie holding a clipboard. He was a city code enforcement inspector who'd finally tracked me down to sign off on the new hot-water heater. I'd delayed an appointment time and again while my pot grew in the adjacent room, and now that the coast was clear, he'd arrived to take care of the final outstanding bit of paperwork.

While the marijuana may have been gone, the grow room was still somewhat put together, and for anyone who'd seen one before, it wasn't any big mystery as to what I'd been up to. In fact, there were still a few branches littering the floor. The biggest giveaway was the poster I'd forgotten to take down, one my wife had bought online, a picture of a pot leaf with the title "What White People Like: Marijuana." The inspector eyeballed the lights hanging from the ceiling and puzzled over the shower pan, which was now stacked with Rubbermaid tubs full of winter coats and sweaters.

"What's all this?" he asked.

With nothing to risk anymore, I told him I'd been growing marijuana.

"Oh," he said. "But not anymore?"

What followed was a thirty-minute conversation about his own experiences with marijuana, and a general lambasting of the federal government for its intractable stance regarding its legality. While we talked, I was sure to reiterate that I was a legal medical patient and added that I'd grown only one crop as a research experiment. I still harbored a healthy paranoia and didn't want to take the chance that he was best friends with half the police force.

"Hell, I don't care what you were doing," he said as he handed me my copy of the inspection report. "I'm just here to make sure that water heater doesn't burn your house down."

Generally speaking, he was a good example of how open-minded Fort Collins initially proved to be about medical marijuana, even as other nearby communities reacted hysterically. After the city council had decided in 2009 that the proliferation of dispensaries wasn't worthy of a moratorium, they crafted zoning regulations for future businesses that kept them out of the immediate vicinity of schools, churches, parks, and even one another. The resulting map of where a new dispensary might locate is incredibly narrow, relegating future businesses to far-flung corners of industrial parks and a few run-down strip malls. That led to some grumbling among the medical marijuana backers, but their bigger concern was what would happen to those existing businesses that were already located outside the permissible areas. Even though more than a hundred sales tax applications were requested in the first wild-eyed wave of marijuana-mania in late 2009, only twenty-three were actually up and running in February 2011. Either the rest of the prospective ganjapreneurs couldn't meet the strict state demands on ownership, background checks, and finances required by HB 1284, or the nuances of running a small business proved more arduous than many expected. Of the twenty-three, only three were in compliance with the new zoning standards, and the council could have voted to wipe out the bulk of them, including the one run by my friends at Abundant Healing. Their store was right next door to a park, even though it was used only by hobos, and within a thousand feet of other such businesses, which wasn't allowed under the new local zoning regulations.

The main local opposition group, a teen substance-abuse prevention organization called TEAM Fort Collins, certainly hoped the city would put Abundant Healing and the other noncompliant operations out of business, even though the new rules had been adopted after they'd already been open for months. The group lobbied the council with the same tired bugaboos about how allowing pot to be legitimized as medicine, especially by a government entity like the city council, sent the wrong message to kids, whose "perception of harm" of the drug would make them drop their guard and, presumably, become the hard-core drug addicts that Colorado Attorney General John Suthers predicted would happen to teen pot smokers.

One of the group's researchers, Dawn Nannini, wrote a guest editorial for the local paper that said allowing medical marijuana dispensaries to remain in business "sends a clear message to our youths about the not-so-harmful effects of marijuana."

"The very term 'medical' lends the perception that this is a substance with healing properties when in fact the evidence for such is negligible," she said.[2]

I'd finally had enough of that sort of ignorant nonsense and quickly fired off my own guest editorial, which ran in the same paper a few days later. Up to that point, I'd been proud of how Fort Collins had distinguished itself from its more reactionary neighbors—bans had been instituted in every surrounding community—by dealing with the issue in a comparatively measured and thoughtful fashion. I wanted to get in a counterargument before the vote.

"Arguing against dispensaries because they threaten to correct old and inaccurate perceptions about marijuana is not the kind of drug education I want for my son," I wrote. "I tend to think teens can be trusted with the knowledge of marijuana's real risks relative to other substances—especially alcohol and tobacco—and its real benefits to those suffering debilitating diseases and illnesses. Keeping them from abusing any substance, including marijuana, is a laudable goal, but I prefer an honest debate rather than baseless fear mongering. If as a result my teenager's 'perception of harm' falls from the realm of the absurd to be more in line with reality, I'm all for it."[3]

There were more eloquent voices than mine in this debate, including Abundant Healing's Dave Schwaab and several other dispensary owners who addressed the council during citizen participation. They apparently resonated with the council members, who voted in February 2011 to allow existing businesses to remain open.

That gave a sigh of relief to the Abundant Healing owners, who'd ridden a roller coaster of uncertainty since their inception. The biggest drain on their peace of mind, they agreed, was the continuing uncertainty of doing business. The 2011 legislative session saw a few nerve-racking bills introduced, including one that sought to ban edible pot products like brownies and cookies, huge money-makers for dispensaries but also critical for people with lung or respiratory ailments who can't smoke pot. Not surprisingly, the bill's sponsor, Rep. Cindy Acree, was motivated by a desire to protect the children.

"You can't tell the difference between Rice Krispies treats you buy at Target and some of these other ones," she told Denver's alternative newspaper, *Westword*. "They look just alike. And we're seeing suckers packaged in a way that they could easily end up in the hands of children on school grounds."[4]

Against great outcry, she eventually withdrew the bill.

Another nail-biter was one that sought to set a THC blood limit for determining when motorists could be legally considered too stoned to drive. Rep. Claire Levy's bill set the THC limit at five nanograms per milliliter of blood—if the bill passed, it would make no difference whether one was driving perfectly or erratically. Testing over the limit meant getting charged with a DUI, Driving Under the Influence, and could result in fines and a loss of license.

"There are reports that as many as 20 percent of the people stopped who have their blood tested are under the influence of marijuana," Levy said in explanation of her bill. "I don't have my own personal data on that, and I acknowledge that a lot of that is anecdotal. But in general, the reason for the bill is that with more widespread use and increasing public tolerance for the use of marijuana, it's important to be sure public safety is protected on the highways.

"I don't have any objection to more liberal laws on marijuana use and possession, and I don't have any objection whatsoever to the medicinal use of marijuana," she continued. "I've been one of the most friendly legislators on this issue. But I think we also have to make sure that we're keeping up with the need for public safety."[5]

Marijuana advocates like Laura Kriho raked the bill over the coals, calling the five-nanograms-per-milliliter limit "arbitrary" and an attempt by the legislature to undermine the medical marijuana amendment by targeting patients. She papered newspapers throughout the state with press releases saying that chronic users usually have more than five nanograms per milliliter in their bloodstream when they're perfectly sober.

Levy disagreed, telling *Westword* with confidence that only those who are actively stoned would test over the limit.

"I'd point people to some of the studies that show that unless people are actively consuming medical marijuana while they're driving, or right before they're driving, either by inhaling it or eating it, they will not have 5 nanograms per milliliter in their system," she said. "If people really dig into the research and compare apples to apples, I think they'll see that their concern is not legitimate."

In any other newspaper, a claim like this would likely go untested. But *Westword* has the country's very first pot critic on its payroll, a twenty-nine-year-old who uses the pen name William Breathes.[6] Breathes suffers from severe stomach problems that cause nausea and sometimes make it difficult for him to keep food down. His condition—and his job—requires constant medication.

In April 2011, he decided to test Levy's theory. He abstained from marijuana for fifteen hours, then went to get his blood drawn. He also asked his doctor to evaluate his level of intoxication. Dr. Alan Shackelford confirmed that Breathes was "in no way incapacitated." And yet his THC level was off the charts, at least compared to the legal limit Levy hoped to impose: 13.5 nanograms per milliliter, or nearly triple what Levy's bill would impose for a DUI charge. Even the doctor thought the proposed limit was too low.

"They need to vote this sucker down based on that alone," he told his patient.[7] The bill was killed on one of the last days of the 2011 legislative session.

Whatever relief my local dispensaries might have felt at this string of near misses was short-lived. If the past seventy-plus years have taught pot advocates anything, it's that those who are opposed to them aren't easily defeated. In July 2011, the U.S. Department of Justice issued another blockbuster memo regarding medical marijuana, this one written by Deputy Attorney General James Cole. Offered as sort of a follow-up message to the Ogden memo, Cole's was met with much less enthusiasm than the first, at least from the marijuana crowd. He clarified that "persons who are in the business of cultivating, selling, or distributing marijuana, and those who knowingly facilitate such activities, are in violation of the Controlled Substances Act, regardless of state law." This was seen as a direct shot at the sort of dispensaries Colorado had legalized—one that also implicated the politicians who had done so—and it wasn't long before anti-pot activists in Fort Collins used it as a tool to gather enough signatures to place an item on November's ballot calling for a dispensary ban. Once again, the charge was led by TEAM Fort Collins and a cabal of businessmen, former politicians, and law enforcement officials under the umbrella of a group called Concerned Fort Collins Citizens. Their concern, in the words of a former mayor, was that Fort Collins would become known as "a city of potheads."

In contrast to the first time I'd seen the city's dispensary owners together, in the council chambers where they regarded one another warily, the threat to their livelihood banded them together as never before. They formed a group called the Fort Collins Medical Cannabis Association and raised nearly ten times the amount of money to oppose the measure than the backers raised to promote it. War was waged on the op-ed page of the local newspaper, with proponents displaying an alarming ignorance of what they were calling for. They worried about crime and their kids getting their hands on medical marijuana, but apparently failed to realize, or simply didn't care, that banning dispensaries would also ban the tight web of law enforcement oversight and official regulation. Voters could ban dispensaries, but it couldn't ban patients' and caregivers' rights to grow for themselves and others, driving the entire industry underground, back into neighborhood basements where it would be invisible to regulators and tax collectors.

In the end, the scare tactics worked. The measure to ban dispensaries passed and businesses like Abundant Healing had ninety days to close. As of this writing, in November 2011, the members of Fort Collins Medical Cannabis Association were still weighing their legal options.

It's this sort of yo-yo effect that makes the front line in the marijuana war seem like an accordion: here one day, there the next, impossible to predict, and with no telling from one day to the next what's permissible and what's not. The shifting sands were what caught poor Chris Bartkowicz unprepared—he thought he was legal growing forests of pot and felt safe telling the world. His biggest mistake was that he was too optimistic. The forces on the battlefield had suddenly changed in his favor with the issuance of the Ogden memo, and he staked out a forward position without realizing it was behind enemy lines and not yet defensible. In the end, it wound up costing him five years in the federal penitentiary and another eight years of supervised probation when he's released, a plea deal he'd agreed to after it became obvious that his only other choice was going to trial—where he wouldn't be allowed to raise a medical defense, meaning his conviction was all but a foregone conclusion—and risk a forty-year maximum sentence. He began serving his time in January 2011.

As for the man who put him there, DEA bureau chief Jeff Sweetin was promoted and reassigned to Quantico, Virginia, in July 2010, where he now trains new DEA agents as they come on the job. There's no telling whether his removal from Colorado had to do with the threats on his life or the complaints made by pro-pot lawyers and politicians angered at his comments about how the time will come when "we arrest everybody" dealing in medical marijuana. Sweetin told me that if such motivations played a factor in his reassignment, they weren't mentioned to him, and he made similar comments to *Westword* as he began his new job.

"It certainly wouldn't surprise me" if his opponents in the medical marijuana movement felt their outcry had something to do with his being in a new home far from the Rockies, he told the paper, without sounding at all regretful. "If everybody in that industry who wants marijuana to be available to everyone is happy with me, that's a bad sign. The fact that there's some frustration—and I get that there is—is probably a good sign, because it means we've continued to do our mission. . . .

"I don't flatter myself into thinking that the president moved me," he continued. "I don't think I'm on his radar screen. And most people aren't punished by being promoted. I don't think they'd have me training the next generation of new agents otherwise."[8]

The image that conjures, of a vast parade ground where battalions of newly minted federal narcotics agents are given their marching order to rip up ditchweed and be on the lookout for "reefer men," reminds me of the scene in *Pink Floyd The Wall* when the dogs are loosed and the unworthy are rounded up. No matter how far the movement has progressed the general acceptance of marijuana since the Great Green Rush of 2009—in terms of both its medical efficacy and its relative safety compared to the old conceptions—the war is not over.

In fact, it may just be starting in earnest. Although defeated at the polls in 2010, California pot proponents have hardly given up their efforts to legalize marijuana there. Those who take a long view of the fight toward legalization have seen it as something of a victory; no other effort has come as close as Prop 19, and since practically the day after the 2010 election, they've been strategizing for a new run at the ballot box in 2012.

Colorado will also be a likely battleground for legalization. As of this writing in May 2011, there are at least two "Legalize 2012" measures being assembled, one being spearheaded by Laura Kriho representing the hard-core activists—who would prefer nothing more onerous than adults being required to show their ID to buy pot for any purpose—and another by seasoned campaigners, including Mason Tvert. The question is whether the groups behind these efforts, who have different styles and opinions about how to best accomplish their goals, can work as a unified force without succumbing to infighting that has doomed the movement at various times throughout the country.

In terms of warfare, the all-out legalization measures can be thought of as the forward lines where the pitched battles are fought. But there are other fronts being advanced that are no less important. Six states have medical marijuana measures pending as of September 2011: Illinois, Massachusetts, New Hampshire, New York, Ohio, and Pennsylvania. Although history has proven that many laws are introduced but only a few are successful, if each of these states joins the club, nearly half of America will have seen the light. The wonder, then, is how long it will take Congress and the White House to catch up.

Until they do, no one will be able to "live the dream" like Bartkowicz prematurely envisioned. For far too many people around the country, the dream is still fleeting. The best reassurance for those living in fear and discomfort comes in knowing they're on the right side of history, no matter how long that history takes to play out.

Michael Corral, the co-owner of a Santa Cruz, California, medical marijuana cooperative raided by the DEA, summed it up best. In the immediate wake of the raid, he was asked what he would do since the agents tore up his patients' plants and destroyed all of the cooperative's marijuana. He said he would simply replant and start over, undeterred.

"There is no turning back for us," he said. "We know we are right. We know the federal government is wrong."[9]

That was in 2002, but the sentiment is as true as ever.

ACKNOWLEDGMENTS

It will come as little surprise that most people involved in a book like this want no acknowledgment whatsoever of having assisted with it. "Marijuana?" they would say. "Never touched the stuff." So this will necessarily be a short list. Know that those of you who are unmentioned here—and there are many—are thanked in my heart.

Of those who should be publicly acknowledged, none deserve to be at the top of the list more than my wonderful, patient, and extraordinarily tolerant wife, Rebecca. I'm thinking now of the time when I tried to make pot brownies, which, I learned after messing up the pot tea, requires that you first make cannabis butter, a recipe that should come with a warning to wear a gas mask. The first step is to heat some oil or butter and sauté as much marijuana as you want to sacrifice to the project. I had a paper bag full of THC-rich trimmings from the harvest still in the freezer, so I dumped the whole thing in, about an ounce's worth. According to instructions I got from some stoner's video on YouTube, you're supposed to let this cook for a good fifteen to twenty minutes so that the THC can infuse into the oil, with the result being a plume of the foulest-smelling charred smoke imaginable infesting the kitchen, as if from burning tires. When Rebecca came home from work, the house smelled like I'd been sacrificing Rastafarians over an open pit. Thank you, honey, for not cutting down my plants in the middle of the night or calling the cops.

A close second is my son, Turner, who endured these experiments and the crimp they put in his summertime social life like a real trooper. Thank you, buddy, for all you put up with from me.

As ever, my outstanding literary agent and friend, Ayesha Pande of Pande Literary, deserves special thanks for helping me take this idea from the harebrained stage to the getting-a-contract stage and for maintaining a level of enthusiasm for it throughout that was simply priceless. One couldn't ask for a better champion in my pursuits, and she has my eternal thanks.

At Sterling Publishing, thanks is owed to Iris Blasi for recognizing the potential of this book and going to bat for it, to Caroline Mann for her creative and tireless efforts in publicity, and to Carlo Devito for reassembling the world when it fell apart. Thanks to Loretta Mowat for the skilled copyediting and critical eye.

As for my editor, Jill Rothenberg, I can't say enough. Jill worked with me on the book *Blood Diamonds* ten years ago and has remained a close friend ever since—having her by my side in the final weeks of writing and editing was a godsend. Her insights, her intuition, and her vast reserve of wit and enthusiasm have helped shape this book in ways that can't be overstated. More important, having a friend when I needed one the most—during a crunch time that was more insane than usual, with much upheaval going on around me—is a debt I can't repay. Thanks, Jill, from the bottom of my heart. There's no one else who could have guided me through this and made this book what it is.

For research, I owe a debt to Gregory Daurer and his librarian's knowledge of Colorado pot history, as well as to Mike Gibbons for arcane information I couldn't have found elsewhere. Thanks to Richard Cowan of Cannabis Sciences Inc.; Laura Kriho of Cannabis Therapy Institute; attorneys Rob and Jessica Corry; DEA SAC Jeff Sweetin; Mike Turner of the DEA; former Larimer County Sheriff Jim Alderden; Drew Brown, Dave Schwaab, and Sonja Gibbons of Abundant Healing; Joey Simental; Bruce Perlowin of Medical Marijuana Inc.; Robert "Bobby Tuna" Platshorn; Mason Tvert of SAFER; Brian Vicente of Sensible Colorado; and William Breathes, the pseudonymous pot reviewer for *Westword*, who appears in this book only briefly but who helped me understand the sensitivities over different nomenclature—*pothead* vs. *stoner* and the like—by giving me the greatest quote of all time, which I could not find a place for elsewhere. Describing different people's sensibilities over the terminology, he gave as an example his own distaste for the word *cannabis*. "Whenever I hear the word *cannabis*, all I can think of is Woody Harrelson's pants," he said. I have no idea what that means, but I thank him for making me laugh every time I think about it.

I owe an unpayable debt of gratitude to my closest and dearest friend, the late Chris Hondros, who never wavered in his support and enthusiasm for any of my writing endeavors and who was especially looking forward to the release of this book. I'm glad we had the chance to explore this unusual new industry together a few times not long before his untimely death in April 2011, but that he can't read the finished product makes this a bittersweet accomplishment. Rest in peace, my dear friend. I'll read it to you myself, in my prayers.

Finally, deserving of more thanks than I can properly convey are the uncountable scores of people with life-altering (and in some cases, life-ending) illnesses and disabilities who've braved public opinion and an inhumane law to seek relief with cannabis and to speak out publicly about it. No less a degree of gratitude is extended to those who risked their freedom, their livelihoods, and—it's no stretch to say—their lives to supply them with medical marijuana. It's my hope that those who are reading this and suffering in silence in areas of the country where medical marijuana is still a dream on the horizon won't have to wait much longer.

I dedicated this book to the memory of my cousin, Cynthia Malara, whose suffering was relieved as well as it could be, thanks to the grace and courage of those who brought her respite in the form of a plant. It's extended to them as well, in gratitude for displaying a humanity that is clearly lacking among those who are capable of making a difference in Washington, D.C.

—GREG CAMPBELL, November 2011

ENDNOTES

Epigraph

1   *New State Ice Co. v. Liebmann*, 285 U.S. 262, 311 (1932)

Prologue

1   Jorge Cervantes, *Marijuana Horticulture: The Indoor/Outdoor Medical Grower's Bible* (Vancouver, WA: Van Patten Publishing, 2006).

2   The quotes come from a compilation of Obama's statements on the campaign trail provided by the Marijuana Policy Project, http://www.youtube.com/watch?v=9flhDmz 7Kwo&feature=related.

3   http://www.coloradopols.com/diary/12367/sen-scott-renfroe-call-out-national-guard-on-potheads.

4   Marijuana Policy Project, "Victim Stories," http://www.mpp.org/victims/jimmy-montgomery.html.

5   Eric Schlosser, *Reefer Madness: Sex, Drugs, and Cheap Labor in the American Black Market.* New York: Mariner Books, 2004), 28.

6   Human Rights and the Drug War, http://www.hr95.org/geddesj.html. For an interview with Geddes, see http://www.youtube.com/watch?v=hLOHK66pQ-8. He was eventually released in 2003 after serving eleven years.

7   Years later, while fighting the case through the court system, Foster's lawyers filed a motion for the prosecutors to produce the confidential informant in court. Foster wanted to face his accuser. Before the appointed court date, however, the confidential informant allegedly committed suicide. To this day, Foster doesn't know who provided the information for the search warrant.

8   Foster's girlfriend avoided jail time when Foster convinced her to testify against him; she had two children when she was arrested, one of whom was five years old, and Foster didn't want to risk her losing the children.

9   Foster had never been arrested before the raid on his home, but in the mid-1980s, he was cited for simple possession of a small amount of marijuana. It was a petty offense on par with a traffic ticket and did not go on his criminal record.

10 These famous commercials were produced by Partnership for a Drug-Free America, which from the early 1980s to the early 1990s received the bulk of its funding from alcohol, cigarette, and pharmaceutical companies. Fairness and Accuracy in Reporting, http://www.fair.org/index.php?page=1390. The group holds a special place under the Office of National Drug Control Policy Reauthorization Act of 2006, wherein it can receive up to $2 million per year in federal funding for anti-drug media campaigns. United States Code, Title 21, Chapter 22 § 1708.

11 "Crime in the United States 2009," FBI Uniform Crime Report (Washington, DC: U.S. Department of Justice, September 2010), Table 29, http://www2.fbi.gov/ucr/cius2009/data/table_29.html, and Arrest Table: Arrests for Drug Abuse Violations, http://www2.fbi.gov/ucr/cius2009/arrests/index.html.

12 U.S. Department of Health and Human Services, 2008 National Survey on Drug Use and Health, http://www.oas.samhsa.gov/NSDUH/2K8NSDUH/tabs/toc.htm.

13 U.S. Department of Justice, National Drug Intelligence Center, "National Drug Threat Assessment 2010," http://www.justice.gov/ndic/pubs38/38661/marijuana.htm.

14 Eric Baily, "Pot Is Called Biggest Cash Crop," *Los Angeles Times*, December 18, 2006, http://articles.latimes.com/2006/dec/18/local/me-pot18.

15　Pew Research Centers, "Public Support for Legalizing Medical Marijuana," April 4, 2010, http://people-press.org/2010/04/01/public-support-for-legalizing-medical-marijuana/.

Chapter 1

1　The word *recommend* is key here; doctors can't "prescribe" marijuana, just as they can't prescribe heroin. Both are Schedule I controlled substances, defined as having no medical benefit and no safe usage, even under medical supervision.

2　CNBC, "Marijuana Inc.: Inside America's Pot Industry," July 17, 2009.

3　Dispensaries had been in operation for years in California before the passage of SB 420 and the issuance of the state attorney general's guidance on interpreting it. According to that document: "Although medical marijuana 'dispensaries' have been operating in California for years, dispensaries, as such, are not recognized under the law. As noted above, the only recognized group entities are cooperatives and collectives (§ 11362.775). It is the opinion of this Office that a properly organized and operated collective or cooperative that dispenses medical marijuana through a storefront may be lawful under California law, but that dispensaries that do not substantially comply with the guidelines set forth in sections IV(A) and (B), above, are likely operating outside the protections of Proposition 215 and the MMP, and that the individuals operating such entities may be subject to arrest and criminal prosecution under California law." See the attorney general's guidance in its entirety at http://ag.ca.gov/cms_attachments/press/pdfs/n1601_medicalmarijuanaguidelines.pdf.

4　"President Clinton States Marijuana Should Be Decriminalized," December 7, 2000, http://norml.org/index.cfm?Group_ID=4235.

5　Alberto R. Gonzales, Attorney General, et al., *Petitioners v. Angel McClary Raich et al.*, on Writ of Certiorari to the United States Court of Appeals for the Ninth Circuit, Supreme Court of the United States, June 6, 2005.

6　*Raich v. Gonzales*, Complaint for Declaratory Relief and for Preliminary and Permanent Injunctive Relief, filed October 9, 2002, in the U.S. District Court for the Northern District of California. The suit was originally filed against U.S. Attorney General John Ashcroft, but later changed to U.S. Attorney Alberto Gonzales when Gonzales replaced Ashcroft.

7　Wayne Buchanan, "Pot Club Owners' Home Raided in SoMa; Plants and Cash Seized, but No Arrests Made," *San Francisco Chronicle*, December 20, 2005.

8　Ann Harrison, "DEA Raids San Francisco Medical Cannabis Cooperative and Grow Sites," *Cannabis Culture*, December 21, 2005, http://www.cannabisculture.com/v2/articles/4610.html.

9　Phillip Smith, "More California Medical Marijuana Raids: The New Status Quo?" *Drug War Chronicle*, October 5, 2006, http://stopthedrugwar.org/chronicle/2006/oct/05/feature_more_california_medical.

10　Americans for Safe Access fact sheet, "Recent Escalation of DEA Intervention in Medical Marijuana States," http://www.safeaccessnow.org/downloads/dea_escalation.pdf.

11　It's an important distinction that *decriminalized* isn't the same as *legalized*. To decriminalize marijuana simply means to reduce the penalties to where they're mere nuisances, typically carrying a small fine with no jail time and no criminal record. In many states, getting caught and cited for carrying a few joints carries the same weight as getting caught speeding. The states that have decriminalized marijuana are Alaska, California, Colorado, Maine, Massachusetts, Minnesota, Mississippi, Nebraska, Nevada, New York, North Carolina, Ohio, and Oregon.

12　Joel Stein, "The New Politics of Pot: Can It Go Legit? How the People Who Brought You Medical Marijuana Have Set Their Sights on Lifting the Ban for Everyone," *Time*, October 27, 2002, http://www.time.com/time/covers/1101021104/story.html.

13　Christine A. Kolosov, "Evaluating the Public Interest: Regulation of Industrial Hemp Under the Controlled Substances Act," *UCLA Law Review*, 244 (2000).

14   Drug Enforcement Agency statistics compiled by *Sourcebook for Criminal Justice Statistics,* http://www.albany.edu/sourcebook/pdf/t4382005.pdf.

15   In 2010, with debate raging in the Capitol over new regulations for medical marijuana, House Bill 1352 passed through the legislature with barely any comment. It doubled the amount of pot a nonpatient could possess (from one ounce to two ounces) and still be charged with only a petty crime, meaning the penalty is no more than $100. Since two ounces is the maximum allowable amount a patient can possess, an argument could be made that it's cheaper not to enroll in the medical program, even if you get caught and fined, considering the cost of applying for a license and paying for a doctor's visit. The only downside would be the need to score street weed rather than dispensary weed. Gov. Bill Ritter signed the bill into law.

16   Originally, the backers wanted the measure on the 1998 ballot, but they'd supposedly not collected enough valid signatures, at least according to the Colorado Secretary of State at the time, Victoria Buckley. But Buckley died of cancer unexpectedly in 1999, and a file full of valid signatures was found in her desk; thus, the measure was put on the 2000 ballot.

Chapter 2

1   U.S. Bureau of Labor Statistics.

2   The loophole about taxes, at least on the state and local level, is one that would be the first lawmakers would close when new regulations were adopted in 2010. The matter of reporting income to the IRS on federal tax returns is a stickier concept—with marijuana being illegal, it's like a hit man reporting his blood money as taxable income. There is likely a wave of audits on the horizon for many marijuana purveyors, but as of this writing, in the spring of 2011, it hasn't hit yet.

3   "Sensible Colorado Press Release: Historic Lawsuit Overturns State's Medical Marijuana Policy," November 19, 2007, http://stopthedrugwar.org/trenches/2007/nov/19/sensible_colorado_press_release.

4   Quote from Jeff Woods, "Bernie Ellis: Marijuana Martyr," *Nashville Scene,* April 26, 2007. The other details in this section are drawn from a telephone interview with Ellis on July 20, 2010; e-mail correspondence with Ellis; and his Web site, http://www.saveberniesfarm.com.

5   Gary Johnson would later run for the Republican nomination for president on a platform that includes legalizing and regulating marijuana.

6   Letters are found at http://www.saveberniesfarm.com.

7   Defendants must meet all five "safety valve" requirements set out by Congress in 1994. They include: (1) the defendant does not have more than one criminal history point, as determined under the sentencing guidelines; (2) the defendant did not use violence or credible threats of violence or possess a firearm or other dangerous weapon (or induce another participant to do so) in connection with the offense; (3) the offense did not result in death or serious bodily injury to any person; (4) the defendant was not an organizer, leader, manager, or supervisor of others in the offense, as determined under the sentencing guidelines and was not engaged in a continuing criminal enterprise, as defined in section 408 of the Controlled Substances Act; and (5) not later than the time of the sentencing hearing, the defendant has truthfully provided to the Government all information and evidence the defendant has concerning the offense or offenses that were part of the same course of conduct or of a common scheme or plan, but the fact that the defendant has no relevant or useful other information to provide or that the Government is already aware of the information shall not preclude a determination by the court that the defendant has complied with this requirement.

8   Telephone interview with Will Foster, July 16, 2010.

9   Telephone interview with Mark Sully, spokesman for the Colorado Department of Public Health and Environment, June 8, 2010.

10   I discreetly timed the appointment using the stopwatch on my iPhone.

Chapter 3

1   From the text of a radio address by Harry J. Anslinger, Columbia Broadcasting Network, October 23, 1937.

2   Testimony of H.J. Anslinger, Taxation of Marihuana hearing before the Committee on Ways and Means, House of Representatives, first session on H.R. 6385, April 27–30 and May 4, 1937.

3   Harry J. Anslinger and Courtney Ryley Cooper, "Marijuana: Assassin of Youth," *The American Magazine*, vol. 124, no. 1, July 1937.

4   This bastardization of "La Cucaracha" is the most enduring version of the song; it was even featured in the 1962 Looney Tunes cartoon "Mexican Boarders," in which it's sung (in Spanish) by Speedy Gonzales's cousin Slowpoke Rodriguez, who certainly gives every impression of being stoned.

5   "Hearst Lauded for Campaign on Dope Evil," *Washington Herald*, July 31, 1934.

6   Annie Laurie, "Marijuana Makes Fiends of Boys in 30 Days: Hasheesh Goads Users to Blood-Lust," *San Francisco Examiner*, January 31, 1923.

7   *Reefer Madness* (originally titled *Tell Your Children*), directed by Louis Gasnier, 1936.

8   State of Florida Inquisition of Lunacy for Victor Fiorito Licata, October 25, 1933, http://www.unclemikesresearch.com.

9   "Denver Court Imposes First U.S. Marihuana Law Penalties," *The Denver Post*, October 8, 1937.

10   Ibid.

11   The 1986 Crime Bill was meant to address the crack epidemic and assessed a mandatory minimum prison sentence of five years for possession of five grams of crack. For powder cocaine, one would need to be caught with five hundred grams to trigger the same sentence. By 1992, 91.3 percent of people sentenced under the new crack laws were black, even though the Department of Health and Human Services estimated that 64 percent of crack users were white. More broadly, by the mid-1990s, blacks accounted for 35 percent of all arrests for drug possession, 55 percent of all drug convictions, and 74 percent of all those receiving drug-related prison sentences. This is despite research that shows that blacks constitute only 13 percent of all monthly drug users. See Joel Dyer, *The Perpetual Prisoner Machine; How America Profits From Crime* (Boulder, CO: Westview Press, 2000), 182–183.

12   Henry O. Whiteside, *Menace in the West: Colorado and the American Experience with Drugs, 1873–1963* (Denver: Colorado Historical Society, 1997), 3–6.

13   D.F. Musto, *The American Disease* (New Haven: Yale University Press, 1973), 43.

14   The racism shown toward Mexicans is the origin of modern advocates' belief that the very word *marijuana* is pejorative and should be stricken from the vocabulary. Indeed, pot was called many things by many people before marijuana became the accepted name, including muggles, moocha, Indian hay, and ganja (which originated in Jamaica), among many others. However, the belief that marijuana rose to dominance because it was meant to be racist is still just a guess; it may well have sounded more exotic to headline writers, but whether its selection for common usage was based on racism or a desire to sell newspapers (or a combination) is unknown.

15   Martin Booth, *Cannabis: A History* (New York: St. Martin's Press, 2005).

16   Testimony of H.J. Anslinger, Taxation of Marihuana hearing before the Committee on Ways and Means, House of Representatives, first session on H.R. 6385, April 27–30 and May 4, 1937.

17   Nixon was notoriously inarticulate when speaking off the cuff, so quotes in this section have been mildly edited for clarity, eliminating instances of "uh" and "er" and numerous interruptions in conversation by others present. The full transcripts relied upon to reconstruct this section can be found at http://www.csdp.org/research/nixonpot.txt.

18   Radley Balko, "The Forfeiture Racket: Police and Prosecutors Won't Give Up Their License to Steal," *Reason*, February 2010.

19   The Shafer commission was composed of Raymond P. Shafer, chairman; Dana L. Farnsworth, M.D., vice chairman; Henry Brill, M.D.; Rep. Tim Lee Carter (R-Kentucky);

Mrs. Joan Ganz Cooney; Charles O. Galvin, S.J.D.; John A. Howard, Ph.D.; Sen. Harold E. Hughes (D-Iowa); Sen. Jacob K. Javits (R-New York); Rep. Paul G. Rogers (R-Florida); Maurice H. Seevers, M.D., Ph.D.; J. Thomas Ungerleider, M.D.; and Mitchell Ware, J.D.

20 There's an interesting bit of stoner lore regarding *Sesame Street*. Big Bird's friend, the elephantine Snuffleupagus, was thought by some to be a characterization of drug users, with his lidded eyes, droopy nose, pothead enunciation, tendency to forget what he's doing, and nickname, Snuffy. *Sesame Street*'s creators always denied this.

21 "Marihuana: A Signal of Misunderstanding," report of the National Commission on Marihuana and Drug Abuse, commissioned by President Richard M. Nixon and presented to Congress in March 1972.

Chapter 4

1 President Ronald Reagan and Nancy Reagan's Address to the Nation, September 14, 1986, from the White House, Washington, D.C., http://www.cnn.com/SPECIALS/2004/reagan/stories/speech.archive/just.say.no.html.

2 *Up in Smoke* (1978) and *Cheech and Chong's Next Movie* (1980), respectively.

3 Michael Pollan, *The Botany of Desire: A Plant's-Eye View of the World* (New York: Random House, 2002).

4 Ibid.

5 Ibid.

6 Janet E. Joy, Stanley J. Watson Jr., and John A. Benson Jr., eds., *Marijuana and Medicine: Assessing the Science Base* (Washington, D.C.: Division of Neuroscience and Behavioral Health, Institute of Medicine, National Academy Press, 1999), 83–84.

Chapter 5

1 J.Q. Xu, K.D. Kochanek, S.L. Murphy, and B. Tejada-Vera, "Deaths: Final Data for 2007," National Vital Statistics Reports (Hyattsville, MD: National Center for Health Statistics, 2010), vol. 58, no. 19, http://www.cdc.gov/nchs/data/nvsr58/nvsr58_19.pdf.

2 Jeffrey A. Miron, "The Budgetary Implications of Drug Prohibition," Department of Economics, Harvard University, February 2010.

3 Janet E. Joy, Stanley J. Watson Jr., and John A. Benson Jr., eds., *Marijuana and Medicine: Assessing the Science Base* (Washington, D.C.: Division of Neuroscience and Behavioral Health, Institute of Medicine, National Academy Press, 1999), 99.

4 "Rand Study Casts Doubt on Claims that Marijuana Acts As 'Gateway' to the Use of Cocaine and Heroin," RAND Corp. news release, December 2002, http://www.rand.org/news/press.02/gateway.html.

5 Sami Sarfaraz, Vaqar M. Adhami, Deeba N. Syed, Farrukh Afaq, and Hasan Mukhtar, "Cannabinoids for Cancer Treatment: Progress and Promise," *Cancer Research* (Philadelphia: American Association for Cancer Research, January 2008) vol. 68, pp. 341–342, http://cancerres.aacrjournals.org/cgi/reprint/68/2/339.pdf.

6 Donald Tashkin, M.D., professor of medicine, David Geffen School of Medicine, University of California at Los Angeles, and Robert Melamede, Ph.D., molecular biologist, University of Colorado at Colorado Springs, American Thoracic Society 102nd International Conference, San Diego, May 23, 2006. See also Salynn Boyles, "Marijuana Does Not Raise Lung Cancer Risk," WebMD, May 23, 2006, http://www.foxnews.com/story/0,2933,196678,00.html.

7 "Treatment Episode Data Set (TEDS) Highlights—2004," National Admissions to Substance Abuse Treatment Services, Department of Health and Human Services, Substance Abuse and Mental Health Services Administration, Office of Applied Studies, February 2006.

8 Philip Hilts, "Is Nicotine Addictive? It Depends on Whose Criteria You Use," *The New York Times*, August 2, 1994. Other criteria evaluated were "reinforcement" and

"intoxication." Out of the six substances that were ranked, marijuana came in fifth for reinforcement, over only caffeine, and it came in fourth for intoxication, ahead of caffeine and nicotine.

9   Multidisciplinary Association for Psychedelic Studies. Statement on MAPS website: "NIDA's monopoly on the supply of marijuana for research and the DEA's refusal to allow researchers to grow their own has effectively paralyzed medical marijuana research, and for over ten years MAPS has been involved in legal struggles against the DEA to end this situation." Craker timeline found at http://www.maps.org/research/mmj/.

10 Ali H. Mokdad, Ph.D.; James S. Marks, M.D., M.P.H.; Donna F. Stroup, Ph.D., M.Sc.; and Julie L. Gerberding, M.D., M.P.H., "Actual Causes of Death in the United States, 2000," *Journal of the American Medical Association*, 291 no. 10 (March 2004): pp. 1238, 1240. See also http://www.cdc.gov/h1n1flu/estimates_2009_h1n1.htm#The%20 Numbers.

Chapter 6

1   Robert Scheer, "The Playboy Interview: Jimmy Carter," *Playboy*, November 1976, pp. 63–86.

2   Message to Congress, August 2, 1977.

3   Maxine Cheshire, "Drugs and Washington, D.C.," *Ladies' Home Journal*, December 1978, p. 62.

4   *High Times*, "Legalizing Marijuana: NORML's Keith Stroup Looks Back on 34 Years," February 8, 2005.

5   "Panic over Paraquat," *Time*, May 1, 1978. It's important to note that later studies found no adverse health effects that could be attributed to Paraquat-laced marijuana. The U.S. Environmental Protection Agency found that when Paraquat was combusted while smoking, it degraded into another compound that produced little toxic hazard. See J. Routt Reigart and James R. Roberts, *Recognition and Management of Pesticide Poisonings*, 5th ed. (Washington, DC: United States Environmental Protection Agency, 1999).

6   "Interview: Peter Bourne," *Frontline: Drug Wars*, circa 2000, http://www.pbs.org/wgbh/ pages/frontline/shows/drugs/interviews/bourne.html.

7   *High Times*, "Legalizing Marijuana: NORML's Keith Stroup Looks Back on 34 Years," February 8, 2005.

8   Ibid.

9   "Interview: Peter Bourne," *Frontline: Drug Wars*, circa 2000, http://www.pbs.org/wgbh/ pages/frontline/shows/drugs/interviews/bourne.html.

10 Ibid.

Chapter 7

1   Jon Gettman, "Marijuana Production in the United States," 2006, http://www. drugscience.org/Archive/bcr2/domstprod.html.

2   Ibid.

Chapter 8

1   "Anslinger's Fight Against 'Pot' Reviewed by *Esquire*," *Altoona Mirror*, August 27, 1968.

2   Associated Press, "After 40 Years, $1 Trillion, US War on Drugs Has Failed to Meet Any of Its Goals," May 13, 2010; and Jason Beaubien, "Cash from Marijuana Fuels Mexico's Drug War," National Public Radio, May 19, 2010, http://www.npr.org/templates/story/ story.php?storyId=126978142.

3   Ralph E. Tarter, Ph.D.; Michael Vanyukov, Ph.D.; Levent Kirisci, Ph.D.; Maureen Reynolds, Ph.D.; and Duncan B. Clark, M.D., Ph.D., "Predictors of Marijuana Use in Adolescents Before and After Licit Drug Use: Examination of the Gateway Hypothesis," *American Journal of Psychiatry* 163, (December 2006) pp. 2134–2140.

4   L. Degenhardt et al., "Evaluating the Drug Use 'Gateway' Theory Using Cross-National

Data: Consistency and Associations of the Order of Initiation of Drug Use Among Participants in the WHO World Mental Health Surveys," National Drug and Alcohol Research Centre, University of New South Wales, Sydney, Australia, April 1, 2010.

5   "National Survey of American Attitudes on Substance Abuse XIV: Teens and Parents," National Center on Addiction and Substance Abuse at Columbia University, August 2009, p. 11.

6   Originally, NORML asked the DEA to remove marijuana from the schedule of controlled substances altogether, which would have had the effect of legalizing it completely. During preliminary hearings in 1987, NORML amended its petition asking for consideration of placement in Schedule II.

7   Dunsmore's written testimony is included in R.C. Randall's *Cancer Treatment and Marijuana Therapy* (Washington, DC: Galen Press, 1990).

Chapter 9

1   It's important to note that the claim of zero deaths for marijuana relates to overdoses. Pot is a powerful drug that impairs one's ability to drive and operate heavy machinery, but how much that impairment contributes to fatal car crashes is disputed. Estimates of the number of marijuana-related traffic fatalities are difficult to come by; many impaired drivers use more than one substance, combining pot with alcohol, for instance. A reliable study by the Calspan Corporation, sponsored by the U.S. Department of Transportation in 1993, estimated that about 1 percent of all U.S. traffic fatalities involved marijuana only. See K.W. Terhune, C.A. Ippolito, et.al., "The Incidence and Role of Drugs in Fatally Injured Drivers," Calspan Corporation, Washington, D.C., October 1993. Other research has shown that pot smokers are more cautious drivers, tending to go slower than normal, perhaps because they realize their impairment more keenly than drunk drivers. One 1999 study concluded, "There is no evidence that consumption of cannabis alone increases the risk of culpability for traffic crash fatalities or injuries for which hospitalization occurs, and may reduce those risks." See M. Bates and T. Blakely, "Role of Cannabis in Motor Vehicle Crashes," *Epidemiologic Review* 21 (1999): 222-232. For a summary of such research, with references, see www.norml.org/index.cfm?Group_ID=5450.

2   SurveyUSA Poll no. 16937, August 12, 2010, http://www.surveyusa.com/client/PollReport.aspx?g=6154e201-0223-41f2-bcd3-5a3b9a9361b5.

3   R. Gil Kerlikowske, "Why Marijuana Legalization Would Compromise Public Health and Public Safety," Statement to the California Police Chiefs Association Conference, San Jose, California, March 4, 2010.

4   National Center on Addiction and Substance Abuse at Columbia University, "National Survey of American Attitudes on Substance Abuse XIV: Teens and Parents," August 2009, p. 14.

5   R.Gil Kerlikowske, "Why Marijuana Legalization Would Compromise Public Health and Public Safety," Statement to the California Police Chiefs Association Conference, San Jose, California, March 4, 2010.

6   Ibid.

7   Beau Kilmer, Jonathan P. Caulkins, Rosalie Liccardo Pacula, Robert J. MacCoun, and Peter H. Reuter, "Altered State? Assessing How Marijuana Legalization in California Could Influence Marijuana Consumption and Public Budgets," RAND Drug Policy Research Center, Occasional Paper Series, 2010.

8   Jeffrey A. Miron, "The Budgetary Implications of Drug Prohibition," Department of Economics, Harvard University, February 2010.

9   Ibid.

10 Rob Reuteman, "The Cost-and-Benefit Arguments Around Enforcement," CNBC.com, April 20, 2010, http://www.cnbc.com/id/36600923/The_Cost_and_Benefit_Arguments_Around_Enforcement.

11 Jessica Bruder, "Hemp Kingpin Ditches Amsterdam for Denver," CNNMoney.com, June 23, 2010, http://money.cnn.com/2010/06/22/smallbusiness/hemp_empire/index.htm.

12　John Ingold, "Judge Bars Centennial from Closing Medical Marijuana Dispensary," *The Denver Post*, December 31, 2009.
13　Chris Romer, "Medical Marijuana: A Common Sense Policy for Colorado," *The Huffington Post*, December 8, 2009.

Chapter 10

1　Colorado General Assembly, House Bill 10-1284.
2　Colorado General Assembly, Senate Bill 10-109.
3　Interview with John Suthers, Denver, Colorado, April 2, 2010.
4　John Suthers, "The Legislature Should Implement Amendment 20, Not Create a New Industry," *The Huffington Post*, January 12, 2010, http://www.huffingtonpost.com/john-suthers/the-legislature-should-im_b_420114.html.
5　Joel Warner, "Medical Marijuana Dispensary Applications: 700-Plus, Earning Colorado $7 Million," *Westword*, August 3, 2010, http://blogs.westword.com/latestword/2010/08/medical_marijuana_dispensary_applications_700-plus_earning_colorado_7_million.php.
6　"'Dr. Reefer' Says He's Sick of Nevada," Associated Press, April 3, 2009.
7　Jennifer McKee, "Legislative Panel Gets to Work on Pot Law Fix," *Helena Independent Record*, June 29, 2010, http://helenair.com/news/article_ce6be8d8-8345-11df-99de-001cc4c002e0.html.

Chapter 11

1　Dave Bienenstock, "How to Have a Heavy Harvest," *The Official High Times Pot Smoker's Handbook* in *High Times Grow Guide 2010*, special collectors' edition, January 2010, p. 44.
2　Merrill Goozner, *The $800 Million Pill: The Truth Behind the Cost of New Drugs* (Berkeley, CA: University of California Press, 2004).

Epilogue

1　Amy Heckel, "Alcohol Caused CU Pledge's Death; Coroner: Blood-Alcohol Level 0.328," *Boulder Daily Camera*, October 5, 2004.
2　Dawn Nannini, "Let Council Know: Pot Shops Hurt Community," *Fort Collins Coloradoan*, March 3, 2011.
3　Greg Campbell, "About Time Marijuana Truth Is Told," *Fort Collins Coloradoan*, March 8, 2011.
4　Michael Roberts, "Medical Marijuana: Rep. Cindy Acree Says MMJ Edibles Ban Needed to Protect Children, Patients," *Westword*, March 1, 2011.
5　Michael Roberts, "Medical Marijuana: Rep. Claire Levy Talks About HB 1261, Which Sets Driving Limits for THC," *Westword*, February 16, 2011.
6　Breathes asked me to preserve his anonymity by referring to him only by his pseudonym. He'd asked the same thing of producers of *The Daily Show with Jon Stewart*, who got around the obvious visual difficulty of the request by filming him obscured in a cloud of pot smoke and wearing a gas mask bong.
7　William Breathes, "THC Blood Test: Pot Critic William Breathes Nearly 3 Times Over Proposed Limit When Sober," *Westword*, April 18, 2011, http://blogs.westword.com/latestword/2011/04/thc_blood_test_pot_critic_william_breathes_3_times_over_limit_sober.php.
8　Michael Roberts, "Jeffrey Sweetin, Controversial DEA Special Agent, Gets Promoted: Sorry, Haters," *Westword*, June 28, 2010, http://blogs.westword.com/latestword/2010/06/jeffrey_sweetin_controversial_dea_special_agent_gets_promoted_sorry_haters.php.
9　Mark Miller, "DEA Raids WAMM Medical-Marijuana Garden: Activists Are Arrested at Gunpoint; Medicine Seized and Destroyed," *High Times*, September 6, 2002.